FRENCH IN ACTION

FRENCH IN ACTION

A Beginning Course in Language and Culture

The Capretz Method

STUDY GUIDE - Part I

Barry Lydgate
Wellesley College

with

Sylvie Mathé
Université de Provence,
Aix-Marseille

Norman Susskind
Oakland University

John Westlie
William Jewell College

Laurence Wylie
Harvard University

Yale University Press

New Haven and London

French in Action is a co-production of Yale University and the WGBH Educational Foundation, in association with Wellesley College.

Major funding for French in Action was provided by the Annenberg/CPB Project. Additional funding was provided by the Andrew W. Mellon Foundation, the Florence J. Gould Foundation, Inc., the Ministries of External Relations and of Culture and Communication of the French government, the Jesse B. Cox Charitable Trust, and the National Endowment for the Humanities.

The authors wish to express their thanks to Elisabeth Archer, Ann Noack, Kristen Svingen, and the Wellesley College Science Center for help in preparing the French in Action Study Guide.

Published with assistance from the foundation established in memory of Calvin Chapin of the Class of 1788, Yale College.

Printed in the United States of America by Murray Printing Company.

International standard book number: 0-300-03939-5

10 9 8 7

Contents

INTRODUCTION
Using the Study Guide

The purpose of this guide is to show how the video, audio, and print components of *French in Action* fit together into a coherent learning system, and how individual users can get the most out of the course.

Before beginning, you should read lesson 1 in the textbook, which describes the function of the different components of the course. Each lesson is made up of:

- a video program
- an audio program
- a textbook chapter
- a workbook chapter
- a study guide chapter

The study guide will lead you through each lesson, and you should follow it step by step. Briefly, the principal steps are these:

1. Preview the study guide. Read carefully the story summary at the head of each lesson, and review the notes on culture and communication. These will prepare you for the video program.

2. View the video program. You will retain more from each video program if you can view it more than once. If you are using the course via broadcast at home and have access to a videocassette recorder, tape the lesson off-air. If the video programs are available in a language lab or media center, review them there. Remember, though, that the purpose of the video program is to expose you in a preliminary way to the material of the lesson and to help develop your feel for communication in French. You will not need to take notes, and you shouldn't worry if you don't understand everything you hear and see. Your objective is to get the gist of what is going on. You won't be expected to learn any word or structure in depth from the video program alone. More extensive practice in understanding and using French comes later, as you work with the workbook, audio program and textbook.

3. Complete the lesson. After you have watched the video program, you should start immediately with the section of the lesson called *Text work-up*, and proceed through the workbook, audio program, and textbook, with the study guide as your companion and road map.

As you begin *French in Action*, keep the following in mind:

• **The importance of regular study.** You will achieve the best results in this course if you do the lessons regularly. Learning a language is like creating a painting or writing a short story: success depends on consistent, steady effort over time. Avoid letting too much time go by between periods of study. And avoid trying to complete several lessons at one sitting; the day-to-day contact you need in order to develop your listening and speaking skills can't be compressed.

• **Determining what is basic.** At the beginning of each study guide lesson you will find a list of features of the language treated in that lesson. Check marks (√) identify the basic, minimal material of the lesson—material that you will be expected to learn and that you should cover carefully. While the balance of the lesson is not optional (you should complete the entire lesson), you may choose how much to concentrate on the remaining material, according to your interest and the time available.

• **Testing; written and oral assignments.** This course has been designed to help you get into a regular rhythm of study and practice. At the end of the study guide you will find a summary quiz for each lesson. If you are taking *French in Action* as a telecourse, your instructor will very likely assign these quizzes, and you should complete and return them following the information in your course syllabus. The summary quizzes for even-numbered lessons (beginning with lesson 4) contain an oral production section for you to record on an audiocassette and submit to your instructor. In addition, topics for additional written and oral assignments are suggested in each study guide lesson. These are optional, and may or may not be assigned by your instructor; again, check the course syllabus for directions.

• **Dealing with overload.** Most language-learners experience a certain amount of disorientation at their first contact with a new language. If you are new to language-study, or if you have studied language via more conventional approaches, you may find the early lessons of this course particularly challenging and time-consuming. If you do, it is because the course **immerses** you in French and asks you to make sense of the language on its own terms, without the aid of English.

This immersion approach is highly effective, but it is a bit unconventional, and you may find it overwhelming and even frustrating at the beginning. You will quickly get used to it, however. First of all, like any new skill, understanding and speaking French gets easier as you learn the ropes. After a few lessons you will build up a critical mass of familiarity with the course and with the language. From that point on, everything will go faster and more smoothly. Second, and even more importantly, although you may find it frustrating at first to study French without the crutch of English, you are developing survival skills that will serve you well in the long run—skills that you would not be likely to acquire in a conventional course.

• **Using the audio program.** As you work with the audio program, resist the natural inclination to whisper or mumble when you repeat and answer. Your goal is to learn to speak French, and there is no reason to be modest. Get into the habit of saying everything **out loud**, as if you were talking back to a telephone answering machine, or speaking to someone halfway across the room. If it helps, try to mimic the voices you hear, as though you were making fun of them. (Most students are experts at making fun of their teachers, so here is a golden opportunity.)

• **Audio cues.** Most of the workbook exercises have an audio component. You will notice that the phrases you hear on the audio program for many of these exercises are printed in the study guide, just below the instructions for completing each exercise. You should be able to do most of the exercises without looking at these phrases, and you should always try to do so. The printed cues are given for reference if you need them.

• **The importance of participation.** Anyone can learn to communicate in French and discover the satisfaction—and the fun—of being able to say steadily more and more. The speed with which you progress, however, depends on your willingness to take the initiative in speaking. That is why your active, verbal participation—your **performance**—in this course is so important.

As you practice speaking up and speaking out, you will get a great deal of support in the lessons that follow. There are role-playing and interactive exercises in abundance in this course, and for good reason. The ability to imagine yourself as a speaker of French is an indispensable first step toward actually becoming one. By assigning you various French-speaking parts, these role-playing exercises help you get used to lending yourself to the language and projecting yourself as a speaker of it. The faster you can cultivate this skill, the more rapid your progress will be.

Good luck—*bonne chance!* And *bon travail!*

PHONETIC SYMBOLS
The sounds of French

In the workbook and study guide lessons, you will see the sounds of French written as symbols contained between two slashes: / /. These are symbols of the International Phonetic Association. They are used because conventional letters are not reliable guides to the sounds of a language—too many of them can be pronounced differently from language to language, and even within a single language.

Below are the symbols for the basic sounds of French, grouped into categories of related sounds. Next to each sound is a word that contains it. You will learn how to make these sounds, and see which spellings are associated with them, in the lessons that follow.

Oral vowels

/i/	il
/e/	divorcé
/ɛ/	père
/a/	grave
/o/	gros
/ɔ/	personne
/u/	toutou
/y/	tutu
/ø/	deux
/œ/	soeur
/ə/	le

Consonants

/p/, /b/	papa, banc
/t/, /d/	taxi, drame
/k/, /g/	calcul, garçon
/f/, /v/	fille, Véronique
/s/, /z/	poisson, poison
/ʃ/, /ʒ/	chat, jardin
/l/	elle
/r/	mardi
/m/, /n/	madame, Noël
/ɲ/	saignant

Nasal vowels

/ɛ̃/	hein
/ã/	roman
/ɔ̃/	allons
/œ̃/	aucun

Semivowels

/j/	voyons
/ɥ/	huit
/w/	Louis

LESSON 2
Genesis I

Before you begin

• Be sure you have read the **Introduction** at the beginning of this guide.

The story

(*Like all the lessons of* **French in Action**, *this lesson revolves around a* **text**—*a narrative that takes the form of a* **story**, *although at this early stage there is not really much of a plot. The story will take shape gradually through lesson 8 and emerge in lesson 9 as a proper tale, complete with characters, adventures, and, here and there, a few surprises.*)

After an introduction by the French teacher, we meet Mireille, who is in a hurry to get to her Italian class. We see her in a series of brief encounters on her way, all of which involve exchanges of small talk of the "How are you?" "—Fine, thanks. Where are you going?" variety. There is Mme Rosa, and then several friends and schoolmates. Mireille's friend Hubert, tennis racket under his arm, is clearly **not** on his way to school. An encounter with an old professor stands out from the rest in its formality. The last meeting is with Aunt Georgette. She isn't feeling too well, but we are greatly comforted to know that her dog Fido couldn't be better.

We leave Mireille at her Italian class and return to the French teacher who, after eliminating numerous alternatives, gets us to say we are going to learn French.

Notes on culture and communication

• **Le monde francophone.** The French-speaking world extends from Canada and the West Indies to Africa and Europe. French is, after English, the second official language of the United Nations, and is an official language in some twenty-five countries worldwide. In Quebec and other provinces of Canada, it is spoken by ten million people. It is the official language of Guadeloupe, Guyana, Martinique, and Haiti. French is the language of education, administration, and business in a number of African countries, including Morocco, the Ivory Coast, and Senegal (Mireille's friend Ousmane is from Senegal), and in Tahiti. It is widely spoken in Lebanon and Egypt. In Europe, it is the language of daily life in areas of Switzerland and Belgium and, of course, in France. Even in the United States, French is spoken in parts of New England and, as Cajun and Creole, in Louisiana. The dozens of U.S. place-names that are French in origin (Detroit, Baton Rouge, Terre Haute, the Grand Tetons, Prairie du Chien, Havre de Grace, and so forth) bear witness to the historic influence of French in the New World.

• **Salutations à la française.** As you view the video program, you will notice that French greetings and goodbyes are physical as well as verbal. With people one does not know well, whether men or women, the gesture is generally a handshake; with close friends and relatives it is usually a kiss on each cheek. (See the foreword "Greetings and Communication" by Laurence Wylie in the textbook.)

Content and learning objectives of lesson 2

This lesson will show you what to expect and what to say in a number of familiar situations: saying hello and goodbye, and saying where you are going and how you feel.

The following points are highlighted in lesson 2 (you should concentrate on sections marked with a √):

- Expressions for greeting and taking leave of others
- √ Personal subject pronouns (2.6-2.8)
- √ Forms of the verb *aller* in the present tense (2.9, 2.10)
- Two different uses of *aller:*
  - a. talking about going places
  - b. talking about health

ASSIMILATION OF THE TEXT

2.1 Text work-up

The **text** or basic material of this lesson and the following lessons occurs in two very similar forms: a written version in the textbook, and a dramatized version in the video and audio programs.

The **text work-up** highlights the important words and structures of each lesson, and will allow you to consolidate this basic material before you practice using it actively. You are not expected to learn word for word all the material contained in the work-up. Its purpose is rather to single out and help you focus on elements of the text that will be treated in detail later on.

To complete the text work-up you will need only the audio program for lesson 2 and your cassette player. You will not need to refer to any printed text.

• Listen to section 2.1 of the audio program. You will hear key words and phrases of the text repeated several times. At various intervals you will hear a short or a long musical signal, followed by a pause. A **short** musical signal means **repeat**, and during the pause you should repeat the phrase you just heard, out loud, trying to imitate as closely as possible the voices on the recording. A **long** musical signal means **answer**, and during the pause you should answer (in French, of course, and out loud) the question you just heard. After the pause you will hear the correct response for confirmation. Notice that the questions can generally be answered using the very words you have just been repeating.

If you don't feel you have fully grasped any section of the text work-up, go back and listen to it again until it is familiar.

After you have completed the work-up, you should be able to recognize the situations referred to in the questions you heard, and be able to give some kind of answer, even if it is limited to one or two key words.

Listen before you read. To get the most out of the text work-up, you should listen to it at least once **before** looking at the printed version of the text in the textbook.

Note. Beginning in the work-up for this lesson, you will come across a certain number of **questions**; for example:

Est-ce que Hubert va à la fac?

Don't confuse such questions with **positive** statements like

Hubert va à la fac.

or with **negative** statements like

Hubert ne va pas à la fac.

It is relatively easy to spot questions in French. In writing you would recognize them by the telltale "?" after the last word. In speech, they give themselves away by their **intonation**—the way the pitch of the voice moves up or down. In many questions—those that call for a yes-or-no answer—the voice rises in pitch at the end:

Hubert va à la fac ? ↗

Hubert va-t-il à la fac? ↗

Est-ce que Hubert va à la fac? ↗

You will learn how to phrase questions later. For the time being, you need only to be able to recognize one when you hear it.

2.2 Aural comprehension

This exercise will help you develop a skill that is of major importance in this course: associating French phrases with recognizable images of everyday situations.

• With your workbook open to section 2.2, look at the pictures and repeat the phrases you hear on the audio recording. Then match pictures and phrases, following the directions in the workbook.

√ After you have completed phase 2 of the exercise, check your answers in key 2.2 at the back of the workbook. If you find you have mismatched any of the phrases and pictures, repeat phases 1 and 2. Then go on to exercise 2.3.

2.3 Aural comprehension

• Work with the audio recording and your workbook. You will hear the first speaker in each of a series of short exchanges between two people. You won't hear the second person respond. Instead, three alternative responses are listed in your workbook. Choose the one that makes the most sense in the context.

√ When you have completed the exercise, check your answers in key 2.3 at the back of the workbook. If you have made any errors, return to those sections of the exercise and try them again. If on second hearing the reason for a particular answer is still not clear, you may want to view the video program again. Or work with the printed text and the accompanying illustrations in the textbook.

THE "TEXT" AND THE TEXTBOOK

This is the ideal point to open your textbook and read the written version of the text of lesson 2. Pay close attention to the illustrations. As in exercises 2.2 and 2.3, the combination of words and pictures will help you understand and remember important words and phrases.

After you have studied the text and pictures, read through the list of questions that follows the text. These questions will be familiar to you from the text work-up (2.1), and you should be able to answer them without much difficulty.

TOWARD COMMUNICATION

2.4, 2.5 Observation and activation: Pronunciation; division into syllables

The first time you listen to French at normal speed you may get the feeling you are being expected to understand a shapeless mass of sounds all run together. Should you experience a momentary wave of panic, pay no attention to it. Fortunately, the sounds of French **do** have a shape, and you **will** be able to make sense of them.

Vowels and consonants. First of all, the sounds of French, like the sounds of English, can be grouped into two categories: vowel sounds and consonant sounds. **Vowel sounds**, such as /o/, /i/, and /a/, are produced when your vocal cords vibrate without your mouth being completely closed. Different positions of the tongue and lips and different degrees of muscle tension in the mouth produce different vowel sounds. For **consonant sounds** (/b/, /d/, /k/, /r/, /p/, /t/, and so forth), the mouth is partly or totally closed; the vocal cords may or may not be vibrating.

Sounds and letters. Vowels and consonants are **sounds.** In order for language to be written down, these sounds must be represented by visual signs—that is, **letters.** Unfortunately, there is often no simple, one-to-one correspondence between sounds and letters, in French or in English. For instance, suppose we represent consonant sounds by the symbol ⋈ and vowel sounds by the symbol ○. We can visualize the English word *miss* in the following way:

⋈○⋈
miss

Miss consists of **three** separate sounds: two consonant sounds and a vowel sound that is sandwiched in between them. Yet it is written with **four** letters: the two *ss* stand for a single sound, /s/. In *bought* the situation is even more complicated, with the letters *o, u, g,* and *h* standing for a single sound. The same letter can also stand for different sounds: *lin***g***er, han***g***er, dan***g***er.* And the same sound can be represented by different letters: *tou***gh**, *stu***ff**.

The system of correspondences between sounds and letters in French is just as complex as the one that prevails in English. But it is a **different** system. We will investigate it gradually, presenting French first through sound only, and postponing work with **written** words until after you have had a chance to get used to the way they **sound**.

Syllables. Vowels and consonants combine in different ways in French and English to form **syllables**. Syllables are made up of a vowel sound that may be accompanied by one or more consonant sounds. Although you may get the impression at first that a French phrase is a continuous flow of sounds, spoken French is actually divided into syllables. Spoken English is split into syllables too, but along different lines. For some reason, English speakers seem to favor syllables that end in consonant sounds, for example in a word like *Mississippi*:

⋈O⋈ ⋈O⋈ ⋈O⋈ ⋈O
Mis s i s s i p p i

French speakers, on the other hand, prefer syllables that end in a vowel sound. They would divide *Mississippi* like this:

⋈O ⋈O ⋈O ⋈O
Mi ssi ssi ppi

This difference between the ways French speakers and English speakers divide words into syllables is **extremely** important: it helps account for the specific, distinctive sound of each language. English speech, made up of syllables ending in consonants, sounds like *tat-tat-tat* or *at-at-at*. French speech, composed of syllables ending in vowels, sounds more like *ta-ta-ta*.

In order to develop a feel for this pattern, try when you speak French to divide words and groups of words into syllables ending in a vowel. For example, you would divide *allons* into two syllables, as follows:

O ⋈O
a llons

(The *-s* at the end of *allons* is not pronounced, with the result that both syllables end in a vowel sound.) You would divide *nous allons* into three syllables, each ending in a vowel:

⋈O ⋈O ⋈O
nou s a llons

You would divide *malade* into two syllables, the first of which, at least, ends with a vowel:

⊠O ⊠O⊠
ma lade

Learning to divide French words into French rather than English syllables—to say *ma-lade* instead of *mal-ade* and *à-la-fac* rather than *àl-af-ac*—is a critical step in developing good pronunciation, and it is well worth practicing carefully at this early stage.

• Listen to the words on the recording and repeat them, paying close attention to the way sounds are grouped into syllables. (Words and phrases will be said at slower than normal speed to make the division into syllables as clear as possible.)

2.6-2.8 Observation and activation: Personal subject pronouns

Pronouns—in French as in English—are words that replace or stand in for nouns. We use personal pronouns—*you*, *she*, *they*—as handy abbreviations. We use them to designate people whose identity is clear from the context and who therefore don't need to be referred to by name.

The point is to avoid needless repetition. For example, it would quickly become tedious to hear someone say, "**Mireille** va à la fac. **Mireille** est pressée. **Mireille** va apprendre l'italien," so we establish whom we're talking about by saying, "Mireille va à la fac," and then continue with "**Elle** est pressée. **Elle** va apprendre l'italien," and so forth, using the subject pronoun *elle* to stand for Mireille.

First person. *Je* is the pronoun used by the **first person singular**—a speaker who refers to himself or herself. It is used in the singular (when there is only one person speaking). In the plural (when the speaker is referring to more than one person, including himself or herself) the pronoun is *nous*:

Hubert and Ousmane: **Nous** allons à la fac.
Mireille and Colette: **Nous** allons à la fac.

Second persons. The pronouns used by speakers to address others (**second** persons) are *tu* and *vous*. *Tu* refers to one person only, *vous* refers to two or more persons:

Colette to Mireille: Où est-ce que **tu** vas?
Mireille to Marc and Catherine: **Vous** allez où comme ça?

Vous can also be used to refer to one person only, as an alternative to *tu*. Choosing between *tu* and *vous* when speaking to one person serves a very important function. Using *tu* indicates that you feel you have a close or friendly relationship with that person. Using *vous* indicates that you don't know the person or that you wish to be more distant or respectful:

Mireille to Ousmane: **Tu** vas bien?
Mireille to the professor: **Vous** allez bien?

The decision to call someone *tu* rather than *vous*, or at some point to switch irrevocably from *vous* to *tu*, is influenced for each speaker of French by social, cultural, and interpersonal forces. Generally speaking, friends and family members call each other *tu*, and young people use *tu* among themselves. In addition, *tu* is used when speaking to children, whether you know them or not, and to pets:

Mireille to Fido: **Tu** vas bien, toi!

On the other hand, it is always polite, and therefore safe, to use *vous* with adults you meet for the first time and to let them take the initiative of switching to *tu* if and when that is appropriate.

Note that when you are addressing more than one person (the plural *vous*) this distinction between familiar and distant is no longer possible.

Referring to third persons. *Il*, *ils*, *elle*, and *elles* are used by speakers to designate other, **third** persons to whom they are not speaking directly. *Il* is used for one male person; *elle*, for one female. *Ils* is used for groups of males; *elles* for groups of females. One peculiarity: *ils* is used for **mixed** groups of males and females.

• In exercise 2.8, answer each of the questions you hear by saying the people you hear mentioned are fine. Write the appropriate subject pronoun in the workbook. If necessary, consult chart 2.6 as you work.

√ Check your answers in key 2.8 at the back of the workbook. If necessary, review specific points by referring again to the charts and the discussion above. Then proceed to 2.9 and 2.10.

2.9, 2.10 Observation and activation: Forms of the verb *aller*

The six forms *vais*, *vas*, *va*, *vont*, *allons*, and *allez* that you see in 2.9 are the **present indicative** forms of the verb *aller*. They are called **present** because they are used when the action of *aller* is happening in the present (as opposed, say, to the past or the future). They are called **indicative** because they do what their name suggests—they indicate an action as being actual (as opposed, for example, to presenting it as dependent on a condition, or as something that must be done).

Stems and endings. You will notice that the *nous* and *vous* forms (*allons*, *allez*) are similar to the basic infinitive form *aller*, but that the other forms do not resemble the infinitive at all. *Allons* and *allez* share *all-*, which is known as a **stem** of the verb—a part that is common to all or several forms of the verb. *-Ons* and *-ez* are **endings** added to this stem to identify different persons: *-ons* indicates the first person plural, and *-ez* the second person plural (the *nous* and *vous* forms).

(By the way, the endings *-ons* and *-ez* are common to **almost all** French verbs in the present indicative.)

The forms *vais*, *vas*, *va*, and *vont* have a *v-* in common. This *v-* is the stem for those forms of the verb. In other words, there are two different stems for the present indicative of *aller*. This is a fairly rare occurrence: most verbs have only one stem.

-Ais, *-as*, *-a*, and *-ont* are endings that enable you to tell apart the first, second, and third persons singular and the third person plural of *aller*.

• Study chart 2.9, and complete exercise 2.10 in your workbook. Answer the questions out loud and in writing, again saying that everyone you hear mentioned is fine.

√ Check your answers in key 2.10 at the back of the workbook. If you have any trouble at all with these verb forms, study the chart again and redo the exercise, pausing as often as necessary to compare the verb form you have said and written with the pronoun given. Then continue on to 2.11, 2.12, and 2.13.

2.11 Observation: Uses of the verb *aller*

You have probably noticed that the verb *aller* in its various forms (*vais*, *vas*, *va*, *vont*, *allons*, *allez*) is used in two different contexts, with different meanings:

1. when talking about going places
   Example: Je vais à la fac.

2. when talking about health
   Example: Je vais bien.

Chart 2.11 illustrates these two different uses in schematic form.

Note that *où* and *comment* are question words used with these two different meanings of *aller*. *Où* refers to a place ("**Où** vas-tu?" "—Je vais à la fac") and *comment* refers to a way of being or doing ("**Comment** vas-tu?" "—Je vais bien").

2.12 Activation: Verb *aller*

In section 2.12, you have an opportunity to play roles in a series of short dialogues and to practice using *aller*.

To work with this exercise you will need principally the audio recording for this section. The examples and the list of characters in the workbook will be useful for orientation only.

• You will hear each dialogue twice, then once again, this time with a pause before your character answers. You should deliver the appropriate line right away. You will hear the correct answer for confirmation. Repeat this exercise, if need be, until you feel comfortable with the material.

2.13 Activation: Verb *aller*

This exercise will give you practice in recognizing whether different forms of *aller* are used to refer to one's health or to going someplace.

• You will need the audio recording, and your workbook for orientation. Listen to the recorded dialogues, decide whether the question you hear asks about health or destination, and answer accordingly, using expressions from the dialogue. You will get immediate confirmation of your answer. Repeat individual items as necessary. Then proceed to the exercises on writing in 2.14, 2.15, and 2.16.

2.14 Observation: Sounds and letters

One danger for the native speaker of English is to assume that a certain letter or combination of letters in French stands for the same sound it would in English. The list in 2.14 shows how certain sounds are spelled in French.

• Study the list and listen to the corresponding section on the audio recording. This will prepare you for the dictation and writing exercises in 2.15 and 2.16.

2.15 Activation: Dictation

In this course, we will use **dictation** not as the merely mechanical process of transcription its name suggests, but as a useful learning tool.

Dictation will be used not so much to check your spelling as to give you practice in recognizing the words and phrases you hear.

In doing dictation exercises, you should not try to transcribe what you hear sound by sound. Instead, try to identify whole words and phrases and figure out—through the context—what they mean. Then, write them down according to your **memory** of their spelling. If you don't trust your memory for certain words, check the spelling of those words after you have completed the exercise.

• Using your workbook and the audio recording, listen to the dictation and fill in the blanks. If you are working with a cassette player, stop your machine after each sentence if you need more time to write. You may want to play back an occasional word or sentence more than once, but if after three hearings it is still unclear, move on to the next item.

√ Check your answers in key 2.15 at the back of the workbook.

2.16 Activation: Uses of the verb *aller*

• You will not need to use any taped material for this written exercise. Simply fill in the blanks with the appropriate phrase containing a form of *aller*.

√ Check what you've written in key 2.16 at the back of the workbook.

2.17, 2.18 Observation and activation: Talking about health

Chart 2.17 and exercise 2.18 show how French speakers use *aller* and *être*, two different verbs, to talk about health.

In lesson 2, you have come across a number of expressions referring to health that use *aller*.

Example: Je ne **vais** pas bien.

You have also seen a few that use *être*.

Example: Je **suis** fatiguée.

Notice that in expressions that use *aller*, the verb is followed by a particular type of word: *bien*, *mal*. In expressions that use *être*, the verb is followed by a different type of word: *fatiguée*, *malade*.

The first type of word (*bien*, *mal*) is usually called an **adverb.** Adverbs add to the information given by the verb, as the words *well* or *poorly* do in sentences like "He is doing well" and "He is doing poorly," where *well* and *poorly* tell us something about how "he" is doing.

The second type of word (*malade*, *fatiguée*) is called an **adjective.** Adjectives qualify a noun or pronoun, as *bright* and *slow* do in sentences like "He is bright" and "He is slow," where *bright* and *slow* tell us something about this "he" we are talking about.

• Exercise 2.18 is a dictation exercise. Write the form of the verb you hear, stopping your machine as necessary to give yourself enough time to write.

√ Check your answers in key 2.18 at the back of the workbook.

2.19, 2.20 Observation and activation: Negation

In this lesson, you have encountered various negative expressions, such as "ça ne va **pas**" (as opposed to the positive "ça va") and "il n'est **pas** pressé" (as opposed to "il est pressé"). Chart 2.19 focuses on these negative expressions.

Notice that the word *pas* appears in each negative expression, and that the response *non* summarizes a negative answer. We will look at ways of forming and using negatives in later lessons. For now, you need only to recognize them.

• In exercise 2.20, identify negative and positive expressions on the grid in your workbook. (If you hear a *ne* and a *pas* in an expression, you may be certain it is negative.)

√ Check your choices by turning to key 2.20 at the back of the workbook.

2.21 Activation: Dialogue between Mireille and Hubert

This speaking exercise is designed to help you learn short, useful French phrases. Once memorized, these phrases will prove helpful in a variety of situations, either as they are or with variations. Memorization and repetition will also strengthen your pronunciation skills.

• Working with the audio recording, listen to the short dialogue between Hubert and Mireille. Repeat Hubert's lines as often as necessary, until you can answer Mireille confidently yourself. The text of the dialogue is printed in the workbook for reference.

TOWARD FREE EXPRESSION

2.22, 2.23 Role-playing and reinvention of the story

Role-playing and reinvention exercises give you an opportunity to make use of what you have learned in the lesson, and to adapt the story to your own tastes and preferences.

Section 2.22 of the audio program contains two examples of possible approaches to reinventing the story. As you listen to these examples, see how many phrases from the story you can recognize, and notice how they have been rearranged to produce something quite different from the original.

In example 1, character X meets character Y and they have a brief exchange.

In example 2, character X is talking to Fido, Aunt Georgette's dog. Although it is a little one-sided, this conversation has the advantage of giving all the options to character X, since Fido's responses can be interpreted by X as he or she wishes.

In exercise 2.23, it's your turn. Suppose you, character X, run into someone you know—a friend, man or woman, a professor, perhaps your Aunt . . . or her dog Fido (character Y). Imagine what you might say (in French, of course), choosing among the various phrases you have seen in lesson 2. You might decide to play Mireille, or Hubert, or Ousmane; or play yourself and imagine that you are meeting someone you know. Then imagine what the person you meet might say, again choosing among things you've learned in the lesson. Keep the conversation going as long as you can.

Work with your workbook (there is no audio segment to accompany this exercise), and, if possible, a partner. The workbook gives the elements of a possible dialogue between character X and character Y. You and your (real or imaginary) partner take roles and build sentences, choosing from among the options given in each column in the workbook.

In imagining a dialogue, you may choose any rejoinder you wish, provided that the exchange makes sense and that each rejoinder is in correct French. Suppose, for example, you decide that your respondent is going to be a famous actress you don't know personally. If you begin with "Bonjour, Madame . . . ," then you can't follow up with "Tu vas bien?" since the formal address *Madame* goes with the use of the *vous* form. Similarly, if you have character X say, "Je vais à la fac," then you can't very well have character Y respond, "Bon appétit!"

To insure that each rejoinder will be correct, simply limit yourself to what you have already learned. The rule of the game is to choose among the phrases you have encountered in the lesson and to rearrange them in different ways. Above all, avoid concocting an English dialogue—no matter how brilliant—and then translating it into French. Work exclusively with French elements from the start.

Working by yourself. If you work by yourself, take the roles of both X and Y, or have a talk with Fido (see example 2 in 2.22). Say the dialogue aloud. You may also write it down, if you like. Try recording it on a cassette, too, for the pleasure of hearing yourself speak French and as a test run, to get yourself ready for oral production assignments in later lessons. (If you decide to write the dialogue down, notice that when referring to a male person who is in a hurry or tired you would write *pressé*, *fatigué*. When the person is female, however, the correct forms are *pressée*, *fatiguée*. This peculiarity of French will be studied in lesson 4.)

Working with a partner. It will be more fun if you can work with another student (or a friend or family member), each of you taking a part and doing the exercise together. If you adopt the Fido gambit in 2.23 with someone else, try assigning the part of Fido to your partner. (**You** ought to be able to do better than that.) In any case, note that Fido is a French dog. He says "ouah, ouah," not "bow-wow."

DOCUMENT

At the end of lesson 2 in the textbook you will find a short reading passage, *Pessimisme*, that presents key structures of the lesson in yet another combination and context.

As in the case of the text for lesson 2, you are not expected to understand every word of this little exchange between park-bench philosophers. You should, however, be able to get the gist of it without difficulty. Two or three words (*pessimisme*, *hein*, *catastrophe*) do not occur in the main text, and so are new. As you come across them, guess what they probably mean; if the passage continues to make sense, you won't need to investigate them any further. (Quite often they will be words like *pessimisme* that look like English words and mean much the same thing in both languages.) If you still can't make sense of the passage, look up the problem words in the French-English glossary at the back of the textbook.

SELF-TESTING EXERCISES

The self-testing exercises in 2.24, 2.25, and 2.26 will help you measure what you've learned in lesson 2. They are keyed to the principal points covered in the lesson.

Be sure to take a few moments to do these exercises. In addition to being a useful gauge of your own progress, they provide a concise review of the lesson.

• There is no audio component for 2.24 and 2.25. Simply write the appropriate word in the blank provided in your workbook. In 2.26, listen to the questions on the audio recording and circle the appropriate answers in the workbook.

√ Check your answers in keys 2.24, 2.25, and 2.26 at the back of the workbook. At the end of each exercise, you will find references to sections in the workbook and audio program. If you have made errors on a particular point, follow those references for review.

SUMMARY QUIZ

A summary quiz for lesson 2 can be found at the back of this guide. Consult the course syllabus or check with your instructor for information about completing it and handing it in.

LESSON 3
Genesis II

Before you begin

You may want to take another look at the **Introduction** at the beginning of this guide.

The story

(*The story that is the basis of this and subsequent lessons continues to take shape. . . .*)

As the class files in, the French teacher greets the students, individually and in groups, using the appropriate titles. (*Ms.*, it appears, never made it across the Atlantic.) When he identifies himself and begins talking about the purpose of the course, we find that one student already speaks French rather well. What is he doing here? Making conversation possible during these first awkward stages, that's what.

The students are going to learn French by making up a story, which should be a useful and effective way to proceed. The teacher will collaborate in the joint creative effort. After rejecting a few suggested subjects for the story (you can't please everybody), the class settles on a young man and a young woman: boy meets girl. Not very original, but it has all kinds of possibilities. Then, having considered several nationalities, they decide that he will be American and she French—not bad choices for a group setting out to learn French! The students will choose friends and devise adventures for these two. All agree, except for the skeptical (but still hopeful) class ringer and unofficial wiseguy, that this should be both amusing and worthwhile.

Content and learning objectives of lesson 3

This lesson will introduce you to ways of referring to things and talking about activities that are about to take place.

The following points are highlighted in lesson 3 (you should concentrate on sections marked with a √):

√• Definite and indefinite articles (3.13-3.17, 3.19, 3.20)
√• Masculine and feminine forms (3.21-3.23)

- Infinitives of verbs
- √ The immediate future tense (3.26-3.30)

ASSIMILATION OF THE TEXT

3.1 Text work-up

The text work-up will help you identify and focus on what is important in lesson 3. Remember that you are not expected to learn the work-up word for word. Its function is to familiarize you with the basic material of the lesson before you practice using it actively. To get the most out of the work-up you should listen to it **before** consulting the printed text in the textbook.

• Listen to section 3.1 of the audio program for lesson 3. When you hear the short musical signal for **repeat**, followed by a pause, repeat the phrase you just heard, imitating the voices on the recording as closely as possible. When you hear the long signal for **answer**, answer the question you just heard; the correct response will be given after the pause. As you repeat and respond, remember to say everything **out loud**.

3.2 Aural comprehension

This exercise will help you develop the habit of associating French phrases with common situations.

• Listen to section 3.2 on the audio recording and look at the pictures reproduced in your workbook. Match the phrases you hear with the corresponding pictures.

√ Check your answers by turning to the key for exercise 3.2 at the back of the workbook. If you have mismatched any of the pairs, repeat phase 1 and phase 2.

3.3 Oral production

• Work with the audio program in this exercise; the workbook will be useful for orientation only. You will hear a series of short question-answer dialogues. After each dialogue, answer the question as you heard it answered in the dialogue. You will hear the correct answer for confirmation.

If you find you have trouble understanding a question, consult the printed version in the workbook. Repeat the exercise, if need be, until you are familiar with the material.

THE "TEXT" AND THE TEXTBOOK

To consolidate and review what you have learned so far, read the text of lesson 3 in your textbook, paying particular attention to the illustrations. Beneath the captions to a number of these pictures you will find sentences that give you other examples of the word being illustrated. Although they are in French, these sentences are full of well-known names (*Peter Pan, Laurel et Hardy*) and familiar-looking words (*zèbre, orchestre, bridge*) that should make them immediately understandable.

After you have studied the text and illustrations, turn to the questions that follow the text. You should recognize them from the text work-up and exercise 3.3, and you should be able to answer them without much difficulty.

TOWARD COMMUNICATION

3.4, 3.5 Observation and activation: Interrogation

In chart 3.4, you will find four important kinds of questions in French, all of which you have already encountered in the text work-up. For now, you are only expected to be able to understand these questions and to give simple answers. You will learn how to phrase questions yourself in later lessons.

You have probably noticed that *est-ce que* occurs again and again in questions in French. *Est-ce que* is in fact a very common interrogative phrase. It asks for a simple "yes" or "no" answer: "oui" or "non."

The three other types of questions presented in 3.4 require answers that give more information than "yes" or "no":

Qu'est-ce que is usually answered by a noun or pronoun representing a **thing** (*une histoire, des aventures, tout ça*).

Qui est-ce qui is answered by a noun or pronoun representing a **person** (*le professeur, les étudiants, nous, moi, lui*).

A question beginning with *pourquoi est-ce que* asks for an **explanation**, which in the answer may be introduced by *pour* ("**pour** apprendre le français") or by *parce que* ("**parce que** ça va être utile").

• In exercise 3.5, you will hear a series of questions. Decide what kind of answer each requires (simple yes or no, a statement about people, a statement about things, or an explanation), and mark the corresponding answer on the grid in your workbook.

√ Check your answers in key 3.5 at the back of the workbook.

3.6, 3.7 Observation and activation: Pronunciation; tonic stress

This section will sensitize you to a feature of spoken French that makes it very different from spoken English.

You saw in lesson 2 that the flow of speech is divided into syllables. These syllables are grouped in turn into larger units called **rhythmic groups**.

Take the sentence "Pour apprendre le français, nous allons inventer une histoire." It consists of two rhythmic groups. You can tell there are two because you hear a slight pause between *français* and *nous*. Just before that pause, if you listen carefully, you will hear a slight stress at the end of the first group, on the last syllable of *fran***çais**. You will also hear a slight stress at the end of the second group, on the last syllable of *hi***stoire**.

These stresses are known as **tonic stresses.** The final syllables of rhythmic groups have this tonic stress, but the remaining syllables are almost all equal; there are no tonic stresses inside a rhythmic group.

The system of tonic stresses in English is quite different. In English, tonic stresses are attached to one or another of the syllables of each word; the stress belongs to that word, no matter where the word occurs in an utterance. For instance, there is always a stress on the second syllable of the English word *important*:

▽
important

The tonic stress does not change when *important* is used with other words:

▽ ▽
important progress

In the French word *important*, however, there is no stress that is an intrinsic part of the word itself. In the phrase *un important progrès*, there is no stress whatever on *important*, although there is a slight stress on the last syllable of *progrès* because it falls at the end of the rhythmic group:

▽
un important progrès

There **will** be a slight stress on the last syllable of *important* **if** *important* happens to fall at the end of a rhythmic group, or if the word is used by itself (which amounts to the same thing):

∇
c'est impor**tant**

∇
impor**tant**

In English, the syllable being stressed in a word is usually stretched out so that it lasts slightly longer than the other syllables in the word. In addition to being lengthened, it is generally said a little LOUDer. In French, stressed syllables are not necessarily louder, but they are always **longer**.

• Listen to the rhythmic groups in section 3.7 of the audio recording and repeat them, being careful to place a slight stress on the last syllable of each group, but **nowhere else**!

3.8–3.10 Observation and activation: *Il/elle*

The difference between the vowel sounds in the pronouns *il* and *elle* is a critical one in French. It tells you whether the speaker is referring to a masculine noun or a feminine noun, which is very useful in keeping track of what or whom one is talking about.

• These exercises will give you practice in perceiving the difference between *il* and *elle*. First, listen to the examples in section 3.8 of the audio recording. Then test your ability to hear the difference in 3.9, marking which sentences contain *il* and which contain *elle* on the grid in your workbook.

√ Check your answers in key 3.9 at the back of the workbook.

Finally, complete the pronunciation exercise in 3.10, taking care to distinguish clearly between the vowel sounds of *il* and *elle*. Be careful not to let a tonic stress creep into those syllables. Remember, the only tonic stress in the rhythmic group *elle va bien* falls on the last syllable of the group:

∇
elle va **bien**

3.11, 3.12 Observation and activation: The consonant /l/

The French consonant sound /l/ is quite different from the English /l/. To produce a French /l/, keep the back of your tongue down, press the tip against the ridge just above the base of your upper teeth, and release:

il est malade

In English, the back of the tongue is pulled backwards, with the result that the English /l/ is produced further back in the mouth:

he feels ill

When pronouncing an /l/ in French, be careful **not** to let the back of your tongue pull backwards, especially at the end of a word:

mademoiselle

• Study the drawing in section 3.11 of your workbook, then listen to examples of the French /l/ in section 3.12 of the audio recording, repeating each one.

3.13 Observation: Definite and indefinite articles

In French, as in English, definite and indefinite articles are placed before nouns to show whether the noun refers to something or someone in particular, or to something or someone unspecified.

When we say, "Pour l'histoire nous allons choisir une jeune fille française," the expression *une jeune fille française* is **indefinite**. That is, it doesn't say **who** the *jeune fille* is, other than to indicate that she will be *française*. Our candidate could be any one of millions of eligible *jeunes filles françaises*. Accordingly, we might say that *une jeune fille française* is an indefinite expression and that *une* is an **indefinite** article.

On the other hand, in "D'accord, la jeune fille de l'histoire va être française," the expression *la jeune fille de l'histoire* is much more specific. We are no longer talking about just any young woman, but about the particular young woman we have in mind for our story. The phrase *de l'histoire* narrows it down from several million to just one. It defines our *jeune fille*, and so we might say that *la jeune fille de l'histoire* is a **definite** expression and that *la* is a **definite** article.

It follows that in both examples the expression *l'histoire* is definite. (We are not talking about just any story, but about the particular spellbinder we propose to invent in order to learn French.)

3.14, 3.15 Observation and activation: The indefinite article *un, une*

Chart 3.14 and exercise 3.15 will familiarize you with the indefinite article in French.

Notice that *un* comes before masculine nouns, such as *jeune homme, étudiant,* or *ami. Une* precedes feminine nouns, such as *jeune fille, étudiante,* or *amie.*

The masculine *un* is pronounced in two different ways. It doesn't sound the same in *un jeune homme* as it does in *un étudiant.* In *un jeune homme*, *un* is just a nasal vowel sound, with no consonant sound /n/ after it. In *un étudiant* or *un ami*, however, the written *-n* does stand for an /n/ sound.

This /n/ is heard whenever *un* comes before a word beginning with a vowel sound (**a***mi*, **é***tudiant*, and so forth). The /n/ is run together with, or **linked** to, the vowel sound of the following word: *un* /n/*ami*. This phenomenon of linking—*liaison*—is very common in French. You saw several examples of *liaison* in lesson 2, for instance in the expression "Comment allez-vous?", where the /t/ sound of *comment* links up with the vowel sound that begins *allez*: "Comment /t/allez-vous?" There are many other examples. You will find more on *liaison* in lesson 4.

The feminine *une* is pronounced only one way: the vowel sound /y/ followed by the consonant sound /n/. There is always an /n/ sound in *une*, since the written *n* is followed by an *e*.

• In exercise 3.15, decide which phrases contain *un* and which contain *une*, and mark the grid accordingly. (Be especially alert to the difference between *une*, on the one hand, and *un* linked to a following vowel by /n/, on the other.)

√ Check your answers in key 3.15 at the back of the workbook.

3.16, 3.17 Observation and activation: The definite article *le, la, l'*

Chart 3.16 and exercise 3.17 acquaint you with the definite article in French.

You may already have figured out that *le* is used in front of masculine nouns (*jeune homme, professeur, Français*, and the like) and that *la* is used in front of feminine nouns (*jeune fille, Française*, and so forth). Thus, *le* and *la* tell you the gender of the word they precede. You may also have noticed a third form, *l'*, that appears in front of masculine nouns (*ami, étudiant, Américain*) **and** feminine nouns (*amie, étudiante, Américaine*), thus giving you no information at all about the gender of the nouns it precedes.

The words preceded by *l'* do have one thing in common: they all begin with a **vowel sound** (**a***mi*, **é***tudiante*). *L'* is in fact a special form of *le* and *la* in which the *-e* and the *-a* are dropped in front of vowel sounds. They are dropped because French speakers prefer to avoid the clash of two vowel sounds in words that usually occur together, as articles do with nouns. This very common phenomenon in French is called **elision** (*élision*). You will find more on elision in lesson 4.

Note that words for nationality are capitalized in French when they are used as nouns ("l'Italien parle français," "nous allons choisir un jeune Américain"). When they are used as adjectives they are not capitalized ("le jeune homme va être brésilien").

• In exercise 3.17, decide which phrases contain *le* and which contain *la*, and mark the grid accordingly.

√ Check your answers in key 3.17 at the back of the workbook.

3.18 Observation: Singular and plural

Un professeur and *une étudiante* refer to only **one** teacher or **one** student, and are therefore called **singular** expressions.

Des professeurs and *des étudiantes*, on the other hand, refer to **a number** of teachers or students; they are **plural** expressions. There is an *-s* at the end of *de*s as well as at the end of *professeur*s and *étudiante*s. This final *-s* in writing is often a mark of the plural in French, as in English.

Notice that the plural of *la jeune fille* is *les jeunes filles*, as one would expect, but the plural of *le jeune homme* is *les jeunes* **gens** rather than *les jeunes hommes*. *Les jeunes gens* is also the plural form for a mixed group of one or more young women and one or more young men (*la jeune fille française + le jeune homme américain = les* **jeunes gens** *de l'histoire*).

3.19 Observation: Singular and plural of definite and indefinite articles

Look at the chart in section 3.19 of your workbook. You will see that the plural form of *un* and *une* is *des*, and that the plural form of *le, la,* and *l'* is *les*.

Notice that while there is a difference in the singular between the masculine (*un, le*) and the feminine (*une, la*), there is no such difference in the plural. *Des* and *les* are used for both the masculine and the feminine.

The form of the definite or indefinite article allows you to figure out whether a noun in French is singular or plural. In English, plural nouns usually sound different from singular nouns (*teacher, teacher*s) because the final *-s* is pronounced. In French, you can seldom tell if a noun is plural from the sound of the noun itself (although you can see the difference in writing), because the final *-s* is **not** pronounced (*professeur, professeurs*). It is the sound of the **article** that gives the essential information about singular and plural (**le** *professeur*, **les** *professeurs*).

The plural forms *les* and *des* both end in *-s* in writing. In speech, this *-s* isn't pronounced before a consonant sound (*des* **p***rofesseurs, des* **j***eunes filles*).

However, when *des* and *les* occur before a vowel sound (*des* **é***tudiants, les* **a***mis*), the *s* is pronounced as a /z/ sound attached to the word that follows: *des /z/étudiants, les /z/amis*. This is yet another example of *liaison: des* and *étudiants* are pronounced together, as if they were a single word. They are linked by the /z/ sound.

3.20 Activation: *Le, la, l', les*

• Decide which definite article fits each of the incomplete sentences you see, and write it in your workbook.

If the noun is plural, there is no problem: simply write *les*. If the noun is singular and begins with a vowel sound, there is no problem either: write *l'*. However, if the noun is singular and starts with a consonant sound, you have a small problem: to figure out whether it is masculine (in which case, write *le*) or feminine (write *la*).

Note. Certain nouns, such as *Anglais* and *Français*, end in *-s* in the **singular**, and therefore look the same in the singular and in the plural. The written form will not be enough to tell you whether these nouns are singular or plural. Check other elements of the sentence—for instance, the verb or the ending of an accompanying adjective ("_____ Anglais **sont** amusants")—for the evidence you need.

√ Check your answers in key 3.20 at the back of the workbook.

3.21-3.23 Observation and activation: Masculine and feminine endings

Charts 3.21 and 3.22 introduce three families of masculine and feminine words in French, grouping them according to their endings.

Chart 3.21 gives masculine and feminine forms of *anglais*. In speech, the feminine form *anglaise* has a final consonant sound, /z/, that is absent in the masculine *anglais*.

Recall that the final *-s* of *anglais* is not pronounced.

In writing, the feminine form has a final *-e* that is not present in the masculine form. The same is true of other words in the same category as *anglais*, for instance, *français, japonais*.

Chart 3.22 gives masculine and feminine forms of *américain* and *italien*. In speech, there are two differences between the masculine and the feminine.

First, the feminine forms *américaine* and *italienne* end in a consonant sound, /n/, that is absent in the masculine forms.

Second, the last vowel sound is different in the masculine and feminine forms. It is a **nasal** vowel in the masculine forms, while in the feminine forms it is an **oral** vowel followed by an /n/ sound. (A nasal vowel is produced when air is allowed to go through the nose as well as through the mouth; in oral vowels, no air is allowed out the nose. You will find more on oral and nasal vowels in lesson 4.)

Note that the nasal vowel in *américain* and *italien* is not followed by any consonant sound; the *-n* that appears in writing is not pronounced.

In **writing**, the feminine forms *américaine, italienne* have a final *-e* that is absent in the masculine. Notice also that the feminine ending *-ienne* is spelled with a double *n*. This is true of other words in the same category as *italien* (such as *norvégien/norvégienne, canadien/canadienne, chilien, colombien, haïtien,* etc.).

• In exercise 3.23, you will hear a series of questions about which nationalities to give to our two main characters. Each nationality is attributed to the wrong character. Help the questioner get it straight, replacing *le jeune homme* with *la jeune fille* and vice-versa, and changing the form of the adjective, as in the examples. You will hear the correct answer for confirmation.

Audio cues (for reference):
3.23 Activation (oral): Masculine and feminine forms

1. Est-ce que le jeune homme va être français?
2. Est-ce que la jeune fille va être américaine?
3. Est-ce que le jeune homme va être japonais?
4. Est-ce que la jeune fille va être anglaise?
5. Est-ce que le jeune homme va être français?
6. Est-ce que la jeune fille va être italienne?
7. Est-ce que le jeune homme va être norvégien?
8. Est-ce que la jeune fille va être américaine?

3.24, 3.25 Observation and activation: Infinitives

The infinitive is the form under which the verb is listed in a dictionary; it may be considered the **neutral** form of the verb, the form that states the action of the verb without giving any other information.

In English, infinitive forms of verbs are preceded by the preposition *to* (**to** *be*, **to** *go*). In French, no such word is attached to the infinitive itself.

A French infinitive is identified by the sound (and look) of its final syllable. Chart 3.24 will familiarize you with the four endings of the infinitive in French: *-re*, *-ir*, *-er*, and *-oir*. Each French verb has one of these four endings. There are no exceptions.

• Complete the dictation exercise in 3.25, filling in the missing infinitive endings (*-re*, *-er*, *-ir*, or *-oir*) in your workbook.

√ Check your answers in key 3.25 at the back of the workbook.

3.26-3.30 Observation and activation: The immediate future

When at the beginning of the course the teacher announced, "Nous allons apprendre le français," he was not saying that we were in the process of learning French, but that we were **about** to do so. He was referring to a **future** time—more precisely, to an **immediate future** time, since the class was just about to start learning French.

If you compare the following sentences:

Les jeunes gens vont manger.
Les jeunes gens mangent.

you can see they both refer to the same activity (eating), represented in both sentences by the verb *manger*. But there is a major difference between them: a difference of time.

"Les jeunes gens mangent" indicates that the young people are eating as the sentence is being spoken, in the present. "Les jeunes gens **vont manger**," on the other hand, indicates that they are about to eat, that they are going to eat in the near future. (They may be about to eat right where they are or **going** somewhere else to eat.)

We can express this difference in time by saying that *mangent* represents the **present** tense of the verb *manger*, and *vont manger* represents the **immediate future** tense.

Chart 3.27 shows that the immediate future forms we have seen so far (*nous allons apprendre, je vais proposer, vous allez choisir, ils vont avoir*) are all composed of a form of the verb *aller* in the present indicative (*allons, vais, allez, vont*) plus a verb in the infinitive (*apprendre, proposer, choisir, avoir*).

The immediate future of every verb is formed this way in French. You can use any verb in the immediate future tense if you know its infinitive form (and the present of *aller*).

Chart 3.28 gives all the forms of *travailler* in the immediate future. You saw in lesson 2.10 that the form of a verb changes according to the person (the first person singular *je vais*, for example, is different from the third person plural *ils vont*). The various forms of a verb constitute what is usually called its **conjugation**; itemizing these forms is called **conjugating** the verb.

You will notice that in the case of the immediate future tense the part that is actually conjugated—that changes according to the person—is the first part, the part involving *aller*. The second part—the infinitive—remains unchanged.

• In exercise 3.29, you are asked what various people are going to do. Reply that they are going to learn French, using the appropriate infinitive and forms of *aller*.

Audio cues (for reference):
3.29 Activation (oral): Conjugation of the immediate future

1. Qu'est-ce que nous allons faire?
2. Et vous, qu'est-ce que vous allez faire?
3. Qu'est-ce que les jeunes gens vont faire?
4. Qu'est-ce que Jean va faire?
5. Qu'est-ce que tu vas faire, toi?
6. Qu'est-ce que l'Américaine va faire?

• In exercise 3.30, you will hear a series of questions in the immediate future tense. Answer them out loud and write the missing verbs in the spaces in your workbook. (Stop your cassette player as necessary to give yourself enough time to write.)

√ Check your answers in key 3.30 at the back of the workbook.

3.31 Activation: Dialogue between Mireille and Jean-Michel

Listen to the brief dialogue between Mireille and Jean-Michel, repeating Jean-Michel's lines as often as necessary until you can answer Mireille confidently yourself. Try to complete the exercise **without** looking at the written text of the dialogue beforehand. Above all, avoid looking at the written text as you do the exercise.

TOWARD LIBERATED EXPRESSION

3.32, 3.33 Role-playing and reinvention of the story

This exercise is an opportunity to make creative use of what you have learned in lessons 2 and 3.

Listen first to the dialogue between character X and Aunt Georgette's dog Fido in section 3.33 of the audio program. It contains an example of possible recombinations of words and phrases from lessons 2 and 3.

Then, working with a real partner if you can, or an imaginary one, invent an encounter between character X and character Y. Draw upon the material you have studied and use your imagination to recombine it, keeping within the limits of what you have learned in the lessons. Section 3.32 of the workbook will give you some ideas; you may follow it as a model, or simply use it to get started.

DOCUMENT

At the end of lesson 3 in the textbook you will find a drawing by the French cartoonist Jean Effel that affectionately appropriates a famous line from the Bible (*John, I, i:* "Au commencement était le Verbe") and applies it to learning French. The artist is taking advantage of a play on words in French between *verbe* the grammatical unit and *Verbe* the divine creative force.

SELF-TESTING EXERCISES

The self-testing exercises in 3.34, 3.35, and 3.36 will help you measure what you've learned in lesson 3. They also provide a useful review.

- In 3.34, decide which of the answers you see correspond best to the questions you hear, and check the grid in your workbook.

- In 3.35, decide whether the nouns you see are part of definite or indefinite expressions and write in the appropriate article.

- In 3.36, replace the feminine forms of the nouns you see with masculine forms, as in the example.

√ Check your answers in keys 3.34, 3.35, and 3.36. At the end of each exercise you will find references to sections in the workbook and audio program. If you have made errors on a particular point, follow those references for review.

SUMMARY QUIZ

A summary quiz for lesson 3 can be found at the back of this guide. Consult the course syllabus or check with your instructor for information about completing it and handing it in.

LESSON 4
Genesis III

The story

After a recap of the decisions reached in the previous class, the teacher tries to determine just what kind of story he and his students are about to create. He finds it will not be easy to please everyone. Mr. Wiseguy expresses his distaste for several kinds of novels before finally settling on detective stories. Another student proves even more difficult. She doesn't like books at all; she prefers movies.

At last, proceeding with the story, the teacher presents a young American arriving in France, going through official checkpoints at the airport, and finally going off by himself. Other arriving students take public transportation to the Cité Universitaire, where they will stay in dormitories. Our young man's destination is another part of Paris, and he has enough loot to take a cab.

Content and learning objectives of lesson 4

This lesson shows ways in which French speakers give decisive and indecisive responses, express basic likes and dislikes, and talk about nationalities. It also shows how to go through airport customs, and how to talk in general terms about movies and novels.

The following points are highlighted in lesson 4 (you should concentrate on sections marked with a √):

- √ Gender of nouns; agreement in gender and number (4.11-4.14)
- Elision and *liaison*
- √ Masculine and feminine endings, review and extension (4.20-4.24)
- √ Forms of *-er* verbs in the present tense (4.27-4.30)
- √ Forms of *être* in the present tense (4.31-4.35)

ASSIMILATION OF THE TEXT

4.1 Text work-up

• You should begin the text work-up as soon as possible after you have viewed the video program for lesson 4. Repeat and answer as usual. (See lesson 3.1 for details.)

4.2, 4.3 Aural comprehension and oral production

• Match the sentences you hear in 4.2 to the pictures you see, as in previous examples of this exercise (see lesson 3.2).

√ Check your answers in key 4.2 at the back of the workbook.

In 4.3, listen and answer as in previous lessons.

THE "TEXT" AND THE TEXTBOOK

Study the text of lesson 4 and the accompanying illustrations in the textbook. Read the *mise en oeuvre* questions and answer them out loud, as usual. (Refer to lesson 3 for details.)

TOWARD COMMUNICATION

4.4, 4.5 Observation and activation: Pronunciation; *le, la, les*

As you listen and speak, it is important to differentiate clearly among the vowel sounds of *le, la* and *les*.

Hearing the difference between the sounds of *le* and *la* is critical because it enables you to tell a masculine noun (**le** *jeune homme*) from a feminine noun (**la** *jeune fille*). Likewise, it is important to distinguish between the sounds of *le/la*, on the one hand, and *les*, on the other, since this distinction tells you whether the noun that follows is singular (**le** *jeune homme*, **la** *jeune fille*) or plural (**les** *jeunes gens*).

Saying these sounds with precision is equally important. If you substitute one sound for the other or fudge with some sort of vague vowel sound for all three of them, you will end up confusing your French-speaking listeners instead of communicating with them.

• In exercise 4.5, listen and repeat, distinguishing carefully among *le, la,* and *les*.

4.6, 4.7 Observation and activation: Pronunciation; nasal vowels

As you speak, air from your lungs is channeled through two passages to give the vowels you utter their characteristic sound.

One of these passages is the mouth. An **oral vowel** is a vowel sound made by letting air out through the mouth. All vowel sounds involve air going out the mouth, but in the case of some that is not its only exit point.

The other is the nose. Just as a nasal spray is a spray that goes through your nose, a **nasal vowel** is a vowel sound that is pronounced by letting some air go through your nose (in the opposite direction, of course). When you hum you are making a pure nasal sound; people who whine also produce strongly nasalized vowels.

Nasal vowels are produced by lowering the soft palate—the back of the roof of your mouth—to allow air out the nose. If you stand close to a mirror, open your mouth wide and say "aah, ung, aah, ung, aah, ung" you can see a downward movement of the soft palate in the back of your mouth as the oral vowel ("aah," /a/) becomes nasalized (/ã/).

In English, the distinction between a nasal and an oral (nonnasal) vowel occasionally determines the meaning of a word (for example, the difference between *trap*, where air does not pass through the nose, and *tramp*, where it does). In general, though, nasalization of vowels does not affect meaning in English, and many native speakers of English routinely nasalize vowels that occur next to *n*s and *m*s in words like *man, don't, plane.*

In French, the distinction between oral and nasal vowels is clear-cut and **extremely** important, because the meaning of many words depends on it. Section 4.6 presents the four nasal vowels that occur in French. Note that all four are associated in writing with the letters *n* or *m*. You must be careful, however, **not** to pronounce an /n/ or /m/ **sound** after nasal vowels.

The distinction between the nasal vowels in *an* (/ã/) and *on* (/ɔ̃/) is particularly critical, and it is well worth practicing these two carefully. When you say *an*, the mouth is open and the lips are neither rounded nor spread. There is more tension in *on*: the lips are rounded, the mouth is less open, and the tongue is pulled toward the back of the mouth.

To pronounce the nasal vowels in *un* (/œ̃/) and *hein* (/ɛ̃/), the tongue is placed further forward in the mouth than it is for /ã/ and /ɔ̃/. For *un* the mouth is less open than for *hein*, and the lips protrude slightly. The distinction between them is not critical, and many native speakers of French do not observe it. You should not worry if you can't always hear and reproduce the difference between /œ̃/ and /ɛ̃/. Distinguishing between /ã/ and /ɔ̃/ is, however, essential.

Finally, remember to distinguish carefully between *un* and *un***e**. *Un* is one sound: a single nasal vowel. *Une* is two separate sounds: a clear, non-nasal /u/ (as in *t***u**) followed by the consonant sound /n/.

• Listen and repeat the examples in section 4.7, distinguishing as precisely as you can among the four nasal vowels you hear. Repeat 4.7 if need be until you feel confident about identifying and making these sounds.

4.8 Activation: Pronunciation; final consonants

You have noticed that words in French often end with letters that **seem** to represent consonant sounds but are not actually pronounced. (See, for example, all the words ending in nasal vowel sounds in 4.6, above.) A great many words in French have this written ending that is not pronounced **except** when it is linked to the beginning vowel of the next word. By contrast, most final consonants in English **are** pronounced, which is why English speakers are constantly tempted to produce consonant sounds at the end of French words. You should resist this temptation strenuously.

• Look at the words in exercise 4.8 as you listen to them and say them. Note the consonants that you see but don't hear. When you have completed the exercise, read the words out loud again to yourself. If you are not sure how to pronounce the final syllable of each one, listen again to the examples on the audio recording.

4.9, 4.10 Observation and activation: Decision and indecision

Grammar is the set of rules according to which words are put together in ways that make sense. Thus, any act of speech reflects grammar to some extent. However, people do not speak in order to display their mastery of the rules of grammar. As a matter of fact, most people are completely unaware of the grammatical rules they apply every time they speak. They use grammar without knowing it.

People speak in order to achieve certain aims: being polite, agreeing, disagreeing, inquiring, informing, persuading, ordering, refusing, and the like. They pick out, adapt, and recombine the words and phrases in their repertory that seem appropriate to the situation at hand. In this course, you will find a number of repertories of phrases useful in various situations, as well as explanations that help you discover the general grammatical patterns of French.

Section 4.9 is such a repertory. The chart illustrates two ways of expressing reactions: decisively and indecisively. *Oui!, Non!, Bien sûr!* are strong, decisive answers, used to express a definite opinion. By comparison, answers like *Peut-être . . . , (il) faut voir . . . , on va voir* are weaker; they indicate hesitation, uncertainty.

• In exercise 4.10, decide which of the statements you hear are decisive and which are indecisive, marking your choices on the grid in your workbook.

√ Check your answers in key 4.10 at the back of the workbook.

4.11-4.14 Observation and activation: Gender of nouns; agreement in gender

The fact that all nouns have **gender**—masculine or feminine—is an essential feature of French. Charts 4.11 and 4.12 give examples of masculine and feminine nouns and show how to determine the gender of a noun from the other words that accompany it.

You have noticed that certain nouns, such as *jeune homme*, are often preceded by *un* or *le*, while others, such as *jeune fille*, are often preceded by *une* or *la*. Nouns preceded by *un* or *le* are **masculine** nouns; those preceded by *une* or *la* are **feminine** nouns.

Un jeune homme is masculine, and it happens to refer to a male person. *Une jeune fille* is feminine, and happens to refer to a female person. You might be tempted to conclude from this that the gender of a noun corresponds systematically to the sex of the person it refers to. Don't. It doesn't.

Suppose a man is murdered or run over by a car. The newspapers will call him *la victime*, because *victime* happens to be a feminine word. It does not matter whether the person it designates is male or female; the word itself is feminine. Similarly, a woman who teaches at a *lycée* or university is called *un professeur* because the word *professeur* is masculine regardless of whether it refers to a male or a female.

In other words, while the gender of a noun often corresponds to the sex of the person it refers to, this is not always the case. Gender is attached to the word itself, not to what it represents.

Nouns also refer to things, of course, not only to people, and in French those nouns too have gender. *Un roman* is masculine and *une maison* is feminine, even though the sex of a house or a novel isn't immediately apparent. Since there is no foolproof way to predict from the noun itself what its gender will be, you have to look elsewhere for clues, in particular at the words that accompany nouns.

The articles *un, une, le* and *la* are the most reliable gender giveaways because they have separate forms for the masculine and the feminine. It is **very important**, therefore, when you learn a new noun, to learn the articles that go with it.

If you need to figure out the gender of an unknown word you hear and there is no article, listen for adjectives. The gender of a noun will probably be reflected in the adjectives that accompany it, since the feminine and masculine forms of most adjectives are slightly different.

• Exercises 4.13 and 4.14 are designed to give you practice recognizing the gender of nouns. In 4.13, listen for the article that precedes each of the nouns you hear, decide whether the noun is masculine or feminine, and mark the grid accordingly.

In 4.14, listen and supply the missing articles for each of the nouns you see.

√ Check your answers in keys 4.13 and 4.14 at the back of the workbook.

4.15-4.19 Observation and activation: Elision and liaison

Lesson 3 introduced you to two important phenomena in French pronunciation: elision and *liaison*. Charts 4.15 and 4.17 go into more detail, showing how elision and *liaison* work with nouns that begin with vowel sounds.

The examples in chart 4.17 show *liaison* occurring after certain very common words (*un, les*) and in common expressions (*comment /t/allez-vous?*). In this lesson and following lessons you will come across many additional situations (*nous /z/allons, vous /z/aimez*, for example) in which all French speakers would automatically supply a *liaison*; in these cases, *liaison* is **obligatory**. There are, however, many instances where it is **optional**, where you may or may not hear a *liaison*, depending on who is speaking and in what circumstances. Thus, you might hear *nous sommes /z/américains, je vais /z/au Quartier Latin*, with *liaison*, or *nous sommes américains, je vais au Quartier Latin*, without *liaison*.

In *nous allons inventer une histoire*, there are examples of both kinds of *liaison*. You will find that *nous* and *allons* will always be linked: *nous /z/allons*. But you will also find that *allons* and *inventer* are sometimes linked (*nous /z/allons /z/inventer*), sometimes not (*nous /z/allons inventer*). When they are linked, it is usually perceived as a slightly more refined way of speaking, but it does not change the basic meaning of the sentence.

Note. One word that is **never** linked with a following vowel is *et*. In speaking, be careful to distinguish *et* from *est* (the *il/elle* form of the verb *être*). The *-t* of *est* **is** generally linked: *il est /t/américain*. But the *-t* of *et* **is not**: *il est grand et américain*.

4.20–4.24 Observation and activation: Masculine and feminine endings *-ais/-aise, -ois/-oise, -ain/-aine,* and *-ien/-ienne* (review and extension)

Charts 4.20 and 4.21 review groups of masculine and feminine forms that were first introduced in lesson 3, and show how words new to lesson 4 fit into these familiar categories.

• Exercise 4.22 is designed to give you training in figuring out whether people being talked about are male or female. Listen for two kinds of telltale distinctions: the form of the personal pronoun (*il* or *elle*), and the ending of the adjective. If you hear the consonant sound /n/ or /z/ at the end of a word (*américai***ne**, *françai***se**), you know it is the feminine form. If you hear no /n/ but a nasal vowel, you know it is the masculine. When you hear a feminine form, check *une jeune fille* on the grid in your workbook. When you hear a masculine form, check *un jeune homme*.

√ Check your answers in key 4.22 at the back of the workbook.

• Exercise 4.23 will give you practice in perceiving the difference between masculine and feminine forms and in producing them on your own. Suppose you are in a contrary mood. You hear people of various nationalities proposed for the story. Where a woman is proposed, you'd rather choose a man of the same nationality, and vice-versa. Express your preferences, using masculine and feminine forms, as in the examples.

Audio cues (for reference):

4.23 Activation (oral): Un/une; -ais/-aise; -ain/-aine; -ois/-oise; -ien/-ienne

1. Je préfère un Français.
2. Je préfère une Danoise.
3. Je préfère un Japonais.
4. Je préfère un Américain.
5. Je préfère une Mexicaine.
6. Je préfère un Italien.
7. Je préfère une Brésilienne.
8. Je préfère une Suédoise.
9. Je préfère un Danois.
10. Je préfère une Algérienne.
11. Je préfère un Cubain.
12. Je préfère une Anglaise.
13. Je préfère un Vietnamien.

• In 4.24, listen, decide whether the individuals referred to are male or female, and complete the sentences in your workbook accordingly.

√ Check your answers in key 4.24 at the back of the workbook.

4.25, 4.26 Observation and activation: Agreement in number

You saw in 4.14 that articles and adjectives reflect the masculine or feminine gender of the nouns they accompany; it can be said that they **agree in gender**.

Similarly, the singular or plural quality of nouns is reflected in the form of articles, adjectives, and verb forms (singular: *elle* **va** *bien*; plural: *elles* **vont** *bien*). The difference between singular and plural is a difference of number; consequently, it can be said that all these elements of the sentence **agree in number.**

• Exercise 4.26 will give you practice recognizing and writing singular and plural forms. Listen and decide whether the sentences you hear refer to one person or several people. Then complete the written versions, adding the missing articles and appropriate endings.

√ Check your answers in key 4.26 at the back of the workbook.

4.27-4.30 Observation and activation: Present indicative of *-er* verbs

In lesson 3, you saw the four endings found in the infinitives of French verbs: *-re*, *-er*, *-ir*, and *-oir*. Infinitives in *-er* are by far the most numerous: they make up more than three quarters of all verbs in the language. It's useful to know this because the majority of *-er* verbs (not including *aller*) are conjugated in the same way. Charts 4.27 and 4.28 show the conjugation of most *-er* verbs in the present indicative.

• Study the charts and explanations carefully. Then complete exercises 4.29 and 4.30. In each exercise you will hear a series of questions. Answer yes, using the appropriate form of the *-er* verb you heard in the question, as in the examples.

Note. Don't forget that the *-ent* ending of the *ils/elles* form is **not pronounced.**

Audio cues (for reference):
4.29 Activation (oral): Present indicative of parler

1. Est-ce que vous parlez bien français, vous deux?
2. Est-ce que tu parles français?
3. Est-ce que vous parlez français, Madame?
4. Est-ce que Mireille parle français?
5. Est-ce que Robert parle français?
6. Est-ce que les étudiants parlent français?
7. Et moi, est-ce que je parle français?

4.30 Activation (oral): Present indicative of -er verbs

1. Est-ce que tu arrives?
2. Est-ce que tu parles français?
3. Est-ce que tu étudies?
4. Est-ce que tu commences?
5. Est-ce que vous écoutez, tous les deux?
6. Est-ce que vous aimez parler français, tous les deux?
7. Est-ce que Robert parle bien français?
8. Est-ce que Mireille aime discuter?
9. Est-ce qu'ils aiment ça?

4.31-4.34 Observation and activation: Present indicative of *être*

The verb *être*, like the verb *aller*, is an irregular verb. Unlike most other verbs in the language, its various forms differ greatly from one another and do not conform to any **regular** pattern. Nonetheless, you will notice that *suis, sommes,* and *sont* have an element in common (an initial *s*-), and that *es, est,* and *êtes* resemble each other.

• Exercises 4.32, 4.33, and 4.34 will familiarize you with the forms of *être* in the present tense. In 4.32, you will be asked whether various people are French. Say no, they are American, as in the example.

Audio cues (for reference):
4.32 Activation (oral): Present indicative of être

1. Vous êtes français, tous les deux?
2. Vous êtes françaises, toutes les deux?
3. Et toi, tu es français?
4. Et toi, tu es française?
5. Les jeunes gens sont français?
6. Et moi, je suis français?

• In 4.33, you will be asked whether various people are in good health. Say no, they are sick, as in the example.

Audio cues (for reference):
4.33 Activation (oral): Present indicative of être

1. Georges va bien?
2. Tu vas bien?
3. Philippe va bien?
4. Colette et Alice vont bien?
5. Vous allez bien, vous deux?
6. Tu vas bien?
7. Et moi, je vais bien?

• In 4.34, write the missing forms of *être* in your workbook.

√ Check your answers in key 4.34 at the back of the workbook.

4.35 Activation: Masculine/feminine; singular/plural; *être*

This is a writing exercise that combines practice on three points covered in lesson 4. To encourage you to go out on a limb and apply what you have learned to new situations, a number of new words that belong to familiar categories have been introduced in this exercise. *Alsacien*, for instance: *un Alsacien* is a man from Alsace, a province in northeastern France. *Une histoire balzacienne* is a tale that evokes the complex world of characters to be found in the novels of Honoré de Balzac, the nineteenth-century author of *La Comédie humaine.* Even though you may not know or fully understand words such as these, you should be able to categorize them in terms of similar words you already know. *Alsac***ien**, for example, looks like *ital***ien**, so you can presume its feminine form will be similar to *ital***ienne**. Similarly, you would associate *portug***aise** and *marseill***aise** with *franç***aise**, *charm***ant** and *fascin***ant** with *étudi***ant**.

4.36 Activation: Dialogue between Robert and Mireille

Listen to the dialogue between Robert and Mireille. Memorize Mireille's lines, repeating them as often as necessary until you can answer Robert confidently yourself. Try to complete the exercise **without** looking at the written text of the dialogue beforehand. Above all, avoid looking at the written text as you do the exercise.

TOWARD LIBERATED EXPRESSION

4.37 Words at large

Words at large is a game that lets you pull together the various elements of French you have learned and use them on your own. It is a first step toward self-expression in French.

The purpose of Words at large is to help you create a mental inventory of useful expressions so that you'll have them at your disposal when you reinvent the story (exercises 4.38 and 4.39, below). It calls for a global search of all the words or phrases you know that can be used with a certain expression: in this case, after the verb *être*, in the phrase "On peut être. . . ." One can be French or American, so you would look for adjectives of nationality like *français*, *américain*, and so forth, either in the masculine or the feminine. One can be sick, or in a hurry, so adjectives like *malade* and *pressé* are likely candidates. One can be a teacher or a customs official, so nouns used as adjectives to indicate a profession or activity like *douanier* and *étudiant* are also fair game.

Choosing among the words you know from lessons 2, 3, and 4 in the above categories, complete the phrase in as many different ways as you can. If you work with another student, have a contest to find as many examples as possible. Limit yourselves to expressions you have seen in lessons 2-4; in case of doubt about a particular item, check through the lessons to find an example that justifies including it in your list.

4.38, 4.39 Role-playing and reinvention of the story

The exercise is in three parts. In the first two parts, play various roles familiar from lesson 4, making up conversations between yourself and the people you encounter. You may keep close to the exchanges given in the text for lesson 4, or make as many substitutions as you wish, provided you feel confident that what you say is correct.

In the third part, invent a new version of the story to take the place of the episode of lesson 4. A number of options are listed in the workbook. You are not limited to them, however; use any of the material from lessons 2, 3, and 4 so long as you can find some basis in the lessons for what you do. Section 4.39 on the audio program contains a sample reinvention, in the form of a conversation between you and Aunt Georgette's dog, Fido. Listen to it before beginning your own reinvention.

These exercises should be done orally, although you may want to write down what you say as well. If you work with a partner, take roles, complete the exercise, then switch roles and do it again. If you work by yourself, imagine and play both parts of the dialogues, or use the Fido gambit, as in the sample conversation in 4.39.

DOCUMENTS

At the end of lesson 4 in the textbook you will find photographs of some of the Parisian settings referred to in this lesson: the Ile de la Cité, an island in the Seine river in the center of Paris; the Latin Quarter, facing the Ile de la Cité on the Left Bank of the Seine; and the International House and Japanese House at the Cité Universitaire in the southern part of town.

The Ile de la Cité, site of the cathedral of Notre-Dame, and the Latin Quarter, where many institutions of higher learning are located, are historically the center of Paris. Traditionally the home of students and scholars, the Latin Quarter gets its name from the fact that Latin was the dominant language spoken there in the Middle Ages.

The Cité Universitaire is not a city but a group of residences maintained by various countries for students of those countries, with the support of the City of Paris. The various residences, or houses, vary greatly in style; some are modern and cosmopolitan, others reflect the traditional architecture of the sponsoring country.

SELF-TESTING EXERCISES

• Complete exercises 4.40 and 4.41 as usual.

√ Check your answers in keys 4.40 and 4.41 at the back of the workbook. If you have made errors, follow the references at the end of each exercise to sections of the workbook and audio program for review.

SUMMARY QUIZ

A summary quiz for lesson 4 can be found at the back of this guide. Consult the course syllabus or check with your instructor for information about completing it and handing it in.

LESSON 5
Families

Before you begin

• **A word of encouragement.** As you begin this new lesson, you should be aware that the hardest part of the course is now behind you. It is true that there is much more material to be covered in lessons 5-52 than you have seen in lessons 2-4. But like a diver hitting the water, you have survived the initial impact: the plunge into a new language and a new teaching method. In a learning situation where not everything is spelled out for you right away, you have learned to live with partial understanding, make educated guesses, use the tools you are given to make sense of what you can, and reserve the rest for later. These are indispensable survival skills in language learning, and you can take considerable satisfaction from having mastered them. They will make it much easier—and more enjoyable—to work with the lessons to come, and to use your French to communicate with French speakers.

• **Directions in French.** Starting with this lesson, titles and instructions in the workbook appear in French. By now you are familiar enough with the approach of this course and know enough French to be able to figure out directions in French. The study guide will continue to provide explanations in English.

The story

Goaded by Mr. Wiseguy, the teacher astutely remarks that since everyone has a first name, we must bestow one each on our hero and heroine. (It also makes telling a story a great deal easier.) She will be Mireille—a pretty name, but not very easy for our learners to pronounce. He will be Robert—an ideal name because it is both French and English (but not easy to pronounce in French either).

Mireille gets a financially comfortable family, neither poor nor rich. Her mother is a department head at the Ministry of Health; her father, an engineer with Renault. Her older sister is married, but her younger sister, age ten, hasn't found the right man yet.

Robert's family is quite different—perhaps not filthy rich, but at least soiled by contact with money. (Remember that Robert, of all the students in lesson 4, had enough to take a taxi.) He is an only child and his parents are divorced, his mother remarried. Mr. Wiseguy licks his lips at the thought of giving Robert hang-ups. It's probably just as well that the class runs out of time.

Content and learning objectives of lesson 5

This lesson shows how French speakers say numbers, give commands, talk about things they have to do and use negative expressions. It presents ways of talking about people's first names and ages and describing family relationships.

The following points are highlighted in lesson 5 (you should concentrate on sections marked with a √):

√• Numbers from 1 to 29 (5.6-5.11)
√• Forms of *avoir* in the present tense (5.12, 5.13)
√• *Avoir* and age (5.14-5.16)
√• Imperative of *-er* verbs (5.18-5.22)
√• *Il faut* and infinitives (5.23-5.25)
√• Negative expressions with *ne . . . pas* (5.26-5.28)
• Negative of *un, des*

ASSIMILATION OF THE TEXT

5.1 Text work-up

• Begin the text work-up (now called *mise en oeuvre*) as soon as possible after you have viewed the video program for lesson 5. Repeat and answer as usual. (See lesson 3.1 for details.)

5.2, 5.3 Aural comprehension and oral production

• Match the sentences you hear in 5.2 to the pictures you see, as in previous examples of this exercise (see lesson 3.2).

√ Check your answers in key 5.2 at the back of the workbook.

In 5.3, listen and answer as usual.

THE "TEXT" AND THE TEXTBOOK

Study the text of lesson 5 and the accompanying illustrations in the textbook. Read the *mise en oeuvre* questions and answer them out loud, as usual. (Refer to lesson 3 for details.)

TOWARD COMMUNICATION

5.4, 5.5 Observation and activation: Pronunciation; the sound /r/

If you compare the way *Robert* is pronounced in French and in English you cannot help but conclude that the French /r/ is substantially different from the English /r/. The French /r/ is not hard to pronounce, but you have to retrain your mouth and tongue to some extent to produce it. Since it is such a distinctively French sound, getting it right is an important step toward sounding authentically French.

Pronunciation of the French /r/ is centered in the **back** of the mouth; pronunciation of the English /r/ is focused in the **front**. In the English /r/, the tip of the tongue is curved toward the rear of the mouth; in the French /r/, the tip of the tongue lies against the lower teeth, and the **back** of the tongue is arched up against the rear of the mouth, slowing down the flow of air and thus causing a bit of friction.

Saying a French /r/ is a little like gargling without mouthwash. Air under pressure from your lungs pushes against the uvula (the paddle-shaped appendage hanging down at the back of your throat), which vibrates when it encounters resistance in the mouth. In the case of a gargle, the resistance is mouthwash; in the case of /r/, it is the arched back of your tongue.

Another way to understand the French /r/ is to think of the familiar expression of distaste, *yuchhh!* The /r/ sound is made in the same place as the last sound in *yuchhh!*, although /r/ does not last quite as long and the friction is not as great.

• Look at the drawing in section 5.4 of the workbook. Take a few moments to figure out where your tongue should be to pronounce /r/, and how different it **feels** from an English /r/, then repeat the examples you hear in section 5.5 of the audio program.

5.6-5.8 Observation and activation: Numbers from 1 to 29

Sections 5.6 and 5.7 in the workbook present two kinds of numbers: **cardinal** numbers and **ordinal** numbers.

Cardinal numbers refer to the arithmetical progression of numbers from zero to infinity (one, two, three, etc.); ordinal numbers rank them in order (first, second, third).

Cardinal numbers do not reflect gender, except for the number 1 in its spoken and written forms: *1 frère* = **un** *frère*, *1 soeur* = **une** *soeur*. (Note that the number 1 and the indefinite article *un, une* are identical.)

Ordinal numbers act like adjectives; that is, they modify nouns (*la* **deuxième** *leçon*). Except for *premier/première* their masculine and feminine forms are identical (*le* **deuxième** *roman*, *la* **deuxième** *leçon*).

Except for *premier*, ordinal numerals are formed by adding *-ième* to the cardinal form.

• Exercise 5.8 will give you practice recognizing numbers. Write the numbers you hear, using figures.

√ Check your answers in key 5.8 at the back of the workbook.

5.9-5.11 Observation and activation: Pronunciation of numbers

The endings of certain numbers are pronounced in more than one way, depending on what follows them.

Six and *dix* are highly interesting numbers from the standpoint of pronunciation. Depending on what comes after them, they are pronounced in three different ways.

1. If nothing follows them—that is, if they occur at the end of a rhythmic group (*ils sont six*), or if the number is said by itself (*Dix!*), then the *-x* at the end is pronounced /s/.

2. If *six* or *dix* is followed by a vowel sound (*six* ***e****nfants*), then the *-x* is **linked** to the following vowel and pronounced /z/: *six /z/enfants* (an example of *liaison*).

3. If *dix* or *six* is followed by a consonant sound (*dix* ***f****illes, six* ***g****arçons*), the *-x* is not pronounced at all; *six* and *dix* end in the vowel sound /i/.

Cinq and *huit* are pronounced in two different ways.

1. The final consonant is pronounced when these numbers occur at the end of a rhythmic group, or by themselves, or in front of a vowel: *Cinq*/k/*!*, *huit* /t/*enfants*.

2. The final consonant is **not** pronounced when these numbers are followed by a word beginning with a consonant sound: *cin[q] livres, hui[t] personnes*.

Sept has a final *-t* that is always pronounced. (Note that the *-p-* of *sept* is never pronounced.)

Vingt has a final *-t* that is not pronounced when the number occurs by itself or at the end of a rhythmic group. This *-t* is pronounced before words beginning with a vowel sound (*vingt* /t/*et un*), and in numbers from 22 to 29 (*vingt-*/t/*deux, vingt-*/t/*trois . . . vingt-*/t/*neuf*). (Note that the *-g-* of *vingt* is never pronounced.)

Neuf has a final *-f* that is pronounced /f/ under all circumstances **except** before the words *ans* and *heures*, where it is pronounced /v/: *neu[f]* /v/*ans*, *neu[f]* /v/*heures*.

• In exercise 5.11, repeat the numbers you hear as you look at their written forms.

5.12, 5.13 Observation and activation: Present indicative of the verb *avoir*

The chart in section 5.12 shows the present tense of the verb *avoir*. *Avoir* is, with *aller* (lesson 2) and *être* (lesson 4), one of the most commonly used verbs in the language. The infinitive ending is *-oir*, and the stem is *av-*. The stem *av-* appears in *avons* and *avez*, but not in the other forms of the present.

• In exercise 5.13, you will be asked about the probable nationality of various people's first names. Answer yes to each question, using *avoir*, as in the example.

Audio cues (for reference):
5.13 Activation orale: Verbe avoir

1. Est-ce que j'ai un prénom français?
2. Est-ce que Mireille a un prénom français?
3. Et toi, tu as un prénom américain?
4. Est-ce que le jeune homme a un prénom américain?
5. Est-ce que la jeune fille a un prénom français?
6. Et nous, est-ce que nous avons des prénoms américains?
7. Est-ce que vous avez des prénoms américains?
8. Est-ce que les soeurs de Mireille ont des prénoms français?
9. Est-ce que les parents de Mireille ont des prénoms français?

5.14, 5.15 Observation and activation: Talking about age

To say someone's age in French, the verb *avoir* is used, followed by the number of years. Notice that the word *an* (*un an*) or its plural *ans* is always used after the number. "He's twenty-nine," we say in English; in French, "Il a vingt-neuf **ans**."

You have seen how the verb *être* is normally used with adjectives ("Il est malade/fatigué/pressé/amusant/français/espagnol"). Chart 5.14 shows how *être* plus certain adjectives can express age in general terms ("Il est jeune/plus âgé," etc.). But remember: *être* is **never** used to give someone's age in terms of years.

• In exercise 5.15, you will be asked how old various people are. Answer using appropriate forms of *avoir*, and write each form in your workbook.

√ Check your answers in key 5.15 at the back of the workbook.

5.16 Activation: The verb *avoir*

• This exercise reviews the various uses of *avoir* that you have seen in 5.12-5.15. You will hear a number of questions, all of which will be familiar from the *mise en oeuvre*. Answer, using the expression given in parentheses in the workbook, plus the appropriate form of *avoir*.

Audio cues (for reference):
5.16 Activation orale: Verbe avoir, présent

1. Vous êtes fils unique?
2. Pourquoi est-ce qu'il faut donner un prénom aux jeunes gens?
3. Est-ce que Mireille est fille unique?
4. Est-ce que Marie-Laure est plus âgée que Mireille?
5. Est-ce que les parents de Robert sont riches?
6. Vous voulez parler des complexes de Robert?

5.17 Activation: Numbers

• This exercise will give you practice in saying numbers—especially numbers whose endings are pronounced differently depending on whether they are followed by a consonant sound or a vowel sound. Look at the phrases in your workbook and listen to the audio recording. You will hear a letter for each of the sentences you see. During the pause that follows, read the sentence out loud. You will then hear the correct pronunciation for confirmation. If necessary, repeat this exercise until you can read each figure without hesitation.

5.18-5.22 Observation and activation: The imperative

The imperative is the command form of the verb—the form used to give orders.

Recall that in French, as in English, verbs have **tenses** and **moods.**

Past, present, and future are **tenses**. Tenses tell you where an action is located in the stream of time: "you **went**" (past), "she's **going**" (present), "I'll **go**" (future).

The imperative is a **mood**. The indicative and the infinitive are also moods. Moods tell you what the purpose of the utterance is—for instance, to make a statement ("she's going," **indicative**), to speak in generalities ("to go or not to go, that is the question," **infinitive**), or to give a command: ("Go!", **imperative**).

Note that subject pronouns are **not** used in an imperative.

For the majority of verbs the forms of the imperative are pronounced in exactly the same way as the corresponding forms of the indicative. Practically speaking, then, if you know a form of the imperative you know its counterpart in the indicative, and vice versa. (There is one minor difference and it concerns only writing: the second person singular of the indicative of verbs in *-er* is spelled with a final *-s* (*tu écoute***s**, *tu va***s**), while in the imperative there is no *-s* (*Ecoute!, Va!*).

• In exercises 5.20 and 5.21, you will hear someone suggesting various activities. Change each suggestion into a firm command, using the imperative of each infinitive you hear, as in the examples.

Audio cues (for reference):

5.20 Activation orale: Impératif, 2ème personne du singulier

1. Toi, tu vas inventer une histoire.
2. Toi, tu vas écouter.
3. Toi, tu vas parler français.
4. Toi, tu vas continuer l'exercice.
5. Toi, tu vas proposer une histoire.
6. Toi, tu vas aller à la bibli.
7. Toi, tu vas aller à la cité.

5.21 Activation orale: Impératif, 1ère personne du pluriel

1. Nous allons inventer une histoire.
2. Nous allons parler français.
3. Nous allons répéter ensemble.
4. Nous allons continuer l'invention de l'histoire.
5. Nous allons écouter le professeur.
6. Nous allons aller au restau-U.
7. Nous allons proposer une histoire.

• In 5.22, you will hear someone giving permission to do various things. Change each statement into a command, using the imperative.

5.23-5.25 Observation and activation: *Il faut* + infinitives

The expression *il faut* plus a verb in the infinitive is used to indicate obligation or necessity.

You have just been working with the imperative, which is a **personal** way of expressing necessity or obligation: people use it to tell each other what to do. The phrase *il faut* is an **impersonal** expression used to express necessity without specifying the person or situation that imposes that necessity. If you say, "Get started!" or "Let's get started!", you are calling the shots; the necessity originates with you. If you say, "We've got to get started!", you are simply the spokesperson for a necessity that originates elsewhere. This is the distinction in French between "Commence!/ Commencez!/Commençons!" and "Il faut commencer."

Notice that the expression *il faut* does not change, no matter whom you are addressing. The *il* of *il faut* is an impersonal pronoun, much like the *it* of *it's raining* in English.

• In exercise 5.24, various actions are characterized as necessary; respond by calling for action with an imperative, as in the example.

Audio cues (for reference):
5.24 Activation orale: L'impératif (révision)

1. Il faut commencer.
2. Il faut parler français.
3. Il faut écouter.
4. Il faut travailler.
5. Il faut inventer une histoire.
6. Il faut essayer.
7. Il faut discuter.
8. Il faut espérer.

• In 5.25, the process is reversed: you hear calls for action, and you respond by agreeing to act since it's necessary, using *il faut* and an infinitive.

Audio cues (for reference):
5.25 Activation orale: Il faut + infinitif

1. Continuons.
2. Essayons.
3. Travaillons.
4. Allons à la fac.
5. Parlons français.
6. Ecoutons.
7. Apprenons le français.
8. Choisissons des prénoms.

5.26-5.28 Observation and activation: Negation with *ne . . . pas*

You saw how to recognize negative expressions in lesson 2 (2.19, 2.20). The most frequent negative expression in French is *ne . . . pas*. Its two parts surround the verb: *ça* **ne** *va* **pas**. Notice that *ne* is written *n'* when it occurs before a vowel sound: *nous* **n'***avons pas de frères*. (This is yet another instance of **elision**.)

In everyday spoken French the *ne* is often omitted. You will hear "Ça va pas" instead of "Ça ne va pas," for instance. In writing, however, the *ne* is always present, unless the written form is intended to be an illustration of what colloquial speech actually sounds like (as in writing "I dunno" for "I don't know" in English).

• Exercise 5.27 will give you practice in distinguishing between negative and affirmative statements. For each sentence you hear, mark a box on the *oui* line if it is affirmative, on the *non* line if it is negative. Listen for the telltale presence of *ne . . . pas*.

√ Check your answers in key 5.27 at the back of the workbook.

• Exercise 5.28 will give you practice making negative statements. Answer no to the questions you hear, using *ne* in front of the verb and *pas* after it.

Audio cues (for reference):
5.28 Activation orale: Négation; ne...pas

1. Ça va?
2. C'est amusant?
3. C'est facile?
4. C'est un joli prénom?
5. Il est marié?
6. Il est divorcé?
7. Il est riche?
8. Il est ingénieur?
9. Il travaille?
10. Il aime ça?
11. Vous parlez français?
12. Vous êtes français?

5.29, 5.30 Observation and activation: Negative of *un, des*

You saw in lesson 3 that nouns can be preceded by the indefinite articles *un, une* in the singular, *des* in the plural (3.13). In **negative** expressions like the ones in lesson 5, *un, une,* and *des* are each replaced by *pas de:* "je n'ai **pas de** frère." (Before a vowel sound, the *de* is written *d':* "il n'a **pas d'**enfants"—a further example of elision.)

• The point of exercise 5.30 is to give you practice in making negative answers, specifically in using *pas de* in negative phrases. Answer no to the questions you hear, replacing the *un*, *une*, or *des* in the question with *pas de* (*pas d'* in front of a vowel sound). Don't forget to place a *ne* in front of the verb.

Audio cues (for reference):
5.30 Activation orale: Un, des et négation

1. Vous avez des enfants?
2. Est-ce que Robert a un frère?
3. Est-ce que Robert a une soeur?
4. Est-ce que Robert a des enfants?
5. Vous avez un chien?
6. Vous avez des amis japonais?
7. Vous avez des complexes?

5.31 Activation: Dialogue between Mireille and Jean-Michel

Listen to the dialogue between Mireille and Jean-Michel. Memorize Jean-Michel's lines, imitating and repeating until you can answer Mireille yourself.

TOWARD FREE EXPRESSION

5.32 Words at large

The two questions and the open-ended statement you see in the workbook can be completed in a variety of ways using words and phrases you have learned in lesson 5. A number of alternatives are given in the workbook to get you started. By coming up with others and combining them in various ways you can create an almost endless supply of possibilities.

Give as many answers to each question—out loud—as you can. If you work with a partner, have a contest to see who can find the most examples. Limit yourselves, however, to expressions you have seen in lessons 2-5. In case of doubt about a particular item, check to see if you can find an example in the lessons that justifies including it on your list.

5.33, 5.34 Role-playing and reinvention of the story

Exercise 5.33 is in four parts. In A and B, choose your favorites among the men's and women's first names listed. In C, pick out the names that can be both French and American, that you find easiest to pronounce, that you think are prettiest.

In D, make up a dialogue between you and someone else (character X), using the elements provided in the workbook as a starting point. Don't limit yourself to what you find in the workbook, however. You may draw from all the material in lessons 2-5 as long as you feel sure you are using it correctly. Section 5.34 of the audio program contains a sample dialogue for you to listen to before embarking on your own version.

Do each part of the exercise orally. If you work with a partner in the dialogue, take parts, complete the exercise, then switch roles and do it again. If you work by yourself, imagine and play both parts.

• **Suggested written assignment.** Write a version of the reinvention exercise in part D of 5.33. Write one sentence for each of the exchanges between you and X, selecting among the options given in the workbook. Send this assignment to your instructor along with summary quiz 5. (Consult the course syllabus for details.)

DOCUMENT

At the end of lesson 5 in the textbook you will find a brief poem by Jacques Prévert for reading practice.

Prévert (1900-1977), a poet who also wrote cabaret songs and scenarios for films and animated cartoons, delighted in playing with words. In this excerpt from "Dans ma maison" (published in *Paroles* in 1946), Prévert toys with the most interesting words of all—people's names. The names of two of the most famous figures in French history—the writer Victor-Marie Hugo and the general, later emperor, Napoleon Bonaparte—strike Prévert as especially odd. There is a curious ambiguity and lack of logic in them. Do names influence the character or destiny of the people who carry them? How do they get chosen in the first place?

SELF-TESTING EXERCISES

• In 5.35, listen to the recording and write the numbers you hear in figures in the spaces provided in the workbook.

• In 5.36, complete the sentences you see with the missing forms of *avoir*.

• In 5.37, write the imperative that corresponds to each infinitive you see, as in the example.

• In 5.38, give negative answers to the questions you see, remembering that *un, une,* and *des* become *pas de* in negative sentences.

√ Check your answers in keys 5.35, 5.36, and 5.37 at the back of the workbook. If you have made errors, follow the references at the end of each exercise to sections of the workbook and audio program for review.

SUMMARY QUIZ

A summary quiz for lesson 5 can be found at the back of this guide. Consult the course syllabus or check with your instructor for information about completing it and handing it in.

LESSON 6
Portraits I

The story

What should Mireille look like? We've already determined her name and that she's a young French woman. Now we further decide that she will be neither a giant nor a midget but relatively petite, perhaps even fragile-looking, although that is deceptive since she is strong and healthy. (Of course! Remember that her mother works at the Ministry of Health.) Active in sports that range from tiddlywinks to the decathlon, Mireille is slender, has a long graceful neck and a narrow waist. She also has long legs and fingers.

Now for the face. Round? No. Long? No. What about oval? And in spite of Mr. Wiseguy's preference for brunettes and redheads, we'll give her long, blonde hair. Her eyes, both of them, will be blue. A matched pair does indeed appear more desirable than any assortment, and blue definitely beats red.

We'll want her mind to be lively and quick. In cameo appearances, her parents confirm these exemplary traits, although her mother and her younger sister do find one or two flaws. . . .

Content and learning objectives of lesson 6

This lesson shows how French speakers describe themselves and others, express the distinction between appearances and reality, talk about sports, ask questions requiring a "yes" or "no" answer, and say numbers from 20 to 69.

The following points are highlighted in lesson 6 (you should concentrate on sections marked with a √):

√• Masculine and feminine forms (6.9-6.16)
• *Avoir l'air* versus *être* with adjectives
√• *Faire*, present indicative (6.19)
√• *Faire* and sports (6.17, 6.20, 6.21)
• *Du, de la, de l'/pas de, pas d'*
• Questions with *est-ce que*
√• Numbers from 20 to 69 (6.24, 6.25)

ASSIMILATION OF THE TEXT

6.1 Text work-up

You should begin the *mise en oeuvre* as soon as possible after you have viewed the video program for lesson 6. Repeat and answer as usual.

6.2, 6.3 Aural comprehension and oral production

• In 6.2, look at the photograph of Mireille in your workbook as you listen to the sentences on the audio recording. You will hear pairs of opposite descriptions. One sentence in each pair describes Mireille accurately; the other does not. Repeat the sentence that does apply to Mireille; you will hear the correct answer for confirmation.

• In 6.3, you will hear sentences describing one of Mireille's cousins who just happens to be her exact opposite. After each sentence describing the cousin, give the contrasting description that corresponds to Mireille.

THE "TEXT" AND THE TEXTBOOK

Work with the text and illustrations in the textbook, as in previous lessons.

TOWARD COMMUNICATION

6.4, 6.5 Pronunciation: The vowel /y/

The French sound /y/ (as in *salut* and *tu*) has no counterpart in English. Consequently, you may find you have trouble hearing it accurately at first. As you listen to the words and phrases in 6.4, notice how the vowel sound represented by *-u-* in the French *sal***u***t*, *am***u***sant*, *exc***u***se-moi*, and *b***u***s* differs from the vowel sounds represented by *-u-* in the English *salute*, *amusing*, *excuse me*, and *bus*.

The French /y/ is no harder to pronounce than any other sound, but since /y/ does not exist in English, it takes some experimenting to find the right position of tongue and lips to produce it.

In French, /y/ is produced in the very front of the mouth. It takes a combination of tightly rounded lips and very forward tongue to make it. To find the right position, begin by running the tip of your tongue over the inner edge of your lower teeth. When you have found the edge, let the tip of your tongue rest almost against it. Then, freezing your tongue where it is, pucker your lips tightly, as if you were about kiss someone. **Do not allow your tongue to budge.** You will see that your lips are tightly rounded, tense and slightly protruding, that the airspace between them is very narrow, and that your tongue is in the very front of your mouth, almost blocking off the space between your teeth. Then, without letting anything change position, make a sound. Chances are it will be /y/.

Note. The kiss you start with should be a very tight pucker. A French kiss, despite its name, is of no use as a starting point for pronouncing a French /y/.

• Take a few moments to practice the sound and get used to its feel. Then repeat the expressions you hear in 6.5 until you feel familiar with the sound.

6.6-6.8 Observation and activation: Being and appearance: ***avoir l'air/être***

In describing people and things, French speakers distinguish (as English speakers do) between what appears to them to be true ("he **looks** nice") and what they think really is true ("he **is** nice"). Appearances can be expressed in French by *avoir l'air* used with an adjective. Actual fact can be expressed by the verb *être* and an adjective.

When used with *être*, the adjective describes the person, so it will be masculine or feminine according to the individual it describes ("**elle** est gentill**e**"). When used with *avoir l'air*, the adjective describes the person's appearance (*air*) rather than the person, and so is masculine, since *air* is a masculine noun ("elle a l'**air** gentil"). (This distinction, while generally observed, is not absolute, and so you may occasionally come across an expression like "**elle** a l'air gentill**e**," where *gentille* agrees with *elle*.)

• In 6.7, you will hear someone say that various people, pets, and things look one way or another. Confirm these statements by saying that that's the way they really are, using *être* and the adjective you hear. Remember that with *être* the form of the adjective will be masculine **or** feminine depending on the person or thing described.

Audio cues (for reference):
6.7 Activation orale: Avoir l'air/être

1. Mireille a l'air gentil.
2. Vous avez l'air fatigué.
3. Mireille a l'air malade.
4. Fido a l'air méchant.
5. Les jeunes gens ont l'air sportif.
6. Le professeur a l'air jeune.
7. Les comédies italiennes ont l'air amusantes.
8. La leçon a l'air facile.

• In 6.8, you will again hear people and pets described in terms of appearances. But appearances can be deceptive. Set the speaker straight by pointing out that these individuals are not at all the way they look, using *être* in negative sentences. Again, remember that the form of the adjective will be masculine **or** feminine depending on who or what is being described.

Audio cues (for reference):
6.8 Activation orale: Avoir l'air/être et négation

1. Mireille a l'air gentil.
2. Vous avez l'air fatigué.
3. Elle a l'air fragile.
4. Les jeunes gens ont l'air sportif.
5. Elle a l'air fatigué.
6. Il a l'air méchant.
7. Vous avez l'air malade.
8. Fido a l'air méchant.

6.9-6.11 Observation and activation: Masculine/feminine

You saw in lesson 4 that adjectives are often a reliable way to tell whether the noun they accompany is masculine or feminine, since the masculine and feminine forms of a great many adjectives look and sound different. The charts in 6.9 illustrate these differences in several groups of adjectives.

All the adjectives in these groups have the same characteristic: in speech, there is a consonant sound in the feminine that is not heard in the masculine. The letter that corresponds to the consonant sound of the feminine is present in the **written** form of the masculine (*peti*t, *épai*s), but it is **not pronounced**. (Recall that many words in French are written with consonant letters at the end that are not pronounced.)

In the case of adjectives that end in *-f* like *vi*f, the *-f* of the masculine form **is** pronounced, but the consonant sound in the feminine is different: /v/ (*vi*ve).

Notice that all the feminine forms given here are written with an *-e* at the end. This final *-e* is a very common ending for feminine words in French.

• In 6.10 and 6.11, decide whether the sentences you hear refer to masculine or feminine nouns, and check the appropriate box on the grid in your workbook. Pay close attention to the adjective in each sentence: its ending contains all the information you need.

√ Check your answers in keys 6.10 and 6.11 at the back of the workbook.

6.12, 6.13 Observation and activation: Masculine/feminine

In certain adjectives, there is no difference at all between the masculine and feminine forms, either in sound or in writing. Chart 6.12 contains examples of this group of adjectives.

• Exercise 6.13 gives you practice in distinguishing between masculine and feminine forms, and in switching from one to the other. You will hear sentences that describe either a man or a woman. Take each description and make it apply to the opposite sex, replacing *il* with *elle* and masculine forms with with feminine forms, and vice versa.

Audio cues (for reference):
6.13 Activation orale: Masculin/féminin

1. Il est un peu fort.
2. Elle est malade.
3. Elle est très grande.
4. Il est solide.
5. Il est rapide.
6. Elle est rousse.
7. Il est très sportif.
8. Elle est assez vive.
9. Elle est fragile.
10. Elle est raisonnable.
11. Il est blond.
12. Elle est petite.
13. Il est sympathique.

6.14-6.16 Observation and activation: Adjectives and personal description

You have seen the verb *être* used with an adjective to refer to general qualities ("Mireille est **mince,**" "elle est **vive**"). If, however, you want to point to some more specific physical or moral feature, you can use the verb *avoir* and name the feature in question, in addition to describing it with an adjective: "Elle a **la taille mince,**" "elle a **l'esprit vif.**" Chart 6.14 illustrates these two basic ways of describing people. Notice that in this kind of description the **definite article** is used: "Elle a **les** cheveux blonds."

Chart 6.15 presents an exception to the general rule of agreement in French. Most adjectives are singular or plural, masculine or feminine depending on the noun they describe. This is not true of the adjective *marron*; it has only one form, which never changes.

• In exercise 6.16, read each sentence carefully and fill in the missing adjective. Two factors should guide your choice. The form of the adjective you select will of course depend on who is being described (*Mireille, le jeune Américain, il, elle*). But the choice of adjective will depend upon the context of the sentence. For example, if you see *aussi,* a parallel is being drawn between two people, and you will want to use a different form of the **same** adjective ("Robert est grand. Mireille est <u>grande</u> aussi"). Alternatively, if you see *au contraire*, a distinction is being drawn, and you will want to look for an adjective that describes the **opposite** feature ("Est-ce que Mireille va être grande ou, au contraire, est-ce qu'elle va être petite ?").

√ Check your answers in key 6.16 at the back of the workbook.

6.17-6.21 Observation and activation: *Faire* and sports

Faire is commonly used in French to say one plays a certain sport. Chart 6.17 shows the distinction between ways of talking about sports with *faire* and with verbs that simply indicate an attitude ("I love soccer," "I hate skiing," and so forth). With verbs of attitude like *aimer, adorer, détester,* and the like a definite article precedes the name of the sport. With *faire,* however, another kind of article is used.

In positive expressions with *faire* and sports, the articles used are *du, de la,* or *de l',* depending on the gender of the noun (**le** *ski* ⇒ **du** *ski,* **la** *voile* ⇒ **de la** *voile*) and whether or not it begins with a vowel sound (**l'** escalade ⇒ **de l'***escalade*). In negative expressions, however, as chart 6.18 demonstrates, these three forms are replaced by a single one: **de** (**d'** before vowel sounds).

Chart 6.19 gives the conjugation of *faire.* Note that the three singular forms are pronounced in exactly the same way. Notice that the *-ai-* of the *nous* form, *faisons*, is pronounced like the *-e* of *j***e** or *l***e**. The *-s-* is pronounced /z/.

• In exercise 6.20, you will find out that various people do or do not like certain sports. Add that they do or don't play those sports, using appropriate forms of *faire* and the article *du, de la, de l'* in positive expressions, or *pas de* (*pas d'*) in negative ones.

Audio cues (for reference):
6.20 Activation orale: Faire du sport

1. J'aime le ski.
2. Les soeurs de Mireille adorent la natation.
3. Mireille n'aime pas la natation.
4. Mireille aime le karaté.
5. Robert n'aime pas la voile.
6. Nous aimons l'alpinisme.
7. Vous aimez l'escalade?
8. J'adore la moto.
9. Le père de Mireille n'aime pas le tennis.
10. Les soeurs de Mireille aiment la planche à voile.
11. Robert aime le canoë.
12. La mère de Mireille n'aime pas le sport.
13. Robert aime l'aviron.

• In the writing exercise in 6.21, supply the missing words according to the context of each the sentence. Remember that *faire* on the one hand, and attitude verbs like *aimer* and *adorer* on the other, are followed by different articles.

√ Check your answers in key 6.21 at the back of the workbook.

6.22, 6.23 Observation and activation: Questions; *est-ce que*

There are a number of ways to ask questions in French. You saw in lesson 2 that one of the simplest is to let your voice rise in pitch at the end of a statement. Another, nearly as simple, is to use the expression *est-ce que* in front of a statement, adding the rising pitch in the voice at the end. (*Est-ce que* becomes *est-ce qu'* when used with a word beginning with a vowel sound.)

• In exercise 6.23, you will hear a series of statements. Change them into questions using *est-ce que*, as in the example.

Audio cues (for reference):
6.23 Activation orale: Interrogation; est-ce que

1. Elle est malade.
2. Robert est américain.
3. Il est fils unique.
4. Les parents de Robert ont de l'argent.
5. Ils sont divorcés.
6. La mère de Robert est remariée.
7. Robert va avoir des complexes.

6.24, 6.25 Observation and activation: Numbers from 20 to 69

Numbers from 20 to 69 in French follow a consistent pattern, as chart 6.23 demonstrates. Each multiple of ten is a single word (*vingt*, *trente*, etc.), and all other numbers are compound words formed by adding *un*, *deux*, *trois*, and so forth to the multiple of ten. *Un* is linked by *et* (*trente* **et** *un*, *quarante* **et** *un*), and all other numbers are linked with a hyphen (*vingt-deux*, *cinquante-neuf*).

You will recall from lesson 5 that the final *-t* of *vingt* is not pronounced when the number occurs by itself or at the end of a rhythmic group. This *-t* **is** pronounced when *vingt* is combined with other numbers (*vingt* /t/*et un*, *vingt*-/t/*quatre*, etc.).

• In exercise 6.25, look at the addition and multiplication problems in your workbook as you hear and complete them. You will hear the correct answer for each item.

Give yourself plenty of time with exercise 6.25, repeating it as often as necessary until you are familiar with the material. And be patient. Most learners find it disorienting at first to use numbers in a foreign language. In part this is so because numbers seem basic and easy, but aren't. The sums and multiplications in this exercise look simple until you realize that, although the math involved is child's play, the French is not. Each number has a name that is the equivalent of an individual vocabulary word, to be learned separately. Furthermore, since the figures used to write numbers are common to many languages, they never really **look** as foreign as the words of a foreign language. As a result, it is hard to think of them in anything but your native tongue. Long after native speakers of English have learned to say "Elle ne fait pas de ski" in perfect French when they see it written, their instinct when they see "52" is to say not *cinquante-deux* but *fifty-two*.

• **Suggested oral assignment.** Record a spoken version of the addition problems in phase 1 of 6.25. Say each sum as in the example ("trois et quatre, sept"). Send this assignment to your instructor on the same cassette you use for the oral production part of summary quiz 6. (See the course syllabus for details.)

6.26 Activation: Dialogue between M. and Mme Belleau

Listen to the conversation between M. and Mme Belleau and memorize Mme Belleau's lines, imitating and repeating as usual.

TOWARD FREE EXPRESSION

6.27 Words at large

Read the question in 6.27 and the dozen possible answers given in the workbook. You should be able to find ten more responses without difficulty. Say your answers out loud. If you work with a partner, go back and forth and see how long you can keep the alternatives coming.

6.28-6.30 Role-playing and reinvention of the story

In 6.28, describe a person you would like to see in the story, using the alternatives listed in the workbook as a starting point and drawing from all the material you have seen in lessons 2-6. Section 6.29 of the audio program contains a sample dialogue; listen to it before creating your own version.

In 6.30, imagine you are a famous person being interviewed by a journalist (or that you are a journalist interviewing a famous person). Conduct your interview out loud, using the suggestions in the workbook as a point of departure. If you work with a partner, take parts and complete the exercise, then switch roles and do it again. If you work by yourself, take both roles.

DOCUMENT

At the end of lesson 6 in the textbook you will find a short poem by Boris Vian and a quotation for reading practice.

Vian (1920-1959) is best known as a novelist whose books combine humor, fantasy, and tenderness, but he was also an amateur trumpet-player and an ardent fan of American jazz who liked to jam with bands in the nightclubs of Saint-Germain-des-Prés. He wrote songs as well. In this little lyric, he asserts that whether one is a blonde, a brunette, or a redhead, each has its own advantages.

As the title of her famous book *Gentlemen Prefer Blondes* suggests, Anita Loos might have disagreed with Vian.

SELF-TESTING EXERCISES

- Complete and check exercises 6.31-6.33 as usual.

SUMMARY QUIZ

Consult the course syllabus or check with your instructor for information about completing and handing in summary quiz 6.

LESSON 7
Portraits II

The story

Now that we have discussed Mireille, it's Robert's turn. What should he look like? Let's say he's solid. No, Mr. Wiseguy, not fat! Robert is of medium height, and slim. He's slightly taller than Mireille; consequently, Mireille is slightly shorter than he. That sounds reasonable. Like Mireille, Robert is very active in sports. Though slim, he is broad-shouldered. He has a square chin, dark hair, and dark eyebrows. No moustache. No beard. (That's fine with Robert; beards itch!) His eyes, finally, are brown.

Mr. Wiseguy prefers a Robert who's dim, but we're going to make him smart; a little less quick than Mireille, perhaps, but bright nonetheless. He's sociable and less sarcastic than she; he's calmer, more tolerant.

These two are quite different. What will happen when they meet? Mutual but reserved attraction? Passion at first sight? Indifference? Violent dislike? Stay tuned. All things are possible.

Content and learning objectives of lesson 7

This lesson shows how French speakers say numbers from 70 to 100, and how they describe people and things and ask for information about them. It will also familiarize you with a new way of asking questions that can be answered "yes" or "no."

The following points are highlighted in lesson 7 (you should concentrate on sections marked with a √):

√ • Numbers from 70 to 100 (7.7-7.9)
- Masculine and feminine endings, review and extension

√ • Questions using intonation, inversion, and *est-ce que* (7.20-7.25)
- *Qu'est-ce que c'est?*, *qui est-ce que c'est?*
- Questions with *qu'est-ce que . . . ?*, *qui est-ce qui . . . ?*

ASSIMILATION OF THE TEXT

7.1-7.4 Text work-up, aural comprehension, and oral production

• Proceed as usual in sections 7.1-7.4. (Refer to lesson 3.1-3.3 and lesson 4.3 for directions, if necessary.) Then work with the text and illustrations in the textbook, as in previous lessons.

TOWARD COMMUNICATION

7.5, 7.6 Observation and activation: Pronunciation; *é* and *è*

These sections present the distinction between two important vowel sounds in French, both contained in *préfère:* the vowel sound represented by *é* (*pr***é***fère*), and the vowel sound represented by *è* (*préf***è***re*).

The vowel sound of *é* is called a **closed** vowel sound, since to pronounce it the tongue must be higher in the mouth, closing off the space in the front of the mouth. Similarly, *è* is referred to as an **open** vowel sound because the tongue is a little lower in the mouth, and the space in the front of the mouth is more open. (As you lower your tongue, you lower your jaw slightly as well.)

Syllables, too, are said to be **closed** or **open**, although for different reasons. For example, the first syllable of *préfère*, *pré-*, is considered open because it ends in a vowel sound; the second syllable, *-fère*, is considered closed because it ends in a consonant sound, which **closes off** the stream of air coming from the mouth.

The **closed** vowel sound of *é* is written here as an *e* with an acute accent (´), *e accent aigu*, and the **open** vowel of *è* by an *e* with a grave accent (`), *e accent grave*. But there are other ways to write these two sounds, as section 7.6 shows.

• Listen to the examples of words with *é* and *è* given in the first part of 7.6 and repeat them, noting the different positions of your tongue for the **closed** and the **open** vowel sound. In the second part of the exercise you will see different ways of writing these two contrasting sounds; look at the words in your workbook as you repeat them.

7.7-7.9 Observation and activation: Numbers from 70 to 100

You saw in lesson 6 that, from 20 to 69, the names for numbers in French follow a regular progression: each multiple of 10 from twenty to sixty is a different word (*vingt, trente, quarante, cinquante*); all other numbers are compound words formed by adding *un*, *deux*, *trois*, and so forth up to *neuf* to the multiple of ten. *Un* is linked by *et* (*trente* **et** *un*, *quarante* **et** *un*), and *deux* through *neuf* are linked with a hyphen (*vingt-deux*, *cinquante-neuf*).

Beginning with sixty, there is a peculiarity. The basic name given to each multiple of ten changes not every ten digits, as it had from ten to sixty, but every twenty digits. *Quarante* and *cinquante* appear in only ten numbers, but *soixante* and *quatre-vingt* cover twenty numbers each. In other words, the basic form *soixante* is used for each of the twenty numbers from sixty to seventy-nine; the basic form *quatre-vingt* is present in each of the twenty numbers from eighty to ninety-nine.

Each new number within the group is formed by adding 1 to 19 to the basic word: 61 = 60 + 1 (*soixante et* **un**), 70 = 60 + **10** (*soixante*-**dix**), 71 = 60 + **11** (*soixante et* **onze**), 72 = 60 + **12** (*soixante*-**douze**) . . . 78 = 60 + **18** (*soixante*-**dix-huit**), and so forth. Notice that *onze* behaves like *un:* both are linked by *et*.

Apart from this, the system works as it did for 20 to 60, with the exception that the +1 and +11 numbers in the *quatre-vingt* series are **not** combined forms with *et un* or *et onze*, as one would expect. The *et* is replaced by a hyphen: *quatre-vingt-un, quatre-vingt-onze*. Notice that the *t* of *vingt* is **not** pronounced here.

Finally, *quatre-vingts* (which is already a multiple of *vingt*) and multiples of *cent* are written with a final *-s*, **except** when they are followed by another number: *deux cent***s**, but *deux cent quarante*.

• Exercise 7.8 on addresses and exercise 7.9 on ages give you practice in identifying numbers from 10 to 100. In each exercise, listen and write the figures that correspond to the numbers you hear.

√ Check your answers in keys 7.8 and 7.9 at the back of the workbook.

7.10-7.12 Observation and activation: Masculine/feminine

In lesson 6 you saw a series of words whose feminine forms differed from the masculine forms by having a consonant sound that was not present in the masculine (*petite* versus *petit*, *épaisse* versus *épais*). Chart 7.10 reintroduces a variation on that pattern that you encountered in lesson 4: words whose masculine forms end in a nasal vowel, and whose feminine forms end in the same vowel in its **oral** (nonnasal) form followed by the consonant sound /n/. (If you need a reminder of what nasal and oral vowel sounds are, review 4.6 and 4.7.)

In *bon, brun, africain,* there is **no** /n/ sound at the end; each word ends in a nasal **vowel**. In *bonne, brune, africaine,* there is an /n/ sound at the end, and the vowel that precedes it is oral, not nasal.

• Exercise 7.11 will give you practice in detecting whether a word is masculine or feminine. Listen for a nasal vowel at the end of the word (which indicates the word is masculine), or an oral vowel + /n/ (indicating it is feminine). Mark the appropriate space on the grid in your workbook.

√ Check your answers in key 7.11 in the workbook.

• Exercise 7.12 will give you practice in producing masculine and feminine forms. You will hear a series of sentences about male persons. Make each sentence apply to the corresponding female person, replacing masculine forms that end in nasal vowels with feminine forms that end in oral vowels + /n/. Don't forget to change all other masculine words into the equivalent feminine forms as well.

Audio cues (for reference):
7.12 Activation orale: Formes masculines et féminines.

1. Le père est américain.
2. J'ai un cousin.
3. Il est canadien.
4. C'est un Indien.
5. Il est bon.
6. J'ai un frère tunisien.
7. Il est brun.
8. Il est très fin.
9. Le père est algérien.

7.13-7.15 Observation and activation: Masculine/feminine

Here are further examples of masculine and feminine forms in which there is a final consonant sound present in the feminine that is absent in the masculine.

In the examples in chart 7.13, the final consonant of the feminine is reflected in the written form of the masculine (with a slight variation in *blanc, blanche*), although of course it is **not pronounced**.

The three examples in chart 7.14 have the same consonant sound in the feminine: /z/, written *-se*. The corresponding masculine forms, however, each have a different ending.

• Exercise 7.15 will give you practice in producing masculine forms. Robert and Mireille are now identical twins. You will hear a series of sentences about Mireille; make each sentence apply to Robert. Essentially this means dropping the consonant sound at the end of feminine adjectives to produce the masculine form. Remember, however, that *moqueuse* does not work in quite the same way. And don't forget the oral/nasal vowel change in the case of *brune*.

Audio cues (for reference):
7.15 Activation orale: Formes masculines et féminines

1. Mireille va être petite.
2. Mireille va être grande.
3. Mireille va être grosse.
4. Mireille va être rousse.
5. Mireille va être brune.
6. Mireille va être blonde.
7. Mireille va être intelligente.
8. Mireille va être idiote.
9. Mireille va être sérieuse.
10. Mireille va être moqueuse.
11. Mireille va être méchante.

7.16–7.19 Observation and activation: Masculine/feminine

Charts 7.16 and 7.17 add new examples to a category of masculine/feminine forms you first encountered in lesson 6: words in which the feminine and masculine forms are pronounced the same way.

In chart 7.16, this identical pronunciation is reflected in identical spelling.

In chart 7.17, the feminine forms given are indistinguishable in pronunciation from the masculine forms, but there is a difference in spelling: the feminine forms are written with an *-e* at the end.

• In exercise 7.18, you will see a series of complete sentences describing one of our two main characters, followed by incomplete sentences describing the other in the same way. Fill in the incomplete sentences with the appropriate masculine or feminine forms. Note that *patineur*, *skieur*, *nageur*, and *voyageur* all work like *moqueur*. Remember, too, that adjectives agree in gender and number with the nouns they modify.

• In the dictation exercise in 7.19, listen and write the missing words, looking for evidence in the sentence that the form you need is masculine or feminine, singular or plural.

√ Check your answers in keys 7.18 and 7.19.

7.20, 7.21 Observation and activation: Questions

Chart 7.20 illustrates three ways of asking a yes-or-no question in French:

(1) by tone of voice (**intonation**) alone: any statement can be made into a question if the voice is made to rise in pitch at the end;

(2) with **est-ce que**: any statement becomes a question when preceded by *est-ce que*, and accompanied by a rise in the pitch of the voice at the end;

(3) through **inversion**: the subject pronoun, which normally comes **before** the verb, is placed **after** it, and the voice rises in pitch.

These three forms are equally good ways of asking questions. The difference among them is that they correspond to different **levels** of speech. Inversion reflects a higher level of speech than the other two; French speakers who ask questions using inversion are making a conscious effort to speak in a polished, elegant way. In everyday speech, the most common way of asking a question is through intonation. The second most common is by using *est-ce que*. Inversion is not used in familiar speech except in certain very frequent, ready-made expressions, such as "Comment vas-tu?" and "Quelle heure est-il?"

• The purpose of exercise 7.21 is to give you practice in recognizing the telltale rise in pitch at the end of a sentence, indicating a question. Listen carefully and determine whether the sentences you hear are declarative (that is, statements) or interrogative (questions). Then mark the appropriate space on the grid in your workbook.

√ Check your answers in key 7.21 at the back of the workbook.

7.22-7.25 Observation and activation: Questions with inversion

As chart 7.22 illustrates, to form a question by inversion the subject pronoun is placed after the verb, and the two are linked by a hyphen.

When the subject of the question is a proper name (*Robert*) or a noun (*la jeune fille*), it is left in position in front of the verb, and the corresponding subject pronoun is added after the verb.

Notice that since the third person subject pronouns (*il, elle, ils, elles*) begin with a vowel sound, when the verb ends in a consonant sound there will be **liaison**. The consonant sound of the verb will be linked in pronunciation to the vowel sound of the pronoun: *est-*/t/*il . . . ?*, *fait-*/t/*elle . . . ?*

Some very common verbs do not end in consonants in the third person forms, as chart 7.24 shows. Under these circumstances, a *-t* is added between the verb and the pronoun, connected by hyphens on either side.

• Exercise 7.23 will give you practice in using inversion questions. You will hear a series of questions with *est-ce que;* change them into inversion questions, placing the proper subject pronoun after the verb. Don't forget to pronounce the *liaison* where appropriate.

Audio cues (for reference):
7.23 Activation orale: Interrogation et inversion

1. Est-ce que Robert est sportif?
2. Est-ce que Robert est un garçon solide?
3. Est-ce que la mère de Robert est mariée?
4. Est-ce que les parents de Robert sont riches?
5. Est-ce qu'ils ont de l'argent?
6. Est-ce que vous avez des amis?
7. Est-ce que vous êtes américain?
8. Est-ce que vous êtes marié?
9. Est-ce que vous avez des enfants?

• Exercise 7.25 will help you form inversion questions using verbs that add the extra *-t*. You will again hear a series of questions with *est-ce que*, to be changed into inversion questions. Be sure to pronounce a clear /t/ sound between the verb and the subject pronoun.

Audio cues (for reference):
7.25 Activation orale: Interrogation et inversion

1. Est-ce que Robert parle français?
2. Est-ce qu'il parle beaucoup?
3. Est-ce qu'il pèse 80 kilos?
4. Est-ce qu'il a les cheveux noirs?
5. Est-ce qu'il a l'esprit vif?
6. Est-ce qu'il a l'esprit aussi vif que Mireille?
7. Est-ce que Mireille a les cheveux blonds?
8. Est-ce que Robert préfère les blondes?

7.26, 7.27 Observation and activation: Questions; *qu'est-ce que c'est?* and *qui est-ce que c'est?*

Chart 7.26 illustrates ways of asking about the identity of things and persons:

Qu'*est-ce que c'est?* is used to ask the nature of an unknown **thing**.

Qui *est-ce que c'est?* is used to ask the identity of an unknown **person**.

• Exercise 7.27 will give you practice in distinguishing between *qu'est-ce que c'est* and *qui est-ce que c'est*. You will hear a number of questions. Two possible answers to each question, labeled *a.* and *b.*, are listed in the workbook. Choose the most appropriate answer by circling *a.* or *b.*

√ Check your answers in key 7.27 at the back of the workbook.

7.28–7.30 Observation and activation: Questions; *qu'est-ce que* and *qui est-ce qui*

Qu'est-ce que . . . ? and *qui est-ce qui . . . ?* ask for further information about a situation that is already familiar to the questioner.

The answer to a question with *qu'est-ce que . . . ?* is a **thing** that is the **object** of the verb.

The answer to a question with *qui est-ce qui . . . ?* is a **person** who is the **subject** of the verb.

• Exercise 7.29 will give you practice in producing questions with *qu'est-ce que.* You will hear a series of statements about things. Ask a question using *qu'est-ce que* to which the statement you just heard is the answer.

Audio cues (for reference):
7.29 Activation orale: Qu'est-ce que...?

1. Nous allons apprendre le français.
2. Ça va être un jeu.
3. Nous allons inventer une histoire.
4. Le jeune homme va être américain.
5. La jeune fille va être française.
6. Les jeunes gens vont avoir des amis.
7. Le jeune homme va faire du sport.
8. Il va peser 70 kilos.

• In 7.30, you have an opportunity to practice using *qui est-ce qui* to ask who is doing various things. You will hear a series of statements about people. Ask a question using *qui est-ce qui* to which the statement you just heard is the answer.

Audio cues (for reference):
7.30 Activation orale: Qui est-ce qui...?

1. Je vais proposer une histoire.
2. Vous allez discuter l'histoire.
3. Les jeunes gens vont avoir des aventures.
4. Le jeune homme parle français.
5. La jeune fille est française.
6. La mère de Mireille travaille au Ministère de la Santé.
7. Le père de Robert a de l'argent.

7.31 Activation: Dialogue between Hubert and Mireille

Listen to the conversation between Hubert and Mireille and memorize Mireille's lines, imitating and repeating as usual.

TOWARD FREE EXPRESSION

7.32 Words at large

Proceed as usual. (If necessary, refer to lesson 3 for directions.)

7.33-7.35 Role-playing and reinvention of the story

In 7.33, imagine you have just met the perfect man or woman. Describe him or her to a friend.

In 7.34, describe a young (or old) man you have chosen for the story, using the alternatives listed in the workbook as a starting point and drawing on all the material you have seen in lessons 2-7.

Work with a partner, if you can, and build your description together, out loud. If you do the exercise by yourself, you may want to pattern it after the dialogue with Fido in 7.35.

• **Suggested written assignment.** Write out a version of 7.33, the portrait of your ideal man or woman. Be sure to describe physical characteristics **and** character traits. Write six to eight sentences. Send this assignment to your instructor along with the answer sheet for summary quiz 7. (See the course syllabus for details.)

SELF-TESTING EXERCISES

• Complete and check exercises 7.36, 7.37, and 7.38 as usual.

SUMMARY QUIZ

Consult the course syllabus or check with your instructor for information about completing and handing in summary quiz 7.

LESSON 8
Genealogy

The story

To learn about Mireille's family, we turn to her family tree. Climbing about in its branches, we trace the line of her descent—a path strewn with aunts, uncles, cousins by the dozens, and so on.

Then the teacher gets Mireille's attention and persuades her to introduce her family, whom we find at their country home. All cooperate politely, except for Marie-Laure, Mireille's ten-year-old sister, who acts very much like a ten-year-old sister. A favorite of the Belleau children is Uncle Guillaume, a well-to-do bachelor who loves kids and is always giving them gifts. Aunt Georgette, who isn't so well-off, is unimpressed.

Marie-Laure, not without grumbling, brings in an album in which we see photos and birth announcements. Jean-Denis, Cécile's husband, likes a snapshot of cousin Sophie. Finally, when Mireille has taken us all the way back to her great-great-great-grandfather, Marie-Laure pulls out a picture of a prehistoric man and asks if we don't see a family resemblance to Mireille. This kid has possibilities!

Notes on culture and communication

• **A la guerre, en '40.** World War II began on September 1, 1939, when Nazi Germany invaded Poland, prompting France and Great Britain to declare war on Germany. The French were defeated in 1940. The northern half of France, including Paris, was occupied by German troops. An armistice was signed by Marshall Pétain, head of a new government installed in Vichy while resistance was being organized from London by General de Gaulle. The war ended in 1945.

Content and learning objectives of lesson 8

This lesson will familiarize you with ways of asking about the identity of people and things, and talking about kinship and family relationships. It also shows how to use numbers above 100 in basic operations such as addition and subtraction and in dates.

The following points are highlighted in lesson 8 (you should concentrate on sections marked with a √):

√• Numbers from 100 to 999,000,000 (8.6-8.8)
√• Partitive use of definite articles, positive and negative (8.9-8.14)
√• Possessive adjectives, single possessor (8.15-8.22)
• Identity questions with *c'est* and *est-ce*

ASSIMILATION OF THE TEXT

8.1 Text work-up

You should begin the *mise en oeuvre* as soon as possible after you have viewed the video program for lesson 8. Repeat and answer as usual.

8.2, 8.3 Aural comprehension and oral production

These sections will familiarize you with the French terms for family members and relatives.

• First, study the diagram of Mireille's family tree in the textbook. Then, on the family tree, find each of the individuals listed in 8.2 in the workbook, and listen to section 8.2 of the audio program. You will hear twelve pairs of statements. One statement in each pair is correct; the other is not. Say the correct statement.

In exercise 8.3, the relationship between two members of the family is given from the standpoint of one of the two. You are asked to define it from the other's point of view. Listen to each statement and answer the question that follows.

THE "TEXT" AND THE TEXTBOOK

Work with the text and illustrations in the textbook, as in previous lessons.

TOWARD COMMUNICATION

8.4, 8.5 Observation and activation: Pronunciation; /u/ and /y/

The vowel sound in *tutu*, /y/, is quite different from the vowel sound in *toutou*, /u/.

You saw in lesson 6 that the sound /y/ in French is the result of a combination of tightly rounded lips and tongue very far forward. Sections 8.4 and 8.5 give you more practice identifying and making the sound /y/ and distinguishing it from the sound /u/.

The sounds /y/ and /u/, although quite different, have one feature in common: rounded, slightly protruding lips. Once the lips are rounded and extended (as in a pout or a kiss), the /u/ sound in *toutou* is produced with the tongue pulled toward the back of the mouth, much as it would be in pronouncing the vowel sound of *pool* in English. (In the vowel sound of *pool*, however, the lips are not as tense and extended as they must be in *toutou.*) To get from the /u/ of *toutou* to the /y/ sound in *tutu*, the tongue advances toward the rounded lips, and comes to rest just short of the space between the teeth.

• In exercise 8.4, determine whether the sentences you hear contain *tutu* or *toutou*, and mark the appropriate box on the grid in your workbook.

√ Check your answers in key 8.4 at the back of the workbook.

• In exercise 8.5, repeat the phrases you hear.

8.6-8.8 Observation and activation: Numbers from 100 to 999,000,000

Once you are past the intricacies of numbers from sixty to ninety-nine, the remaining numbers in French up to a billion are simplicity itself.

Section 8.6 sets forth the major number groups beyond tens (*cent, mille, million*). Notice the *-s* on *cents* for even multiples of hundred (*deux cent*s, *trois cent*s); notice, too, that the *-s* disappears in all other combined forms (*deux cent un*, *neuf cent quatre-vingt-dix-neuf*). In the case of multiples of *mille*, there is no added *-s*.

Note that although the English expressions for 100 and 1000 are always preceded by *a* or *one*, in French *cent* and *mille* are **never** preceded by *un*.

Section 8.7 shows how French speakers refer to dates. Note that you may either specify the thousands (1623 = one thousand six hundred twenty-three) or convert them into hundreds (1623 = sixteen hundred twenty-three). The first option has none of the old-fashioned ring that it has in English ("in the Year of our Lord one thousand six hundred and twenty-three . . ."). Note also that the most common way of saying dates in English—by dropping the word *hundred* altogether (1623 = sixteen twenty-three)—is not used in French: one always says *seize* **cent** *vingt-trois*.

• Exercise 8.8 gives you practice in using numbers above one hundred in simple problems of addition and subtraction. Look at and say each pair of numbers to be added or subtracted, and the result. The correct answers will be given for confirmation. Go back and repeat this exercise as often as you need to get used to saying these numbers.

8.9-8.14 Observation and activation: *Du, de la, de l', des*

Chart 8.9 shows how the definite articles *le*, *la*, *l'*, and *les* combine with *de* to indicate an unspecified amount or quantity—a notion that in English would be expressed with no article at all: "Uncle Bill has time," "Uncle Bill has friends," and so forth. Notice that *de* combines with *le* to produce a new form, *du*. Similarly, *de* and *les* combine to form *des*. The article you would expect before a word beginning with a vowel sound, *l'*, follows *de* to produce *de l': de l'argent*. The final *-s* of *des* is not pronounced before words beginning with consonants, but before words beginning with vowel sounds it is pronounced /z/: *des /z/amis*.

In negative expressions, *du*, *de la*, *de l'*, and *des* become *pas de* (*pas d'* in front of a word beginning with a vowel sound), as chart 8.10 illustrates.

Exercises 8.11-8.14 give you practice using these combined forms of the definite article.

• In 8.11, deny everything you hear attributed to you, using *pas de* or *pas d'*.

Audio cues (for reference):
8.11 Activation orale: De après négation

1. Vous avez du courage!
2. Vous avez de la chance!
3. Vous avez de la fortune!
4. Vous avez de la famille?
5. Vous avez de l'argent!
6. Vous avez du courage!
7. Vous avez du temps!
8. Vous avez des loisirs!
9. Vous avez des relations!
10. Vous avez des frères?
11. Vous avez des complexes!

• In 8.12, you will be asked a number of questions about Uncle Guillaume and Aunt Georgette. Again, answer each one negatively, as in the example.

Audio cues (for reference):
8.12 Activation orale: De après négation

1. Est-ce que l'oncle Guillaume a des enfants?
2. Est-ce que la tante Georgette a des fils?

3. Est-ce que la tante Georgette a des filles?
4. Est-ce que la tante Georgette a des enfants?
5. Est-ce que la tante Georgette a de l'argent?
6. Est-ce que la tante Georgette a de la chance?
7. Est-ce que la tante Georgette a du courage?
8. Est-ce que la tante Georgette a du temps?
9. Est-ce que la tante Georgette a des loisirs?

• In 8.13, you will hear questions about various people in Mireille's family. Answer yes or no, basing your answers on what you know about them from the story.

Audio cues (for reference):

8.13 Activation orale: Du, de la, de l', des, pas de

1. Est-ce que Henri Pothier a des enfants?
2. Est-ce que Paulette Belleau a des enfants?
3. Est-ce que François Belleau a des filles?
4. Est-ce que Guillaume Belleau a des filles?
5. Est-ce que Guillaume Belleau a des frères?
6. Est-ce que Mireille a des frères?
7. Est-ce que Mireille a des cousins?
8. Est-ce que Mireille a des enfants?
9. Est-ce que Mireille a des oncles?
10. Est-ce que Mireille a des tantes?
11. Est-ce que François Belleau a des fils?

• In 8.14, complete the sentences you see in your workbook by writing the correct form of the verb *avoir* and the appropriate form of the definite article with *de*.

√ Check your answers in key 8.14 at the back of the workbook.

8.15–8.22 Observation and activation: Possessives

Charts 8.15, 8.17, and 8.19 introduce possessive adjectives, which are used with nouns to indicate ownership or, as here, family relationships (*mon père, ta soeur*).

An important difference between possessives in French and in English is that in English the gender of the possessor dictates the choice of adjective: in *his sister*, the word *his* is masculine because the person whose sister it is is male. In *her sister*, *her* is feminine because the person whose sister it is is female.

In French this is not the case: in *sa soeur*, *sa* is feminine because it agrees with *soeur*, which happens to be feminine. *Sa soeur* can refer to the sister of a man or a woman; you can tell which it is from the context.

In English, possessive adjectives are invariable: **his** *brother*, **his** *sister*, **his** *sisters*. In French they agree in gender and number with the noun that is possessed: **son** *frère*, **sa** *soeur*, **ses** *soeurs*.

Chart 8.15 illustrates the **first person** possessive adjectives *mon, ma, mes*. Notice the initial *m-* that these adjectives have in common with the first person pronouns *me* and *moi*. Mon is used in front of masculine nouns. *Ma* is used in front of feminine nouns beginning with a consonant sound (**ma** *cousine*). But *mon*, rather than *ma*, is used in front of feminine nouns beginning with a vowel sound, to avoid the clash of two vowels: *mon /n/arrière-grand-mère*. *Mes* is used in front of all plural nouns; it is linked with a following vowel sound: *mes /z/oncles*.

Chart 8.17 shows the forms for the **second person** possessives *ton, ta, tes*. Notice that they closely parallel the first-person forms *mon, ma, mes*. Note that there is also a family resemblance between the possessive adjectives and the pronouns *te* and *toi*, an initial *t-*. *Ton* is the form used in front of masculine nouns. *Ton* is also used, with *liaison*, in front of feminine nouns that begin with a vowel sound (*ton /n/arrière grand-mère*). *Tes* is used with plural nouns regardless of gender; here, too, there is *liaison* with a following vowel: *tes /z/oncles*.

Chart 8.19 presents the **third person** forms *son, sa, ses*, which behave like the first and second person possessives you have already seen.

For exercises 8.16, 8.18, and 8.20, you will need to refer to the family tree reproduced in the textbook.

• In exercise 8.16, look at the family tree and answer the questions you hear on the audio recording as if you were Mireille, using *mon*, *ma*, or *mes* as in the example. Remember that when you are talking about a plural noun the form of the verb changes along with the form of the possessive: "C'**est** ma soeur," but "Ce **sont** mes soeurs."

Audio cues (for reference):
8.16 Activation orale: Possessifs; mon, ma, mes

1. Qui est Cécile?
2. Qui est Marie-Laure?
3. Qui est Madeleine Belleau?
4. Qui est François Belleau?
5. Qui est Henri Pothier?
6. Qui est Armand Belleau?
7. Qui est Paulette Belleau?
8. Qui est Lucie Pothier?
9. Qui sont Paulette et Georgette Belleau?
10. Qui sont Armand et Guillaume Belleau?
11. Qui sont François et Madeleine Belleau?
12. Qui sont Sophie et Philippe Pothier?

• In exercise 8.18, look at the family tree and answer the questions you hear as though your good friend Mireille were quizzing you directly about her family, using the familiar forms *ton*, *ta*, or *tes*, as in the example.

Audio cues (for reference):
8.18 Activation orale: Possessifs; ton, ta, tes

1. Qui est Cécile?
2. Qui est Marie-Laure?
3. Qui est Madeleine Belleau?
4. Qui est Georgette Belleau?
5. Qui est Jeanne Belleau?
6. Qui est Lucie Pothier?
7. Qui sont Jeanne Belleau et Louise Thomas?
8. Qui est François Belleau?
9. Qui est Anatole Belleau?
10. Qui sont Anatole Belleau et Léon Pothier?
11. Qui sont Guillaume Belleau et Henri Pothier?

• In exercise 8.20, answer the questions you hear as though you were speaking about Mireille's family in her absence, using appropriate forms of the third person possessive adjective.

Audio cues (for reference):
8.20 Activation orale: Possessifs; son, sa, ses

1. Qui est Anatole Belleau?
2. Qui est François Belleau?
3. Qui est Guillaume Belleau?
4. Qui est Philippe Pothier?
5. Qui est Madeleine Belleau?
6. Qui est Louise Pothier?
7. Qui est Julienne Pothier?
8. Qui est Sophie Pothier?
9. Qui est Lucie Pothier?
10. Qui sont Georgette et Paulette Belleau?
11. Qui sont Guillaume et Armand Belleau?
12. Qui sont François et Madeleine Belleau?
13. Qui sont Georges et Yvonne Belleau?

• Finally, review chart 8.21, which gives an overview of the possessives studied in lesson 8, and complete the writing exercise in 8.22. This exercise is divided into two parts. In part A, complete the answers to the questions you see in the workbook. In part B, answer the questions you see as if you were Mireille.

√ Check your answers in key 8.22 at the back of the workbook.

8.23, 8.24 Observation and activation: Questions about identity

Chart 8.23 presents a series of questions used to ask the identity of people and things.

Note that there are various alternatives for the questions in chart 8.23. These alternatives are not automatically interchangeable. The choice of which to use depends on the situation in which communication is taking place.

You saw in lesson 7 that using inversion (*est-il sportif?*) is a more elegant way to ask a question than using *est-ce que* or simple intonation. The expressions in 8.23 also correspond to different **levels** of speech, from the colloquial to the refined.

Level 1 (*c'est quoi?*, *c'est qui?*, *qui c'est?*) corresponds to an offhand, colloquial way of speaking.

Level 2 (*qu'est-ce que c'est?*, *qui est-ce que c'est?*) is a middle level of speech, with no overtones of either street language or refinement.

Level 3 is more proper, more correct. The expression *qu'est-ce?* is even high style, suggesting a certain affectation on the part of the user. As a result, it is rarely heard, which is why in your workbook it appears between parentheses.

Note. You will see for the first time in 8.23 an addition in small type at the end of the chart. This feature, which will appear from time to time in the workbook, is designed to give more detailed information about the workings of the language, for the benefit of the inquisitive or curious learner who wants to go beyond the basics. It is completely optional.

• In exercise 8.24, you will hear a series of statements about persons or things. Ask a question about the subject of each statement as though you had not fully understood the statement, as in the examples.

Audio cues (for reference):
8.24 Activation orale: Questions sur l'identité

1. Ça, c'est mon frère.
2. Ça, c'est une maison en Bretagne.
3. Ça, c'est un arbre généalogique.
4. Ça, c'est Tonton Guillaume.
5. Ça, c'est Tante Georgette.
6. Ça, c'est un album.
7. Ça, c'est une photo.
8. Ça, c'est Mireille.
9. Ça, c'est la grand-mère de Mireille.
10. Ça, c'est une maison en Bretagne.

8.25 Activation: Dialogue between Mireille and Jean-Denis

Listen to the conversation between Mireille and Jean-Denis and memorize Mireille's lines, imitating and repeating as usual.

TOWARD FREE EXPRESSION

8.26 Words at large

Proceed as usual. (If necessary, refer to lesson 3 for directions.)

8.27, 8.28 Role-playing and reinvention of the story

In section 8.27, part A, you play Mireille, answering a friend's questions about your family. (If you wish, you may invent a family that bears no resemblance to the family in the story.)

In part B, play yourself and describe your own family, drawing on all the material you have seen in lessons 2-8.

In section 8.28, you are at the hospital visiting Mireille, who has been in an accident and is suffering from amnesia. Help her rediscover her family (or give her an entirely new one.)

If you work with a partner in these exercises, take parts wherever you can, complete the exercise, then switch roles and do it again.

• **Suggested oral assignment.** Record the portrait of one member of your family—a parent or grandparent, a child, a spouse—as in part B of exercise 8.27. Say six to eight sentences. Send this assignment to your instructor, using the same audiocassette you use for the oral production part of summary quiz 8. (See the course syllabus for details.)

DOCUMENT

At the end of the textbook chapter for lesson 8 you will find a poem for reading practice: "Les Belles familles," by Jacques Prévert.

A fiercely independent writer, distrustful of movements and ideologies, Prévert delighted in poking fun at all forms of pretentiousness and pomposity. In this poem, he enumerates all the kings named Louis from the beginning to the end of the French monarchy. (The line was interrupted abruptly in the 18th century: Louis XVI was beheaded during the French Revolution, Louis XVII never reigned, and Louis XVIII was the last of the dynasty.) The poet closes by wondering irreverently how a family that can't even count to twenty could rule a nation.

SELF-TESTING EXERCISES

• Complete and check exercises 8.29, 8.30, and 8.31 as usual.

SUMMARY QUIZ

Consult the course syllabus or check with your instructor for information about completing and handing in summary quiz 8.

LESSON 9
Vacation in Brittany I

The story

We go back in time now to summer vacation two or three years ago. Mireille, her two sisters, and cousins Yvonne and Georges are at a seaside cottage rented by their two families. Sounds good, but it's been raining for three days and the young people are terribly bored.

Rejecting chess, checkers, and cards, they decide to kill time by playing portraits, a simple game in which one player describes someone in a few sentences and the others try to guess who it is. Uncle Guillaume and Aunt Georgette are easy. Then Mireille does a mildly satirical job on her once-athletic uncle, the father of Yvonne and Georges. Finally, Georges does one, complimentary to Mireille, of someone who must be her mother, but before we can find out, snack time intervenes.

Marie-Laure, dying to know the identity of the last portrait, agrees to serve the snacks in exchange for the information. While she is in the kitchen, the others shout instructions on what to bring. On her way back, in spite of Mireille's warning, she trips, drops a loaded tray, and begins to cry. Cécile tries to comfort her and, through her tears, we hear the child ask once more: "Who is it?"

Notes on culture and communication

• **La Bretagne.** Brittany, the western peninsula of France, is a maritime region bordered by the English Channel to the North and the Atlantic to the West and South. It is a country of wild moors and scenic coastal landscapes, with a mild and rainy climate. Still marked by Celtic traditions, Brittany is also a stronghold of Catholicism; religious art and architecture—especially the striking roadside crosses called *calvaires*—are prominent features of the region. Its main resources are tourism, fishing, and naval activities.

• **Le goûter.** Traditionally, French children eat a light snack between four and five in the afternoon. *Le goûter* usually consists of bread and chocolate, a bun, or a piece of cake.

• **Tension and relaxation.** The young people, stranded and bored in their Breton house on a rainy summer day, look relaxed, but their bodies are tense, and when activity occurs it is abrupt, rapid. Mireille is watching the rain from the window. Suddenly she turns and goes to flop disgustedly on the sofa. But her body is not relaxed. Look at her erect posture and the characteristic French squareness of her shoulders. She and the others seem to express their impatience and their pent-up energy not so much through words as through the decisive bobbing of the head, the rolling of the eyes, the penetrating glances. Notice Mireille's eyes as she argues with her sister, as she acknowledges Georges's flattery, as she warns Marie-Laure not to drop the tray.

Content and learning objectives of lesson 9

This lesson shows how French speakers refer to actions and situations that begin in the past and continue into the present. It will also familiarize you with ways of identifying and describing people, indicating ownership and kinship, and talking about games and sports.

The following points are highlighted in lesson 9 (you should concentrate on sections marked with a √):

√• Present tense with *il y a . . . que, ça fait . . . que* (9.7-9.9)
• Masculine/feminine forms, review and extension
√• Possessive adjectives, plural possessor (9.12-9.17)
• Use of *à:* destination, allocation
√• *Faire de . . .* versus *jouer à . . .* (9.21, 9.22)
√• Stressed pronouns (9.24, 9.25)
• *Quelqu'un/une personne; quelqu'un/personne*
• *En* (*il en reste*)

ASSIMILATION OF THE TEXT

9.1-9.4 Text work-up, aural comprehension, and oral production

• Proceed as usual in sections 9.1-9.4. (Refer to lessons 3.1, 3.2, 4.3, and 3.3 for directions, if necessary.) Work with the text and illustrations in the textbook, as in previous lessons.

TOWARD COMMUNICATION

9.5, 9.6 Observation and activation: Pronunciation; *notre/nos*

The vowel sound in the words *notre* and *votre* is different from the vowel sound of *nos* and *vos*. In *nos/vos*, the lips are tightly rounded and protruding; in *notre/votre*, the mouth is less compressed: the lips are only slightly pursed and protruding, and the mouth is more open.

• Listen to the examples in 9.5 and take a minute or two to get the feel of the two different sounds. Then listen to the expressions in 9.6 and repeat them, distinguishing carefully between the two vowel sounds.

9.7-9.9 Observation and activation: Present tense with *il y a . . . que, ça fait . . . que*

The phrase *il y a* with an expression of time (*dix ans*) refers to the past. *Il y a . . . que* and the related expression *ça fait . . . que* are used with verbs in the present tense to indicate an action that began in the past and is still going on in the present. "Ça fait trois jours qu'il pleut" tell us that this is the third day of rain, that it began raining two days ago and is still raining today.

Notice that French and English have quite different ways of expressing this connection between past and present. French uses the **present tense**; English uses a form of the past tense: "it's been raining for . . . ," "we've been here for. . . ."

• In exercises 9.8 and 9.9 you will hear a series of questions about current situations and activities. Say how long each situation or activity has been going on. Use the expressions of time printed in your workbook, and *il y a . . . que* or *ça fait . . . que*, according to the example.

Audio cues (for reference):
9.8 Activation orale: Le temps qui passe; il y a...que

1. La grand-tante Amélie est veuve?
2. Les Belleau habitent à Paris?
3. M. Belleau est chez Renault?
4. Ton oncle est veuf?
5. Mireille fait du karaté maintenant?
6. Ta mère travaille au Ministère?
7. Il pleut?

9.9 Activation orale: Le temps qui passe; ça fait...que

1. La grand-tante Amélie est veuve?
2. Les parents de Robert sont divorcés?
3. Sa mère est remariée?
4. La mère de Robert habite en Argentine?
5. Ils vont en vacances en Bretagne?
6. Ils jouent aux portraits?

9.10, 9.11 Observation and activation: Masculine and feminine forms (review and extension)

Chart 9.10 presents some new masculine and feminine forms, most of which fall into categories you are already familiar with from lessons 4, 6, and 7. They are grouped by their characteristic endings.

In *sérieux/sérieuse, blanc/blanche,* and *sourd/sourde*, as in *anglais/anglaise* (lesson 4), the feminine forms have a consonant sound at the end that is not present in the masculine. Words of the *fin/fine* type present a variation on that pattern: the masculine forms end in a nasal vowel, the feminine forms end in an oral vowel followed by /n/ (recall *américain/américaine*).

Note that the final *-r* of the masculine *fier* is pronounced.

The feminine form *fraîche* is written with a circumflex (^), *accent circonflexe*, over the *i*.

• In exercise 9.11, you will hear a series of men described. Make each description apply to a woman, substituting feminine forms for masculine forms, as in the example. Remember to change **all** masculine forms into feminine forms: in "son frère est très généreux," for example, the noun *frère* (in addition to the adjective *généreux*) will need to be changed to its feminine counterpart.

9.12-9.17 Observation and activation: Possessives

In lesson 8 you saw possessive adjectives that refer to situations in which a single person is doing the possessing. Chart 9.12 introduces possessives that indicate more than one possessor. Sections 9.14-9.17 will help you review and consolidate all the possessives, singular and plural.

Note that, like the forms of singular possessives, the forms of plural possessives depend on how many things are possessed: **notre** *frère,* **nos** *frères.* (In English, the forms of possessive adjectives aren't affected by this variable: **our** *brother,* **our** *brothers.*)

• In exercise 9.13, you will hear pairs of sentences that describe various people's relatives. Combine each pair of sentences into one sentence using the plural possessives, as in the example.

Audio cues (for reference):

9.13 Activation orale: Possessifs; notre, votre, leur, nos, vos, leurs

1. Nous avons des soeurs. Elles sont mariées.
2. Nous avons des frères. Ils sont mariés.
3. Nous avons un frère. Il est marié.
4. Nous avons une soeur. Elle est divorcée.
5. Vous avez un frère? Il est célibataire?
6. Vous avez des cousins? Ils sont étudiants?
7. Vous avez des cousines? Elles sont sympathiques?
8. Vous avez un cousin? Il est sympathique?

9. Ils ont un oncle. Il est veuf.
10. Ils ont une tante. Elle est veuve.
11. Ils ont des frères. Ils sont idiots.
12. Elles ont des soeurs. Elles sont idiotes.

When you have completed 9.13, review the entire system of singular and plural possessives in chart 9.14, and complete exercises 9.15 and 9.16.

• In 9.15, tell various people that the games they are playing at are dumb, fun, or dangerous, using possessives as in the example.

Audio cues (for reference):
9.15 Activation orale: Possessifs; personnes du singulier et du pluriel

1. Vous jouez à un jeu idiot.
2. Cécile et Mireille jouent à un jeu idiot.
3. Georges joue à un jeu idiot.
4. Tu joues à un jeu idiot.
5. Tu joues à des jeux idiots.
6. Nous jouons à des jeux idiots.
7. Nous jouons à un jeu amusant.
8. Vous jouez à des jeux dangereux.
9. Mes cousins jouent à des jeux dangereux.

• In 9.16, talk about your brother's and sister's friends, using possessives.

Audio cues (for reference):
9.16 Activation orale: Possessifs; personnes du singulier et du pluriel

1. Mon frère a une amie anglaise.
2. Elle a les lèvres minces.
3. Elle a de grandes dents.
4. Elle a la voix pointue.
5. Elle a le nez pointu. [CROCHU?)
6. Elle a un chien policier.
7. Ma soeur a un ami anglais.
8. Il a le crâne chauve.
9. Il a les joues creuses.
10. Il a les jambes courtes.
11. Il a des enfants.
12. Ses enfants ont les cheveux courts.
13. Ils ont les joues rondes et rouges.
14. Ils ont le menton rond.
15. Ils ont l'air moqueur.

• In 9.17, say what you think of various people, using possessives. Listen carefully to the sentences you hear to determine who the possessor is in each case. Then write the possessive forms in the workbook.

√ Check your answers in key 9.17 at the back of the workbook.

Audio cues (for reference):
9.17 Activation orale et écrite: Possessifs; personnes du singulier et du pluriel

1. Vous avez un père très indulgent.
2. Vous avez une mère très indulgente.
3. Nous avons un père très distingué.
4. Nous avons des parents très distingués.
5. Tu as une mère très distinguée.
6. J'ai un grand-père sourd.
7. Marie-Laure et Cécile ont des parents très sympathiques.
8. Elles ont une soeur très sympathique.
9. Mireille a des soeurs très sympathiques.
10. J'ai des cousines agaçantes.
11. J'ai un oncle très généreux.

9.18-9.20 Observation and activation: Use of *à*; destination, allocation, games

Chart 9.18 illustrates three situations in which the preposition *à* is used with a noun: to say where you are going ("elle va **à** la fac"), to identify the recipient of something ("donnons un prénom **à** la jeune fille"), and with games ("jouons **à** la belote").

Notice that, like *de* (lesson 8), *à* combines with the definite articles *le* and *les* to produce new forms: *au* (= *à* + *le*) and *aux* (= *à* + *les*). The final -*x* of *aux* is not pronounced at all before words beginning with a consonant; it is pronounced /z/ before words beginning with a vowel sound: *aux* /z/*Antilles*.

• In exercise 9.19, you will hear about things that various characters in the story don't have. Exercise your right to invent and reinvent the story by suggesting we give them these missing things. Listen first for *le, la, l'* or *les* in front of the name of each character, then use the appropriate form of the article with *à*.

Audio cues (for reference):
9.19 Activation orale: Attribution; à la, à l', au, aux

1. Les jeunes gens n'ont pas de famille.
2. La jeune fille n'a pas de prénom.
3. Le jeune homme n'a pas de prénom.
4. L'ami brésilien de Robert n'a pas de prénom.
5. Les jeunes gens n'ont pas d'amis.
6. Le père de Mireille n'a pas de profession.
7. La mère de Mireille n'a pas de profession.
8. La tante Georgette n'a pas de relations.
9. L'oncle Guillaume n'a pas d'enfants.
10. Les enfants n'ont pas de cadeaux.

• In exercise 9.20, you will hear preferences expressed for certain games. Agree to play these games, again identifying the article that precedes the name of each game and using the combined form with *à*.

Audio cues (for reference):
9.20 Activation orale: Jeu; à la, à l', au, aux

1. Moi, j'adore la pelote basque.
2. Moi, je préfère les cartes.
3. Moi, j'aime bien la belote.
4. Moi, je préfère le bridge.
5. Non, le poker, c'est mieux.
6. Moi, je préfère les dames.
7. Non, les échecs, c'est plus intéressant.
8. Non, les portraits, c'est plus amusant.

9.21, 9.22 Observation and activation: *Faire du sport/ jouer à un jeu*

Chart 9.21 presents the distinction between sports and other physical activities, on the one hand, and games involving rules on the other. As you saw in lesson 6, the verb *faire* is used to talk about physical activities and sports. With games, the verb is *jouer*.

In the case of a game like tennis, which is a sport but is also governed by elaborate rules, either *faire* or *jouer* can be used. When you use *faire*, you are talking about tennis as a physical activity, a means of healthy exercise. When you use *jouer*, you are stressing the regulated, rule-bound side of the game. "Je **fais** du tennis" = I play tennis (to stay in shape, for fun, etc.). "**Jouons** au tennis!" = Let's have a game of tennis (and see who wins).

• In exercise 9.22, you will be asked whether you like various sports, physical activities, and games. Answer yes and say that you participate in each one, too. Determine whether each activity primarily involves exercise and movement or is more a game governed by rules, and use *jouer* or *faire*, as appropriate.

Audio cues (for reference):
9.22 Activation orale: Faire du sport/jouer à un jeu

1. Vous aimez le tennis?
2. Vous aimez l'alpinisme?
3. Vous aimez le ski?
4. Vous aimez l'escrime?
5. Vous aimez le football?
6. Et le cheval, vous aimez ça?
7. Robert aime le basket?
8. Il aime le patin à glace?
9. Et la moto, il aime ça?
10. Est-ce qu'il aime le vélo?
11. Est-ce qu'il aime la planche à voile?
12. Est-ce qu'il aime les échecs?
13. Est-ce que Mireille aime les dames?

9.23 Activation: *A la, à l', au*

The writing exercise in 9.23 reintroduces a pattern that will be familiar to you from lesson 2: the use of *à* with **places** ("Mireille va **à** la fac").

• Decide whether the names of places you see are usually preceded by *la, le,* or *l'*, and write the missing combined forms with *à*.

√ Check your answers in key 9.23 at the back of the workbook.

9.24, 9.25 Observation and activation: Stressed (or disjunctive) pronouns

Stressed pronouns, also known as **disjunctive** pronouns, are used for emphasis and in situations where there is a pronoun but no verb, the pronoun having been in effect cut off—**disjoined**—from a verb. Stressed pronouns are also used after prepositions.

Chart 9.24 gives the forms of stressed pronouns in French, and illustrates the most frequent situations in which they occur. At the beginning of a sentence, just before the subject pronoun ("**Moi**, je trouve ça idiot!"), or at the end of a sentence ("Je trouve ça idiot, **moi**!") their function is most clearly to accentuate or stress.

• Exercise 9.25 concentrates on the use of stressed pronouns with the preposition *à*. You will hear that various people are next in line to do a portrait. Say it is each one's turn, using the appropriate stressed pronoun.

Audio cues (for reference):
9.25 Activation orale: Pronoms accentués

1. Georges va faire le portrait suivant.
2. Tu vas faire le portrait suivant.
3. Marie-Laure va faire le portrait suivant.
4. Jean-Denis va faire le portrait suivant.
5. Nous allons faire le portrait suivant.
6. Mireille et Cécile vont faire le portrait suivant.
7. Georges et Yvonne vont faire le portrait suivant.
8. Vous allez faire le portrait suivant?
9. Je vais faire le portrait suivant.

9.26-9.29 Observation and activation: *Quelqu'un/une personne; quelqu'un/personne*

Charts 9.26, 9.27, and 9.28 illustrate two common terms—*quelqu'un* and *personne*—that designate people without specifying who they are. One of these expressions—*personne*—is also used negatively to indicate the total absence of people.

Chart 9.26 shows that *quelqu'un* can be used for either male or female persons. Though it is a masculine noun, *quelqu'un* may be used to refer to females: "Une dame, c'est **quelqu'un.**"

Similarly, *personne*, a feminine noun, can designate males: "Un monsieur est **une personne.**"

When used in a negative construction, as in chart 9.28, *personne* is the **opposite** of *quelqu'un*. Notice that when *personne* is used negatively, *ne* is placed in front of the verb, and *personne* after it.

• In exercise 9.29, you will hear a series of questions about unspecified people. For each question, the number of people involved is given in parentheses in the workbook. Say the number of people involved, using *quelqu'un* if the number you see is 1, *personnes* if it is larger than 1, and *ne . . . personne* if it is zero.

Audio cues (for reference):
9.29 Activation orale: Quelqu'un, personne

1. Il y a quelqu'un?
2. Vous voyez quelqu'un?
3. Vous voyez quelqu'un?
4. Vous cherchez quelqu'un?
5. Il reste quelqu'un?
6. Il y a quelqu'un?
7. Il cherche quelqu'un?
8. Il reste quelqu'un?
9. Tu cherches quelqu'un?

9.30, 9.31 Observation and activation: *Pleuvoir/pleurer*

Chart 9.30 presents two verbs that look similar at first glance, and that both refer to the behavior of drops of liquid. The two verbs function very differently, however. *Pleurer* is a regular verb that behaves like most other verbs with infinitives ending in *-er*. *Pleuvoir*, on the other hand, is used only for the third person singular *il pleut*, and only with the **impersonal pronoun** *il*. (In English, too, the **it** of *it's raining* is called an impersonal pronoun because it doesn't refer to any identified person or thing.)

• Exercise 9.31 will help you distinguish between these two verbs and know in what circumstances to use which. Read each sentence carefully, and decide whether it is about a person or about the weather. Then write the appropriate form of *pleurer* or *pleuvoir*.

√ Check your answers in key 9.31 at the back of the workbook.

9.32, 9.33 Observation: *Il reste, il en reste*

Charts 9.32 and 9.33 show one way to indicate what is left: using the expression *il reste* (an impersonal expression, like *il pleut*). What is left may be expressed by a noun following *il reste: il reste* **des galettes.**

The noun may also be replaced by *en*. *En* is placed **before** the verb: *il* **en** reste. *En* is used by itself if the amount of what is left is not indicated. If the amount is indicated, an expression of quantity is placed after the verb: *il en reste* **deux.**

9.34 Activation: Dialogue between Georges and Yvonne

Listen to the conversation between Georges and Yvonne and memorize Yvonne's lines, imitating and repeating as usual.

TOWARD FREE EXPRESSION

9.35 Words at large

Proceed as usual. (If necessary, refer to lesson 4 for directions.)

9.36, 9.37 Role-playing and reinvention of the story

You are on vacation in Brittany. Imagine your leisure activities, using the alternatives suggested in section 9.36 as a point of departure. (Where the workbook says *vous*, you will say *je* or *nous*, of course.) Section 9.37 of the audio program contains a sample dialogue with Aunt Georgette's dog Fido; you may want to listen to it for further ideas.

Work with a partner if you can, and do the exercise out loud. One of you can ask questions using *vous* or *tu* ("Vous allez faire du karaté?"), the other can answer yes or no ("Non, nous allons faire du patin à roulettes!"). Then switch roles and repeat the exercise. Or you can compare vacation plans ("Moi, je vais faire du ski nautique!" "—Ah, moi, je vais faire la sieste!").

• **Suggested written assignment.** Write out an imaginary dialogue between you and a friend or relative (or character X) in which you discuss plans for an upcoming vacation. Follow one of the models suggested in the paragraph above, having one speaker ask questions and the other answer, or having the two speakers compare plans. Write a minimum of five exchanges.

Send this assignment to your instructor along with the answer sheet for summary quiz 9. (See the course syllabus for details.)

SELF-TESTING EXERCISES

- Complete and check exercises 9.38, 9.39, and 9.40 as usual.

SUMMARY QUIZ

Consult the course syllabus or check with your instructor for information about completing and handing in summary quiz 9.

LESSON 10
Vacation in Brittany II

The story

Same vacation cottage in Brittany, same characters, same rain. Ironically, as Mireille points out, the weather is fine back in Paris.

Marie-Laure persists in asking about that last portrait. Mireille is, as usual, rather impatient with her, but Cécile helps Marie-Laure to guess correctly by noting resemblances to Mireille.

At the little girl's insistence, they go on with the portraits. Mireille does a quick job on poor Uncle Victor who is, to be sure, a bit cross-eyed. Cécile does Uncle Henri, who shaves his head to hide progressing baldness. Mireille presents the mustached Aunt Amélie. At last, Georges kills the game by describing his unpleasant and unpopular math teacher, whom the others don't even know. No fair!

Amid talk of the current movie at the local film society ("Claire's Knee," by Rohmer), Jean-Denis comes in to say that the rain stopped an hour ago. His invitation to go sailing is declined by Georges but eagerly taken up by Cécile. Mireille comments, a little pointedly, on her sister's sudden interest in sports, but is thoughtful enough to throw the hastily departing young woman a slicker.

Notes on culture and communication

• **Ciné-clubs** are film societies that present movie classics; sometimes screenings are followed by discussions in which the audience is invited to participate.

• **Socialization and sibling rivalry.** Poor little Marie-Laure! Charming, bright, but constantly put down by her older sisters and her cousin. They call her *bête, sourde, bécasse, idiote*. She spills the tray of food in part at least because Mireille shouts so violently at her to be careful. American viewers will tend to perceive this behavior as needlessly cruel sibling rivalry. But the fact of the matter is that by our standards, French socialization is quite harsh. As soon as young children can understand and speak they are expected to live up to adult expectations. If they do not, they are put in their place with a severity that startles us because we do not perceive the love and the socializing purpose behind it. French children sense the love, however, and do not feel rejected. They develop a thick skin that the verbal attacks scarcely penetrate, and, with words and facial expressions, they learn to defend themselves.

Content and learning objectives of lesson 10

This lesson shows how French speakers express agreement and disagreement, talk about particular people and things and about people in general, and speak about time and the weather. It also shows how to express the difference between being acquainted with people or things and knowing something intellectually.

The following points are highlighted in lesson 10 (you should concentrate on sections marked with a √):

√• Stressed pronouns, review and extension; use of stressed pronouns in comparisons (10.12-10.14)
√• Demonstrative adjectives (10.15-10.16)
√• *Venir*, present indicative (10.17-10.18)
√• *Connaître* and *savoir* (10.19-10.21)
• *On*
• Masculine/feminine forms, review and extension

ASSIMILATION OF THE TEXT

10.1, 10.2 Text work-up and aural comprehension

• Proceed as usual in sections 10.1 and 10.2. (Refer to lesson 3.1-3.2 for directions, if necessary.) Work with the text and illustrations in the textbook, as in previous lessons.

TOWARD COMMUNICATION

10.3, 10.4 Observation and activation: Pronunciation: /ø/ and /œ/

Sections 10.3 and 10.4 give you practice recognizing and pronouncing two different vowel sounds: the /ø/ sound of *eux* and the /œ/ sound of *soeur*. The vowel sound in *eux* is the more closed of the two—that is, the lips are more rounded and extended, and there is greater tension focused in the front of the mouth.

Notice that the more closed /ø/ occurs in a syllable ending in a **vowel sound**: *eu[x]*, and that the more open /œ/ occurs in a syllable ending in a **consonant sound**: *soeu*r.

• First practice distinguishing the two sounds by listening to the examples in 10.3. Then practice reproducing them by repeating the phrases you hear in 10.4.

10.5-10.8 Observation and activation: Agreeing and disagreeing

In French, as in English, it is possible to agree and disagree with people when they are being positive as well as when they are being negative. "That's pretty." "—Yes, it is," and "That's not very pretty." "—No, it's not" are both situations in which the two speakers are in **agreement**.

English speakers show disagreement by opposing *no* to a positive statement: "That's pretty." "—**No**, (you're wrong), it's not." And by opposing *yes* to a negative statement: "That's not very pretty." "—**Yes**, (on the contrary), it is."

In French, disagreement with a negative statement is indicated by a special word, *si:* "Ce n'est pas joli! "—**Si**, c'est joli!" Charts 10.5 and 10.6 illustrate this use of *si*.

• Exercises 10.7 and 10.8 give you practice using *oui*, *non*, and *si* to express agreement and disagreement. In 10.7, agree with the statements you hear on the audio recording, as in the examples. In 10.8, disagree. Remember that some of the statements you hear will be positive and some will be negative. And pay close attention to the tone of voice you hear in the examples. Although you might use the same **words** in agreeing with "Life isn't easy!" ("No, it's not!") and disagreeing with "Life is easy!" ("No it's not!"), your responses will **sound** very different. Similarly, "Non, ça ne va pas" will sound different depending on whether you are saying it to agree ("Ça ne va pas." "—Non, ça ne va pas!") or disagree ("Ça va." "—Non, ça ne va pas!").

Audio cues (for reference):
10.7 Activation orale: Accord

1. Ça va.
2. Ça ne va pas.
3. C'est difficile.
4. Ce n'est pas un joli prénom.
5. Il aime ça.
6. Elle est divorcée.
7. Elle n'est pas française.
8. Vous aimez les films italiens.
9. Vous êtes français.
10. Vous ne parlez pas français.

Audio cues (for reference):
10.8 Activation orale: Désaccord

1. Ça va.
2. Ça ne va pas.
3. C'est facile.
4. Ce n'est pas un joli prénom.
5. Elle n'est pas mariée.
6. Elle travaille.
7. Il ne travaille pas.
8. Vous parlez français.
9. Elle ne parle pas français.
10. Elle est française.

10.9, 10.10 Observation and activation: Weather and time

In French, the same word, *temps*, is used to refer to time (*temps chronologique*) and weather (*temps météorologique*). The two terms are seldom confused, since the context in which they occur invariably tells you which is which. (*Temps*-time is often used with the verb *passer*, for instance, while *temps*-weather is often used with the verb *faire*.) Chart 10.9 illustrates these two uses of *temps*.

• In exercise 10.10, you will hear a series of sentences that refer either to weather or to time. Determine which it is, and mark the appropriate box on the grid in your workbook.

√ Check your answers in key 10.10 at the back of the workbook.

10.11 Observation: Degrees

In the story, Georges uses some critical words to describe his math teacher: "Il est bête comme ses pieds, et il n'y a pas plus vache." The expression "il n'y a pas plus vache" indicates that this person is about as mean as they come, that there isn't anyone meaner. On a meanness scale of 0 to 3, he rates a 3.

10.12 Observation: Comparisons

In 10.11, you saw ways of describing individual people's characteristics in graduated terms (*il est vache*, *il est très vache*, and so forth). Those descriptions rated the individual on an absolute scale. Often, however, it is more useful (and much more interesting) to put individuals up against each other, to compare them in terms of a particular quality: who is cuter than whom, who is older than whom, and so forth. Such comparisons can come out essentially in one of three ways: X is either **more candid** than Y, **as candid** as Y, or **less candid** than Y. (With *less* and *more* there can be further nuances: X can be **much more candid** than Y, and so forth.)

Chart 10.12 illustrates comparisons by matching women who are approximately 5'3", 5'5", 5'6", 5'7", and 5'9" with a man who is 5'6" (*1m71 = 1 mètre 71 centimètres*).

Note the use of the **stressed pronoun** in these comparisons ("plus grande que **lui**").

10.13, 10.14 Observation and activation: Stressed pronouns and comparison

You saw in lesson 9 how stressed pronouns are used for emphasis, and after prepositions. Chart 10.13 shows that they are also used after *que* in comparisons.

• In exercise 10.14, you will see a series of sentences in which one person is compared to another. Rewrite them by turning each comparison around, as in the examples. Remember, when you replace the subject of each sentence, that other elements of the sentence (the verb, as in example 1, or an adjective, as in examples 2 and 3) may have to be changed as a result.

√ Check your answers in key 10.14 at the back of the workbook.

10.15, 10.16 Observation and activation: Demonstratives

The demonstratives presented in 10.15 accompany and modify nouns. Their function is to emphasize or focus attention on the noun. Often they serve to specify more precisely which one of a number of possible people or things is being talked about: "**ce** passeport est à moi" = the one I'm holding, as distinct from any others in view. A demonstrative and a noun are also used to convey the intensity of an attitude held toward a person or thing ("qu'il est agaçant, **ce** gamin!"). When special precision or intensity are needed, *-là* can be added after the noun (". . . ce gamin-**là**!").

Like all adjectives, these demonstratives vary in form according to whether the noun they describe is masculine or feminine, singular or plural. Notice that there are two masculine forms in the singular: *ce* in front of words beginning with a consonant sound and *cet* in front of words beginning with a vowel sound. The *-t* of *cet* is pronounced (*cet* /t/*enfant*), avoiding the dreaded clash of two vowel sounds. In the same way, and for the same reason, the *-s* of the plural form *ces*, which is not pronounced in front of consonants, is pronounced /z/ in front of vowels: *ces* /z/*enfants*.

• In exercise 10.16, lay claim to the items you hear mentioned. You will need to figure out whether each item is plural, feminine, or masculine (or masculine beginning with a vowel). Then use *ces, cette, ce,* or *cet* accordingly. Notice that the sentences you hear give you not one but **two** clues to whether the nouns are masculine or feminine: a possessive ("c'est **mon** passeport") and a direct object pronoun ("donne-**le**-moi!").

Audio cues (for reference):
10.16 Activation orale: Démonstratifs

1. C'est mon passeport. Donne-le-moi!
2. C'est ma carte d'identité. Donne-la-moi!
3. C'est mon argent. Donne-le-moi.
4. Ce sont mes cigarettes. Donne-les-moi!
5. C'est ma galette. Donne-la-moi!
6. Ce sont mes lunettes. Donne-les-moi!
7. C'est mon journal. Donne-le-moi.

10.17, 10.18 Observation and activation: Present indicative of *venir*

Chart 10.17 presents the forms of a very common and very useful verb, *venir*, in the present tense.

• In exercise 10.18, you will be asked whether various people work much. Say yes, as a matter of fact they have just come from the library, using appropriate forms of *venir*.

Audio cues (for reference):
10.18 Activation orale: Présent de l'indicatif du verbe venir

1. Tu travailles beaucoup?
2. Mireille travaille beaucoup?
3. Mireille et Robert travaillent beaucoup?
4. Vous travaillez beaucoup, vous deux?
5. Tu travailles beaucoup?

10.19, 10.20 Observation and activation: Knowing; *savoir* and *connaître*

Unlike English, French has different expressions for two separate kinds of knowing: (1) acquaintanceship or familiarity, and (2) intellectual knowledge or certainty. In English, if I am asked a question I can't answer about someone I have never met, and I say, "I don't **know**; I don't **know** him," a single verb expresses both my ignorance and my unfamiliarity with the fellow. In French, these functions are assigned to two different verbs: *savoir* ("je ne **sais** pas . . .") and *connaître* (". . . je ne le **connais** pas"). Chart 10.19 presents the forms of these two verbs.

• Exercise 10.20 gives you practice using *savoir* and *connaître*. You will be asked whether various people think a certain history teacher is nice. Say they don't know, since they don't know him, using appropriate forms of *savoir* and *connaître*, as in the examples.

Audio cues (for reference):

10.20 Activation orale: Connaissance; savoir et connaître

1. Est-ce que tu trouves le prof d'histoire sympathique?
2. Est-ce que Mireille trouve le prof d'histoire sympathique?
3. Est-ce que Robert et Mireille trouvent le prof d'histoire sympathique?
4. Est-ce que vous trouvez le prof d'histoire sympathique, vous deux?
5. Est-ce que Robert trouve le prof d'histoire sympathique?
6. Et toi, est-ce que tu trouves le prof d'histoire sympathique?

10.21 Dictation: *venir, connaître,* and *savoir*

This dictation exercise will give you practice writing forms of the three important verbs you have seen in the last few sections.

• Listen and write the verb forms in the blank spaces in your workbook. If you are working with an individual cassette player, use the pause button where necessary to give yourself more time to write.

√ Check your answers in key 10.21 at the back of the workbook.

10.22, 10.23 Observation and activation: *On*

The pronoun *on* refers to people in a collective, unspecific way. It can be used, like *les gens* or *tout le monde*, to generalize ("en France, **on** parle français"). *On* has an impersonal quality that also makes it appropriate for popular sayings ("quand **on** joue, le temps passe vite").

In informal, everyday speech *on* is often used as a replacement for *nous*.

• In exercise 10.23, you will be asked about various groups of people. In your answers, substitute *on* for the collective expressions you hear in the questions.

Audio cues (for reference):

10.23 Activation orale: On

1. En France, les gens parlent français?
2. Dans votre famille, vous mangez ensemble?
3. A Paris, tout le monde parle français?
4. Vous allez au cinéma, toi et tes amis?
5. Vous jouez au bridge pour passer le temps, vous quatre?
6. Vous êtes à la fac, vous deux?

10.24 Observation: Masculine/feminine forms (review and extension)

The charts in 10.24 group some new and some familiar masculine and feminine forms into categories according to their characteristic endings. Like many others you have encountered, words of the *petit/petite* type have a consonant sound in the feminine that is absent in the masculine. In writing, the feminine forms end in an *-e*.

In the case of words like *rapide* and *chauve*, the written and spoken forms are identical in the masculine and the feminine.

Beau, *nouveau*, and *vieux* end in a vowel sound in the masculine, and a consonant sound in the feminine (in the case of *vieille*, the final sound is halfway between a vowel and a consonant—the semi-vowel /j/).

Note that in front of a masculine noun beginning with a vowel the forms *bel*, *nouvel*, and *vieil* are used to avoid the clash of two vowel sounds.

10.25 Observation: Direction

Chart 10.25 illustrates three alternate ways of referring to geographical direction.

10.26 Activation: Dialogue between Jean-Denis and Georges

Listen to the conversation between Jean-Denis and Georges and memorize Georges's lines, imitating and repeating as usual.

TOWARD FREE EXPRESSION

10.27 Words at large

In 10.27, two kinds of negative or critical comments are asked for: comments you can make about someone you don't like, and comments you can make to be disagreeable with someone you do like. Proceed as in previous lessons.

10.28, 10.29 Role-playing and reinvention of the story

In 10.28, draw on your knowledge of the story and your practice in words at large, above, to express your exasperation at Marie-Laure for dropping the snack tray. Use the alternatives suggested in the workbook as a point of departure.

In 10.29, describe someone you know in as much detail as you can.

Work with a partner in this exercise, if possible, and build the list of possibilities out loud.

DOCUMENT

At the end of the textbook chapter for lesson 10 you will find a brief poem for reading practice: "Paris at Night," from *Paroles*, by Jacques Prévert.

You have seen Prévert in an irreverent vein in lessons 5 and 8; here is a poem that is a little more romantic. Like the bursts of light that dot Paris at night, three matches illuminate a face, first revealing it in its entirety (*ton visage tout entier*), then highlighting its two most striking features. After the last match goes out, darkness cloaks the lovers' embrace (*En te serrant dans mes bras*). But it cannot obscure the image of the face, whose remembered radiance fills the darkness with its light (*l'obscurité tout entière pour me rappeler tout cela*).

• **Suggested oral assignment.** Do a reading of "Paris at Night." Don't rush as you read (remember you are reading a poem), and be sure to make the appropriate *liaisons: trois* /z/allumettes, *tout* /t/*entier*, *tes* /z/*yeux*, *tout* /t/*entière*. Note that the *-c-* of *seconde* is pronounced /g/. Send your reading to your instructor on the same cassette you use for the oral production part of summary quiz 10. (See the course syllabus for details.)

SELF-TESTING EXERCISES

• Complete and check exercises 10.30, 10.31, and 10.32 as usual.

SUMMARY QUIZ

Consult the course syllabus or check with your instructor for information about completing and handing in summary quiz 10.

LESSON 11
Encounters I

The story

Maybe today, May 29, our two characters will meet. It's a lovely spring day, so, predictably, there's a student strike in Paris.

Mireille, an art student at the Sorbonne, is sitting on a chair in the Luxembourg Garden. Robert, who arrived in Paris yesterday, comes out of his hotel for a look around the Latin Quarter. Maybe today. . .

Meanwhile, back at the Luxembourg Garden, an idle young man sees an attractive young woman on a chair. He approaches and tries several opening gambits: the weather, the cloudless sky, even the old "Do you come here often?" He turns out not to be Robert.

The young man stays at bat, though he has obviously struck out. He even tries to guess the source of Mireille's pretty skirt. After he has named most of the top designers, Mireille says her first and only words: "I get all my clothes at the Prisunic" (something like our K-Mart). This guy has to get an A for effort because even that put-down doesn't stop him. He introduces himself. Finally, Mireille just gets up and walks away.

Maybe not today, after all. . . .

Notes on culture and communication

• **Ça vient de chez Dior!** Dior, Fath, Saint-Laurent, Lanvin, Courrèges, Cardin, and Givenchy are fashion designers specializing in *haute couture*, one of the major luxury industries in France.

• **Prisunic**, on the other hand, is a department store chain that sells discount items and inexpensive ready-to-wear clothing.

• **Vanity and comic behavior.** Jean-Pierre Bourdon the pick-up artist is trying to make it with a woman—any woman. Why is he so offensive that he becomes comic? The French philosopher Henri Bergson theorized that the basic cause of comic behavior is human vanity. We laugh at people because they are so dominated by their high opinion of themselves. Jean-Pierre may be a fundamentally weak person who has a compulsion to succeed with women. He is vain enough to think that they will fall for his worn-out tricks. His whole body exudes vanity: his aggression into their personal space, his exaggeratedly self-assured stance, the stiff haughtiness of his movement, his impertinent glance, the expression of disdain around his mouth.

Content and learning objectives of lesson 11

This lesson shows further ways in which speakers of French talk about the weather and the seasons of the year. It also shows how they refer to events that happened in the immediate past.

The following points are highlighted in lesson 11 (you should concentrate on sections marked with a √):

- *Il fait* with weather
- Present tense with *depuis*
- Exclamations with *quel, quelle, quels, quelles*
- √ Immediate past tense: *venir de* + infinitive (11.19-11.22)
- √ Direct object pronouns *le, la, les, me, te, nous, vous* (11.23-11.28)
- √ Reflexive pronouns (11.29-11.33)

ASSIMILATION OF THE TEXT

11.1-11.3 Text work-up, aural comprehension, and oral production

- Proceed as usual in sections 11.1-11.3. (Refer to lesson 3.1-3.3 for directions, if necessary.) Work with the text and illustrations in the textbook, as in previous lessons.

TOWARD COMMUNICATION

11.4-11.7 Observation and activation: Pronunciation; the semi-vowels /w/ and /ɥ/

The two sounds presented in section 11.4 are called **semi-vowels** because they have characteristics of both vowel and consonant sounds.

The semi-vowel /ɥ/ starts with an /y/ sound (as in *tu*), made, as you remember from lesson 6, with tongue in the very front of the mouth and lips extended in a tight pout. The instant you make the /y/ sound, however, you shift to the vowel sound /i/, as in words like *huit* and *lui*. In going from /y/ to /i/ your lips spread slightly, but your tongue should not change position; it stays lightly pressed against your lower front teeth.

Similarly, /w/ is an /u/ sound (as in *vous*), made with lips forward and tongue toward the back of the mouth. As soon as you make the /u/ sound, you shift to the vowel sound /i/, as in the examples given in 11.4.

• Listen to the examples in 11.4, repeating them until you are confident you have found the correct position of tongue and lips for the two sounds. Then complete the exercises, repeating the sounds you hear in 11.5 and 11.6 (11.6 helps you review the /y/ sound).

• In 11.7, determine whether you hear /ɥ/ (*lui*) or /w/ (*Louis*) and check the appropriate boxes on the grid in your workbook.

√ Check your answers in key 11.7 at the back of the workbook.

11.8 Observation: Real time and narrative time

In French, as in English, different expressions are used to designate various moments in time depending on whether the point of reference is or is not the present.

When our point of reference is the present, we use words like *today*, *yesterday*, and *tomorrow;* "I'll call her **tomorrow**," we say. But if our point of reference is the past, we use slightly different expressions: "I called her **the following day.**"

In French, May 29 is *aujourd'hui* when you are speaking to someone on that day; the day before and the day after are *hier* and *demain.* But from the point of view of the story, which took place on a certain May 29 and is being told at a later date, May 28 and May 30 are *la veille* and *le lendemain.*

11.9, 11.10 Observation and activation: Present tense with *depuis*

You saw in lesson 9 that the present tense is used with *il y a . . . que* and *ça fait . . . que* to indicate an action that began in the past and is continuing into the present.

Il y a . . . que and *ça fait . . . que* are used with expressions that tell the total amount of **elapsed time**: "Ça fait **24 heures** que Robert est à Paris."

Chart 11.9 introduces another expression that can be used with the present tense to refer to actions that began in the past and are still going on in the present: *depuis.* Like *ça fait . . . que* and *il y a . . . que*, *depuis* is used with expressions that refer to periods of elapsed time: *un jour, deux semaines, 24 heures.* Unlike the other two, *depuis* is also used with words that indicate a specific **point in time**: *hier, le 29 mai, 3h15,* and so forth.

• In exercise 11.10, you will hear a number of questions about activities and situations. Answer by saying how long each activity or situation has been going on. (You will find the expressions of time you need printed in the workbook.) Use *il y a . . . que, ça fait . . . que,* or *depuis,* as in the example. Remember that *depuis, il y a . . . que,* and *ça fait . . . que* are interchangeable in sentences that mention stretches of **elapsed time**. When a **point** in time (a precise day, date, or hour) is specified, however, only *depuis* is used.

Audio cues (for reference):
11.10 Activation orale: Présent duratif

1. Grand-tante Amélie est veuve?
2. Robert est à Paris?
3. Robert est à Paris?
4. Mireille est étudiante?
5. Mireille se repose sur un banc?
6. Le jeune homme se promène dans le jardin du Luxembourg?
7. Il fait beau?
8. Les étudiants font la grève?
9. Mireille s'habille à Prisunic?

11.11-11.14 Observation and activation: Time, weather, and the seasons

The seasons and their characteristic weather are the subjects of charts 11.11 and 11.12.

• In exercise 11.13, you will hear a dialogue on the audio recording, followed by four questions about the seasons. Listen to the dialogue and answer the questions.

• In 11.14, you will hear a series of incomplete sentences that compare the weather for one season with the weather for another. Complete each comparison using the contrasting expression you see in the workbook, as in the example.

Audio cues (for reference):
11.14 Activation orale: Le temps qu'il fait

1. En été il fait beau, mais en hiver...
2. En janvier il fait froid, mais en août...
3. En juin il fait bon, mais en avril...
4. En été, le ciel est bleu, mais en automne...
5. En automne, il pleut, mais en hiver...
6. En automne il y a des nuages, mais en été...

11.15-11.18 Observation and activation: Exclamations

Chart 11.15 will familiarize you with ways of expressing an intense reaction to a thing or event. *Quel* is used in exclamations with nouns; *que* is used in phrases that include a verb. They may be used to express a positive reaction ("quel beau ciel!") or a negative reaction ("quel sale temps!"), depending on the adjective you use.

Occasionally, you will hear *quel* used with a noun alone, as chart 11.16 demonstrates. In that case, the tone of voice and the context tell you whether the reaction is positive or negative: "Quel ciel!" can refer to a beautiful sky or a threatening sky, depending on what the sky actually looks like.

Quel functions like an adjective, appearing as masculine or feminine, singular or plural according to the noun it accompanies. Notice that there is **no article** between *quel* and the noun.

• In exercise 11.18, you will hear a series of exclamations with *que* and a verb. Respond with an equivalent exclamation containing *quel*. To select the appropriate form of *quel*, you will need to decide whether each exclamation focuses on a word that is masculine or feminine, singular or plural. Write the proper form in the workbook.

√ Check your answers in key 11.18 at the back of the workbook.

Audio cues (for reference):
11.18 Activation orale et écrite: Exclamation; quel

1. Que sa jupe est ravissante!
2. Que le ciel est bleu!
3. Qu'il fait froid!
4. Qu'il fait mauvais!
5. Que son sourire est beau!
6. Que ses yeux sont beaux!
7. Que ses mains sont belles!
8. Que ce garçon est bavard!
9. Qu'il a l'air bête!
10. Que cette rencontre est intéressante!
11. Que cette histoire est fascinante!

11.19, 11.20 Observation and activation: *aller* and *venir*

You saw in lesson 2 how the verb *aller* is used with *à* to indicate the place **toward which** a person is going: "Elle va à la fac." The place **from which** a person or thing is coming is expressed by *venir* used with *de*, as chart 11.19 illustrates.

• Exercise 11.20 gives you practice using *venir* to say where people are coming from. You will hear a series of questions about where people are coming from. Answer each question with the appropriate form of *venir de.* The information about places is given in the workbook. Remember that *de* combines with the definite articles *le* (⇒ **du**) and *les* (⇒ **des**); see lesson 8.

Audio cues (for reference):
11.20 Activation orale: Venir

1. D'où venez-vous, vous deux?
2. D'où viens-tu?
3. D'où vient Robert?
4. D'où venez-vous, vous deux?
5. D'où vient Mireille?
6. D'où vient Robert?
7. D'où viennent tes soeurs?
8. D'où vient Mme Belleau?
9. Et moi, devinez d'où je viens.

11.21, 11.22 Observation and activation: Immediate past with *venir de*

You saw in lesson 3 how *aller* can be used with infinitives to refer to what is about to happen: "nous **allons** apprendre le français." That construction was called the **immediate future**. There is an **immediate past**, too, used to refer to what has just happened. It is expressed by *venir de* with an infinitive: "Elle **vient de sortir** de l'Institut."

• Exercise 11.22 will give you practice using *venir de* to talk about the immediate past. You will be asked whether various people have been where they are for a long time. Answer no, they just arrived, using appropriate forms of *venir de.*

Audio cues (for reference):
11.22 Activation orale: Passé immédiat; venir de

1. Ça fait longtemps que Robert est à Paris?
2. Ça fait longtemps que Robert et Mireille sont là?
3. Ça fait longtemps que vous êtes ici, tous les deux?
4. Ça fait longtemps que Mireille est au Luxembourg?
5. Ça fait longtemps que tu es là, toi?

11.23, 11.24 Observation and activation: Personal pronouns *le, la, les*

Recall from lesson 2 that pronouns can stand in for nouns, identifying people or things that are familiar from the context and no longer need to be referred to by name. The pronouns you saw in lesson 2 replaced **subject** nouns, that is, the agent of the principal action of the sentence: in "**elle** voit le jeune homme," *elle* = Mireille, since Mireille is the one who performs the action of seeing.

Sections 11.23-11.28 introduce another kind of pronoun: one that replaces a **direct object** noun, that is, the target or recipient of the principal action. In "le jeune homme remarque **Mireille**," Mireille is not the one doing the noticing, but rather the one that gets noticed. A noun that has this function is called a **direct object**, because the action of the verb is focused directly on it, and the pronouns that replace such nouns are known as **direct object pronouns**. In "le jeune homme **la** remarque," *la*, which replaces Mireille, is a **direct object pronoun**.

Chart 11.23 presents the **third person** direct object pronouns. Notice that the three pronouns *le, la,* and *les* are indistinguishable from the definite articles *le, la,* and *les*. In addition, the pronouns *le* and *la* (like the articles *le, la*) contract when followed by a word beginning with a vowel sound: *elle* **l'***aime* (*élision*). And like the article *les*, the direct object pronoun *les* links up with a following vowel sound: *elle les /z/aime* (*liaison*).

• In exercise 11.24, you will hear a series of sentences that say what Jean-Pierre notices in his encounter with Mireille. What he notices is expressed by a direct object noun (*Mireille*, *sa jupe*, *son pull*, and so forth). Determine whether each of these nouns is masculine or feminine, singular or plural, and replace it with the appropriate direct object pronoun (*le, la, l'*, or *les*).

Audio cues (for reference):
11.24 Activation orale: Les pronoms personnels le, la, les

1. Jean-Pierre Bourdon remarque Mireille.
2. Il remarque sa jupe rouge.
3. Il remarque son pull blanc.
4. Il remarque sa taille fine.
5. Il remarque ses cheveux blonds.
6. Il remarque ses doigts longs et fins.
7. Il trouve ses jambes jolies.
8. Il trouve son visage agréable.
9. Il aime la jupe de Mireille.
10. Il aime le pull de Mireille.
11. Il aime ses yeux bleus.
12. Il aime beaucoup les jupes rouges.
13. Il aime beaucoup les filles qui ne sont pas bavardes.

11.25, 11.26 Observation and activation: Personal pronouns *me, te, nous, vous*

The diagrams in chart 11.25 introduce direct object pronouns for the **first** and **second persons**, singular and plural. Again, you will notice elision (*je* **m'***ennuie*, *il* **t'***ennuie*) and *liaison* (*il nous /z/ennuie*, *il vous /z/ennuie*) before words beginning with a vowel sound.

• In exercise 11.26, you will be asked whether various people find Jean-Pierre interesting. Say no, he bores them, using the appropriate direct object pronoun.

Audio cues (for reference):
11.26 Activation orale: Pronoms personnels objets directs

1. Vous trouvez Jean-Pierre intéressant?
2. Tu trouves Jean-Pierre intéressant?
3. Mireille trouve Jean-Pierre intéressant?
4. Robert trouve Jean-Pierre intéressant?
5. Ses amis trouvent Jean-Pierre intéressant?
6. Vous trouvez Jean-Pierre intéressant, vous deux?
7. Et moi, est-ce que vous pensez que je trouve Jean-Pierre intéressant?

11.27, 11.28 Observation and activation: Position of personal pronouns

Chart 11.27 shows how direct object pronouns are placed directly in front of the verb, in both positive and negative expressions.

• In exercise 11.28, you will be asked whether Robert or Mireille know various people. Say no, replacing the person they don't know with a direct object pronoun, and being careful to place the pronoun before the verb, just after *ne*.

Audio cues (for reference):
11.28 Activation orale: Place des pronoms personnels objets directs

1. Est-ce que Mireille connaît Robert?
2. Est-ce que Robert connaît Mireille?
3. Est-ce qu'il connaît les parents de Mireille?
4. Est-ce que Robert connaît Hubert?
5. Est-ce que Robert me connaît, moi?
6. Est-ce que Robert nous connaît?

11.29-11.33 Observation and activation: Reflexive pronouns

You have just seen (sections 11.23-11.28) how French speakers use subject and object pronouns that refer to different people: "Mireille voit Jean-Pierre" ⇒ "**elle le** voit," "Jean-Pierre remarque Mireille" ⇒ "**il la** remarque," and so forth.

It is perfectly possible, even common, to encounter a situation in which the **subject** of an action and the **object** of that action are the **same** individual. (This is as true in English as it is in French. In an expression like "Pull yourself together," for instance, the puller and the pulled are the same person.) Verbs used in this way are called **reflexive verbs**, and the object pronouns used in reflexive expressions are called **reflexive pronouns**.

Chart 11.29 contrasts the reflexive and nonreflexive use of two common verbs. Aunt Georgette can take Fido out for a walk, or she can take herself out for a walk. Marie-Laure can dress her doll, or she can dress herself. Virtually any verb that takes a direct object can be used reflexively; the subject simply takes on the additional role of object.

Chart 11.30 presents the forms of the reflexive pronouns. They are simple to use: except for the third person, reflexive pronouns are identical to the nonreflexive object pronouns you saw in 11.23-11.28. And the exception—the third person reflexive pronoun *se*—is the same for masculine and feminine, singular and plural.

Chart 11.31 contains further examples of verbs used reflexively.

• Exercise 11.32 will give you practice using reflexive verbs. It is divided into three sections. In section (1), answer the questions about where people's clothes come from by saying that everyone gets their clothes at a famous designer's (take your pick). Use appropriate forms of *s'habiller*.

• In section (2), you will hear about various people's expectations. Say they're all mistaken, using the proper form of *se tromper*.

• In section (3), some creep is bothering you, Mireille, and her sister. Say that the people being bothered are getting up and leaving, using *se lever* and *s'en aller*.

Audio cues (for reference):
11.32 Activation orale: Verbes réfléchis

1. s'habiller
   1. Vos vêtements viennent de Prisunic?
   2. Ton pull vient de Prisunic?
   3. Le pull de Colette vient de Prisunic?
   4. Les jupes de tes cousines viennent de Prisunic?
   5. La jupe de ta mère vient de Prisunic?
   6. Vous avez de jolies jupes toutes les deux! Elles viennent de Prisunic?
   7. Et moi, vous pensez que ma jupe vient de Prisunic?

2. se tromper
   1. Jean-Pierre pense que Mireille va dire quelque chose.
   2. Mireille espère que Jean-Pierre va s'en aller.
   3. Moi, je crois que Robert va rencontrer Mireille au Luxembourg.
   4. Vous pensez que ça va être un roman d'amour?
   5. Tu crois que nous allons avoir un crime dans l'histoire?

3. se lever et s'en aller
   1. Ce type m'ennuie.
   2. Ce type ennuie Mireille.
   3. Il y a un type qui ennuie Mireille et sa soeur.

• In the written exercise in 11.33, decide whether the missing forms of each verb in parentheses are reflexive (in which case the direct object of the verb will be its subject) or nonreflexive (the direct object will be another person or thing). Write the appropriate form in your workbook.

√ Check your answers in key 11.33 at the back of the workbook.

11.34 Activation: Dialogue between Mireille and Jean-Pierre

Listen to the conversation between Mireille and Jean-Pierre and memorize Jean-Pierre's lines, repeating and imitating as usual.

TOWARD FREE EXPRESSION

11.35 Words at large

Proceed as usual. (If necessary, refer to lesson 3 for directions.)

11.36, 11.37 Role-playing and reinvention of the story

In 11.36, you are Jean-Pierre trying to get acquainted with an uncooperative Mireille in the Luxembourg Garden. See how long you can keep the monologue going.

In 11.37, by contrast, your attempts to strike up a conversation are successful, and Mireille turns out to be very talkative indeed. Reinvent the encounter, making Mireille as pleasant—or as unpleasant—as you wish. You may use the alternatives suggested in section 11.37 of the workbook as a point of departure.

If you work with a partner, take roles and complete the exercise (orally, of course). When you have finished, switch roles and do it again. If you work by yourself, take both roles.

• **Suggested written assignment.** Write out a version of the dialogue in 11.37, above, between Jean-Pierre and a talkative Mireille. Write five complete exchanges between them. Send this assignment to your instructor along with the answer sheet to summary quiz 11. (See the course syllabus for details.)

DOCUMENT

At the end of the textbook chapter for lesson 11 you will find a text for reading practice.

Recette is a recipe for cooking up a story, including step-by-step directions for choosing the ingredients, adding just the right amount of spice (*des hommes et des femmes . . . sinon ce n'est pas amusant*), and stirring everything up into a fine adventure. Not to mention finding someone to serve it all up to. . . .

SELF-TESTING EXERCISES

- Complete and check exercises 11.38-11.41 as usual.

SUMMARY QUIZ

Consult the course syllabus or check with your instructor for information about completing and handing in summary quiz 11.

LESSON 12
Encounters II

The story

The same day, half an hour later. (It may still happen!) We see Robert doing his good deed for the day by helping an old woman whose sack of potatoes has broken. We see Jean-Pierre Bourdon striking out again, and Mireille arriving home. She is surprised to find Marie-Laure, who explains that a sore throat has kept her out of school.

There is a card for Mireille from a friend, Ghislaine, who is vacationing in Brighton, England, with her boyfriend Bruce. Marie-Laure doesn't understand the card very well, and Mireille—not too graciously—explains it to her. Then Mireille phones Ghislaine, and the two discuss the dreadful weather in Brighton and the beautiful Paris spring. Ghislaine keeps catching colds, while Mireille keeps getting sunburned. Ghislaine is spending fortunes on aspirin; Mireille, on suntan oil, and so forth.

After the phone call, Mireille leaves again for school. Marie-Laure, who asks if her sister has any English boyfriends at school, is told to mind her own business.

Events are bringing people closer together. Jean-Pierre strikes out for a third time. Robert, who has followed a group of student demonstrators to the Place de la Sorbonne, runs into Jean-Pierre and asks him about the demonstration. Mireille stops in the Sorbonne to check a bulletin-board and then goes out into the courtyard. This brings her very near Robert, who, noticing her striking good looks, smiles at her. She, a little amused, returns the smile. Contact!

But who is that strange man in black passing behind them?

Notes on culture and communication

• **La Sorbonne.** Founded in 1227 in the heart of the Latin Quarter, the Sorbonne is the oldest university in France. It ranks today among the most prestigious branches of the University of Paris, specializing in arts and letters.

• **Grèves et manifestations.** Student strikes and demonstrations recur cyclically in the history of French academic life, and are a part of its folklore. The most serious and far-reaching protests in recent history occurred in May of 1968 and continued through the early 70's in the aftermath of the "May Events." More recently, student unrest caused significant disruptions in late 1986.

• **The Gallic shrug.** For all his offensiveness, we can be grateful to Jean-Pierre the pick-up artist for demonstrating one of the most beautiful and typical French body movements. If you watch the screen carefully (in slow motion, if possible) you will see a magnificent Gallic shrug when he answers Robert's questions about the nature of the student demonstration. His shrug takes no more than half a second, but you can plainly see the raised shoulders, protruding lips, and the pulling down of the lower facial muscles to express his ignorance of what is going on.

Content and learning objectives of lesson 12

This lesson shows how French speakers talk about health and refer to various parts of the body. It will also familiarize you with ways of asking for more precise information about a general topic, expressing impatience, and giving commands.

The following points are highlighted in lesson 12 (you should concentrate on sections marked with a √):

√• Interrogative adjective *quel* (12.7, 12.8)
• Reciprocal verbs
√• Imperative and personal pronouns; negative imperative (12.13-12.17)
• *Pouvoir*, present indicative
• *Suivre*, present indicative
√• Verb patterns in the present indicative (12.25-12.27)
• Masculine and feminine forms, review and extension

ASSIMILATION OF THE TEXT

12.1-12.3 Text work-up, aural comprehension and oral production

• Proceed as usual in sections 12.1 and 12.2. (Refer to lesson 3.1, 3.2 for directions, if necessary.)

In 12.3, you will hear Ghislaine's lines in her conversation with Mireille about the weather. Take Mireille's part, responding with the opposite of what you hear Ghislaine say, as in the example.

Work with the text and illustrations in the textbook, as in previous lessons.

TOWARD COMMUNICATION

12.4, 12.5 Observation and activation: Pronunciation; vowel alternation

The *e* of the stem of verbs such as *prendre* can be pronounced in two different ways, depending on whether it falls in an open syllable (one that ends in a vowel sound: **pre***nons*) or a closed syllable (one that ends in a consonant sound: **prennent**). In an open syllable, the *e* is pronounced /ə/, like the *e* of *l***e**. In a closed syllable, it is pronounced /ɛ/, like the *e* of **e***lle*.

Notice that the /ɛ/ sound of the closed syllable can be written in two ways: as *è* (*prom***è***ne*) and as *e* followed by a double consonant (*compr***enn***ent*).

• Listen to the examples of /ə/ and /ɛ/ on the audio recording, and repeat each one. Notice the spelling patterns for the /ɛ/ sound.

12.6 Observation: Impatience

This section presents a number of expressions you can use when someone is annoying you. Note the familiar form in many of these reprimands ("Tu m'ennuies . . . ," "Occupe-toi . . . ," "Arrête!"): they are for use only with people you know well enough to call *tu*. (Those are just the ones, of course, who can be the most annoying.)

12.7, 12.8 Observation and activation: Interrogative adjective *quel*

You saw *quel* used with exclamations in lesson 11. *Quel* is also used in questions to ask for more specific information. Its function is to narrow down a range of possible options. Of all the sports you could play, "**quels** sports pratiquez-vous?" Is it nice out? Raining? Snowing? "**Quel** temps fait-il?"

As it does with exclamations, *quel* with questions will vary in form according to the noun it modifies: feminine or masculine, singular or plural.

• In exercise 12.8, determine whether the nouns you see are masculine or feminine, singular or plural, and write the appropriate forms of *quel* in your workbook.

√ Check your answers in key 12.8 at the back of the workbook.

12.9, 12.10 Observation and activation: Health; parts of the body

Chart 12.9 shows how to talk about pain localized in a particular part of the body. General, nonspecific illness is expressed with *être* and the adjective *malade*. When the source of discomfort can be pinpointed in a specific area, however, the expression *avoir mal à* is used, followed by the affected part of the body: "j'ai mal **à la tête**." Note the presence of the definite article: *à* **la** *tête*.

• In exercise 12.10 you will hear a series of exclamations referring to various areas of the body; for each one, ask if that part of the body hurts, using *avoir mal à* as in the examples.

Audio cues (for reference):

12.10 Activation orale; Parties du corps

1. Oh la, mon cou!
2. Oh la, ma tête!
3. Oh la, ma jambe!
4. Oh la, mon doigt!
5. Oh la, mon oreille!
6. Oh la, mes yeux!
7. Oh la, mes dents!
8. Oh la, mon ventre!
9. Oh la, ma gorge!

12.11, 12.12 Observation and activation: Reciprocity

In lesson 11 you saw that verbs used with subjects and objects that are the same are called **reflexive verbs**: "ils se promènent," "elle s'habille."

In their **plural** forms, these verbs can refer to actions directed reciprocally to others as well as to oneself: "ils s'aiment" can designate people who love each other as well as people who love themselves. Generally, any possible ambiguity is resolved by the context: in "ils se rencontrent dans la cour," it is clear that the subjects are meeting each other, not themselves.

• The written exercise in 12.12 contains pairs of sentences that show the two sides of a reciprocal action separately. Combine each pair into a single sentence using appropriate forms of the reflexive verb, as in the example.

√ Check your answers in key 12.12 at the back of the workbook.

12.13-12.17 Observation and activation: Imperative and pronouns

You saw in lesson 11 that the noun objects of verbs can be replaced by pronouns (*le, la, les, me, te, nous, vous*): "il remarque Mireille" ⇒ "il **la** remarque."

The sentences in 11.21 were in the **indicative**, but in the **imperative**, too—the command form of the verb—pronouns can replace direct object nouns: "Regarde Mireille!" ⇒ "Regarde-**la**!" In the indicative, the pronoun comes before the verb. In the imperative, its position is different: it follows the verb, and is linked to it by a hyphen.

Chart 12.13 lists the pronouns that are used with the imperative. Notice that *moi* and *toi* are the same as the **stressed** pronouns.

Notice, too, that *toi* and *vous* become **reflexive** pronouns when used with the command form of the verb, since the subject and object are the same person: "Regarde-**toi**!", "regardez-**vous**!"

Chart 12.15 illustrates the negative use of the command form with pronouns. In negative commands, the pronoun comes before the verb, as it does in the indicative.

• In exercise 12.14, you will hear a series of sentences that express necessity. Follow up with the logical command, using the appropriate imperative and direct object pronoun.

Audio cues (for reference):
12.14 Activation orale: Pronoms personnels et impératif

1. Il faut que tu demandes le numéro de téléphone de Mireille.
2. Il faut vous reposer.
3. Il faut te reposer.
4. Il faut écouter le professeur, vous deux.
5. Toi aussi, il faut écouter le professeur.
6. Il faut vous lever.
7. Et toi aussi, il faut te lever.
8. Il faut nous reposer.

• Changing one's mind and contradicting others are two of the privileges of rational beings. Exercises 12.16 and 12.17 will let you practice exercising these privileges. In 12.16, you will hear various commands. Follow up with the opposite command. Since the original commands are positive, your countercommands will be negative. Remember that the direct object pronouns will come **before** the verb.

Audio cues (for reference):
12.16 Activation orale: Contrordres; impératif et négation

1. Lève-toi.
2. Repose-toi.
3. Regarde-moi.
4. Regardez-moi!
5. Reposez-vous.

• In 12.17, it's just the reverse. Your countercommands will be positive, and the pronouns will come **after** the verb. (Don't forget about *moi* and *toi*.)

Audio cues (for reference):
12.17 Activation orale: Contrordres

1. Ne te lève pas.
2. Ne te repose pas.
3. Ne vous reposez pas.
4. Ne les appelez pas.
5. Ne la regardez pas.

12.18 Observation: Present indicative of *pouvoir*

Chart 12.18 presents the forms of the verb *pouvoir*. Notice that the infinitive stem *pou-* of *pouvoir* appears in the *nous* and *vous* forms of the plural. In all three of the singular forms, and in the *ils/elles* form of the plural, a different vowel sound is present, /ø/. Although they are written differently, the singular forms *peux* and *peut* are pronounced the same way,

12.19, 12.20 Observation and activation: Present indicative of *suivre*

In studying chart 12.19, notice that all three of the plural forms have the consonant sound /v/ that is found in the infinitive. Notice also that this /v/ sound is absent in the singular forms. Although they are written differently, the singular forms *suis* and *suit* are pronounced the same way.

Finally, compare the *je* form of *suivre* with the *je* form of *être:* by pure coincidence, they are identical. (The other forms of the two verbs show no similarity at all.)

• Complete the exercise in 12.20 by writing the appropriate forms of *suivre* in your workbook.

√ Check your answers in key 12.20 at the back of the workbook.

12.21-12.23 Observation and activation: Present indicative of *sortir* and *partir*

As chart 12.21 shows, *sortir* and *partir* follow a pattern similar to that of *suivre:* the three singular forms are identical in sound (though not in writing), and the plural forms have a consonant sound (/t/ in the case of *sortir* and *partir*) that is not found in the singular. (*Il sort* is written with a *t* that is not pronounced.)

• In exercise 12.22, you will be asked whether various people are staying home; say no, they are going out, using appropriate forms of *sortir*.

Audio cues (for reference):
12.22 Activation orale: Sortir; présent de l'indicatif

1. Tu restes à la maison?
2. Robert reste à la maison?
3. Et vous deux, vous restez à la maison?
4. Mireille et Ghislaine restent à la maison?
5. Tu restes à la maison?

• In 12.23, you will be asked whether various people are in a hurry; say they are leaving right away, using *partir* as in the example.

Audio cues (for reference):
12.23 Activation orale: Partir; présent de l'indicatif

1. Tu es pressé?
2. Mireille est pressée?
3. Les Belleau sont pressés?
4. Vous êtes pressés, vous deux?
5. Tu es pressé?

12.24 Observation: Present indicative of *prendre, apprendre, comprendre*

Like the singular forms of *sortir* and *partir*, the singular forms of *prendre* are identical in sound. (The same is true of the related verbs *apprendre* and *comprendre*.) In the plural forms *apprenons, apprenez, apprennent* a consonant sound (/n/) appears that is not heard in the singular.

12.25-12.27 Observation and activation: Singular forms of the present tense

In the last few sections, you have observed a recurring pattern: the *je, tu,* and *il/elle* forms of verbs are pronounced exactly the same. Chart 12.25 confirms and extends this pattern, which can be found in the overwhelming majority of verbs in French. (Obvious exceptions to this rule—as to many other rules—are *aller, être,* and *avoir*.)

• Exercises 12.26 and 12.27 give you practice in saying and writing singular and plural forms of the verbs studied in lesson 12.

In 12.26, you will be asked a number of questions; answer using the *je* form of the verb you heard, as in the example. (The verb form you say should, of course, be the same as the one you hear, since the three singular forms are identical in sound.)

In 12.27, write answers to the questions you see in the workbook. Notice that when the verb form to be written is a singular, the question will also contain a singular; the same is true for the plural. This makes your task easier because of the similarities inside each group. As you write **singular** forms, however, recall that even though all the singular forms of each verb are **pronounced** the same way, they are not **written** the same way.

Audio cues (for reference):

12.26 Activation orale: Présent de l'indicatif; personnes du singulier

1. Tu comprends?
2. Tu sors?
3. Tu fais la sieste?
4. Tu connais la famille de Mireille?
5. Tu prends l'autobus?
6. Tu viens au cinéma?
7. Tu peux venir?
8. Tu apprends le français?

12.28, 12.29 Observation and activation: Masculine and feminine forms (review and extension)

Chart 12.28 presents adjectives encountered in lesson 12 in terms of a pattern you saw in lesson 6: the feminine forms end in a consonant sound that is absent in the masculine. In writing, the feminine forms end in *-e*.

• Listen to the dictation exercise in section 12.29 and complete the sentences in your workbook, using the masculine and feminine forms you hear.

√ Check your answers in key 12.29 at the back of the workbook.

12.30 Activation: Dialogue between Ghislaine and Mireille

Listen to the conversation between Ghislaine and Mireille and memorize Mireille's lines, imitating and repeating as usual.

TOWARD FREE EXPRESSION

12.31 Words at large

Proceed as usual. (If necessary, refer to lesson 3 for directions.)

12.32, 12.33 Role-playing and reinvention of the story

In 12.32, attempt to strike up a conversation with a man or woman whom you don't know and who is apparently rendered speechless by your charm. Take your inspiration from Jean-Pierre Bourdon, drawing on his techniques, modifying them, improving on them in any way you like. Above all, imitate Jean-Pierre's persistence: say everything you can, don't give up, and don't take silence for an answer. If you work with a partner, take turns approaching and being approached.

In 12.33, tell the story of the old woman whom Robert helps in a street in the Latin Quarter when her bag of potatoes falls to the sidewalk. Use the alternatives suggested in your workbook as a point of departure. If you work with someone else, go back and forth and build the story together, or imagine two parallel stories.

• **Suggested oral assignment.** Record a version of the one-sided conversation in 12.32, saying five to eight sentences. Send this assignment to your instructor on the cassette you use for summary quiz 12. (See the course syllabus for details.)

DOCUMENTS

At the end of the textbook chapter for lesson 12 you will find a quotation and a meteorological report for reading practice.

Nathalie Sarraute (b. 1902) is one of the most famous and influential writers of contemporary France. Her comment on chance encounters (she doesn't believe they happen completely by chance—at least, not the ones that count) places her squarely within an old tradition in French writing: the tradition of the aphorism or maxim, that pithy, witty comment, often ironic or paradoxical, that seems to sum up volumes in a few short words. The seventeenth-century writers Pascal, La Fontaine, and La Rochefoucauld are most often associated with this aphoristic tradition in French litterature and thought.

SELF-TESTING EXERCISES

• Complete and check exercises 12.34, 12.35, and 12.36 as usual.

SUMMARY QUIZ

Consult the course syllabus or check with your instructor for information about completing and handing in summary quiz 12.

LESSON 13
Encounters III

The story

Same day; by now it is 11 a.m. In the courtyard of the Sorbonne, Jean-Pierre asks a young woman for a light. Still no luck. Then, up on the third floor, he goes to the head of a line of students, where the target is a young woman with dark hair. Jean-Pierre claims to have met her last summer at St. Tropez. But the young woman has the perfect answer: she hates summer, so she spends all her summers in Patagonia, where it is winter. A general outburst against cutting in sends Jean-Pierre to the end of the line. There he asks another young woman, Annick, for a light. Annick's response is not encouraging, but her friend Jean-Luc is much more patient. He identifies some of the people in the line and even discusses courses of study and careers with Jean-Pierre who, it turns out, is 29 and has no clear idea of what he will be when he grows up.

Jean-Pierre draws Jean-Luc's attention to a redhead in the courtyard who he claims is Garbo's granddaughter. She isn't. Jean-Pierre then delivers a dissertation on the art of the pickup. (His techniques, as Annick points out, are hopelessly simpleminded.) The line is moving very slowly and Jean-Pierre has to leave. He has a date with a "real winner" at a nearby café. Annick finds him and his way of talking about women as if they were racehorses utterly repulsive. Jean-Luc comes halfheartedly to Jean-Pierre's defense, and some of Annick's scorn spills over onto him, prompting a heated exchange about Women's Lib.

Notes on culture and communication

• **L'X.** L'Ecole Polytechnique, familiarly referred to as *L'X*, is an elite scientific and polytechnical institute (affiliated with the French army) to which candidates are admitted after a highly competitive examination.

• **HEC.** L'Ecole des Hautes Etudes Commerciales is one of the most prominent French business schools.

• **L'IDHEC.** L'Institut des Hautes Etudes Cinématographiques is the most renowned school of film studies and film technique in France.

• **Langues O.** L'Institut des Langues Orientales is a branch of the

University of Paris specializing in Slavic, Near-Eastern, Middle-Eastern, and Far-Eastern Studies.

• **"L'Année dernière à Marienbad"** is a reference to Alain Resnais's famous film of that name (1961).

• **Smiling at strangers.** Jean-Pierre, with his pathological need to make conversation with women by any and all means, is pathetic. Nevertheless, his case holds a lesson for American women who are traveling for the first time in other parts of the world. People smile for different reasons in different cultures. Even within a culture there are different customs that govern smiling. (People smile less in upper New York State than they do in western Kentucky, for instance.) Americans in general smile at strangers more than other peoples do. The Japanese differ in smiling when they are embarrassed. In the Mediterranean area generally, women do not smile at unknown men unless they welcome the men's advances. This can become a problem for American women abroad who smile at strangers as they would at home. When American women return the smiles of Mediterranean men, they do not mean to solicit advances, but the men interpret these smiles according to their own cultures, and American women sometimes find themselves more involved than they intended.

Content and learning objectives of lesson 13

This lesson shows how French speakers register protest and indicate that they approve. It also shows how they refer to past and upcoming events and talk about abundance and scarcity.

The following points are highlighted in lesson 13 (you should concentrate on sections marked with a √):

- Masculine and feminine forms, review and extension
- √ Interrogative pronoun *lequel, laquelle, lesquels, lesquelles* (13.21, 13.22)
- √ Demonstrative pronoun *celui, celle, ceux, celles* (13.23-13.26)
- *Attendre*, present indicative

ASSIMILATION OF THE TEXT

13.1-13.4 Text work-up, aural comprehension, and oral production

• Proceed as usual in sections 13.1-13.4. (Refer to lesson 3.1-3.3 and lesson 4.3 for directions, if necessary.) Then work with the text and illustrations in the textbook, as in previous lessons.

TOWARD COMMUNICATION

13.5, 13.6 Observation and activation: Pronunciation; the semi-vowel /j/

You saw semi-vowels at work in words like *Louis* and *huit* in lesson 11. Section 13.5 presents /j/, another of these in-between sounds that have features of both vowels and consonants.

In *rien*, the letters *-ien* represent the semi-vowel sound /j/ followed by the nasal vowel /ɛ̃/. There is no separation between the semi-vowel /j/ and the nasal vowel /ɛ̃/; the two sounds are tightly linked.

• Listen to the examples in section 13.6 and repeat the words you hear, imitating the voices on the recording as carefully as you can.

13.7, 13.8 Observation and activation: Protestations

In 13.7 you will find a list of expressions that French speakers use in two circumstances: to disapprove of what someone else is doing ("**Eh, là! Pas de** resquille!") and to protest someone else's disapproval of what they are doing ("**—Oh, la la! Si on ne peut plus** resquiller!").

Notice that *pas de* can be followed by any one of various nouns, depending on the offending activity. Similarly, *comme tout le monde* could follow any imperative phrase. ("A la queue!" is short for "Allez à la queue!", an imperative phrase). Likewise, *si on ne peut plus* could be followed by any infinitive phrase (*resquiller*, *faire du bruit*, *être insolent*). Note that the sentence "Si on ne peut plus **[infinitive]**, où va-t-on?" is the complete expression from which "où va-t-on?" (or "où allons-nous?") is often dropped.

• Review the list in 13.7 and repeat the examples you hear in section 13.8 of the audio program, imitating the voices as exactly as you can.

13.9, 13.10 Observation and activation: Speaking decisively and indecisively

In lesson 4 you saw a series of phrases that are often associated with decisive and indecisive ways of speaking. Chart 13.9 extends this list.

• Repeat the examples you hear in section 13.10 of the audio recording, mimicking the voices as closely as you can.

13.11, 13.12 Observation and activation: Agreement and approval

Section 13.11 contains a number of expressions French speakers use to express agreement and approval.

• In exercise 13.12, react to the statements you hear with an appropriate expression of agreement or approval.

13.13, 13.14 Observation and activation: Time; *dernier, prochain*

You saw in lesson 11 how to refer to today and to the days before and after today (*aujourd'hui, hier, demain*). Chart 13.13 illustrates ways of referring to weeks, months, and years on either side of the present, using the adjectives *dernier* and *prochain.*

• In exercise 13.14, you will be asked about your plans for the near future. Answer with the appropriate form of *prochain.* Since *prochain* has a masculine form that is different from the feminine, you will need to decide whether the noun it applies to is masculine (like *été*) or feminine (like *semaine*) and select the proper form accordingly.

Audio cues (for reference):

13.14 Activation orale: Le temps qui passe; dernier, prochain

1. C'est cet été que vous allez en Patagonie?
2. C'est cette semaine que vous allez à St. Tropez?
3. C'est cette année que tu commences ta médecine?
4. C'est ce mercredi que tu as rendez-vous avec Mireille?

13.15, 13.16 Observation and activation: Studies

Faire is the verb used to talk about taking a specific academic **subject**. It is also used to say you are attending a specialized **school** such as medical school or business school. As section 13.15 illustrates, *faire* is used slightly differently in each case.

With the names of **subjects** or fields, *faire* is used with *de* and the definite article: "Je vais faire **du** droit."

With specific **schools**, and depending on the name of the school, *faire* is used either with the definite article ("Je vais faire **l'**ENA") or, occasionally, with no article at all ("Je vais faire médecine").

Note. In France, institutions such as HEC, Polytechnique, Normale Sup., and so forth are known as *grandes écoles:* highly selective, prestigious professional schools that admit students solely on the basis of a nationwide competitive exam.

• In exercise 13.16, you will be asked whether various schools or various fields of study interest you. Say yes, you plan to go into them, using *faire* and the name of the field or school you hear. Remember to distinguish between subjects and schools, as in the examples.

Audio cues (for reference):
13.16 Activation orale: Etudes

1. L'informatique, ça vous intéresse?
2. L'ENA, ça vous intéresse?
3. La sociologie, ça t'intéresse?
4. Le russe intéresse Colette?
5. Les Langues O. intéressent Colette?
6. Les maths vous intéressent?
7. L'IDHEC, ça vous intéresse?

13.17, 13.18 Observation and activation: Absence and abundance; *manquer*

Chart 13.17 shows how the verb *manquer* can be used to indicate (1) a relative lack of something or (2) its complete absence.

To indicate that something or someone is missing entirely, *manquer* is used with the impersonal pronoun *il* that you have seen in *il pleut* and *il faut:* "**Il** manque quelqu'un."

To say there is not enough of something, the noun is used as the subject of *manquer:* "**le temps** manque," or, more emphatically, "**c'est le temps qui** manque!" Note that when this kind of emphatic statement is put into the negative, it indicates that there is more than enough: "Ce **n'**est **pas** le temps qui manque!"

• In exercise 13.18, you will hear about various situations in which there is not enough or too much. Comment on each situation, using *manquer* positively or negatively, as in the examples.

13.19, 13.20 Observation and activation: Masculine and feminine forms (review and extension)

Chart 13.19 takes the new masculine and feminine forms you have encountered in the last two or three lessons and groups them with familiar masculine/feminine words from earlier lessons.

As you study the chart, you will see patterns emerging that help you predict the masculine or feminine form of adjectives (and nouns formed from adjectives) that you hear for the first time.

For example, you encountered the feminine forms *fascinante* and *élégante* in lesson 12. You know from that lesson that the masculine forms of these words are identical in sound to the feminine forms **except** that the final consonant sound of the feminine is gone: *fascinant, élégant*. In lesson 13 you see that the noun *passant* follows this pattern, as does the adjective *puant:* their feminine forms end in a /t/ sound that is absent in the masculine. As a result, when you come across "un steak saignant" in lesson 24, you can be reasonably certain that in ordering *une côtelette* you would want to specify that it be *saignante*. Likewise, you will be able to predict that the female counterpart of "un figurant" in lesson 40 is *une figurante*.

• Study the chart, saying each word out loud to get the feel of the difference in pronunciation—or, as in the case of words in the *russe/sexiste/impossible* category, the lack of difference. Then complete exercise 13.20, changing the masculine words in the sentences you hear into feminine words, as in the example.

Audio cues (for reference):
13.20 Activation orale: Formes masculines et féminines

1. Nous allons avoir un nouveau garçon dans l'histoire.
2. C'est un dragueur.
3. Il n'est pas très beau.
4. Il est puant ce garçon!
5. Il est un peu resquilleur.
6. Je ne le trouve pas très malin.
7. On dit qu'il est dangereux.
8. En fait, il est assez inoffensif.
9. C'est un bon copain.

13.21-13.26 Observation and activation: *Lequel, celui*

In lesson 10 you saw the demonstrative *ce*, used with nouns to specify which of a number of possible people or things is being talked about: "**ce passeport** est à moi." In lesson 12, you saw *quel*, the question word also used with nouns to narrow down a range of possible options: "**quels sports** pratiquez-vous?" Chart 13.21 presents the counterparts of *quel* and *ce* for use without nouns: *lequel* and *celui*.

Chart 13.22 contrasts *quel*, which works like an adjective (it **accompanies** a noun), and *lequel*, which works like a pronoun (it **replaces** a noun).

Chart 13.23 contrasts *ce*, which functions like an adjective, and *celui*, which functions like a pronoun.

Chart 13.24 points out that *celui* is not used by itself. It occurs in combination with *-ci* and *-là*, or with a phrase that identifies the specific alternative being talked about: "**celui de** Mireille."

• In exercise 13.25, complete the sentences you see in the workbook, using the appropriate forms of *quel* (with a noun) or *lequel* (without one) for questions, and forms of *celui* for answers.

In 13.26, complete the paragraph by adding the forms of *lequel* or *celui* that make the most sense according to the context of each sentence.

√ Check your answers in keys 13.25 and 13.26 at the back of the workbook.

13.27-13.29 Observation and activation: Reality, appearance, semblance

Charts 13.27 and 13.28 show how the expression *faire semblant de* used with an infinitive indicates an effort to disguise reality by pretense or simulation.

Note the distinction between *faire semblant*, which indicates deliberate deception, and *avoir l'air*, which indicates appearance (whether deceptive or not) but does not suggest any **intent** to deceive.

• In exercise 13.29, you will hear a series of statements that say what is really true about people. Point out that they are pretending otherwise, using *faire semblant de*.

Audio cues (for reference):
13.29 Activation orale: Apparence et simulation

1. Il n'est pas vraiment malade!
2. Ils ne comprennent pas.
3. Nous ne comprenons pas.
4. Il ne tombe pas vraiment.
5. Il ne la connaît pas.
6. Elle n'est pas vraiment pressée.

13.30, 13.31 Observation and activation: Waiting; *attendre, faire la queue*

Chart 13.30 illustrates two ways of expressing the notion of waiting: with the verb *attendre*, which can refer to any kind of waiting, and with the expression *faire la queue*, which refers to waiting in line. (To stand in line in British English is to **queue** up.)

• In exercise 13.31, you will be asked whether various people are waiting. Answer by saying yes, they've been standing in line for quite some time.

Audio cues (for reference):
13.31 Activation orale: Attendre, faire la queue

1. Jean-Luc attend?
2. Annick attend?
3. Les jeunes gens attendent?
4. Tu attends?
5. Vous attendez tous les deux?

13.32 Activation: Dialogue between the teacher and a young woman

Listen to the conversation between the teacher and the young woman and memorize the young woman's lines, imitating and repeating as usual.

TOWARD FREE EXPRESSION

13.33 Words at large

Proceed as usual. (If necessary, refer to lesson 3 for directions.)

13.34-13.36 Role-playing and reinvention of the story

In one of the role-playing exercises in lesson 12, you tried to strike up a conversation with an interesting-looking person who wouldn't answer. In 13.34, your new acquaintance will answer. Imagine a possible dialogue, giving at least three responses for each speaker and carrying on for as long after that as you can. The dialogue may be as zany as you wish, as long as it makes sense. If you work with a partner, take parts and complete the scene, then switch roles and do it again. If you work by yourself, take both parts.

In 13.35, paint a verbal portrait of Jean-Pierre Bourdon: his physical appearance, his principal activities, his character. What will he be when he grows up (if he ever does)? What do **you** think of him?

In 13.36, take another crack at solving the riddle of the Man in Black. Where is he from? What is he doing at the Sorbonne? You may select from among the alternatives suggested in the workbook; you may also invent others. Work with a partner, if you can, and build the description together, out loud, of course.

• **Suggested written assignment.** Write out a version of your portrait of Jean-Pierre (exercise 13.35). Five to eight sentences is about right. Send this assignment to your instructor along with summary quiz 13. (See the course syllabus for details.)

SELF-TESTING EXERCISES

- Complete and check exercises 13.37 and 13.38 as usual.

SUMMARY QUIZ

Consult the course syllabus or check with your instructor for information about completing and handing in summary quiz 13.

LESSON 14
Getting underway I

The story

Yes, today is the day! Robert finally breaks the silence by asking Mireille about the demonstration. Then there's the weather, her student status, his nationality. Finally, a real conversation gets started. They talk about Robert's French mother, where he's staying in Paris, the frequency of his trips to France (this is his first). Mireille learns that Robert's father didn't like France, so the family vacationed in Bermuda or Latin America, where the father, a bank vice-president, had "interests." She also learns about the divorce and his mother's remarriage.

Mireille is more than once amused by Robert's ceremoniousness and his inability to understand student slang. She likes him well enough to walk back to the Luxembourg Garden with him on her way home. She leaves him only when she realizes that she was supposed to take Marie-Laure to a dancing lesson an hour ago. Robert is on cloud nine.

That evening, on the same cloud but in a café, he orders an espresso and writes a card to his mother. When he goes to the post office for stamps, he finds the place closed. Well, something had to be less than perfect on the first day, didn't it?

Notes on culture and communication

• **Le Jardin du Luxembourg, Le Sénat.** The Luxembourg Garden, at the edge of the Latin Quarter, is a beautiful park in the French classical style with a central pond where children sail boats, a shaded fountain (Fontaine Médicis), flower beds, and horse-chestnut trees harmoniously laid out in front of the Luxembourg Palace. The Palace, built in the seventeenth century for King Louis XIII's mother, Marie de Médicis, has been the seat of the French Senate since 1879.

• **Speech, sympathy, and the one-second rhythm.** When Robert and Mireille speak, their speech comes out in bursts, with slight pauses between the bursts:

Robert: C'est que [**pause**] je ne veux pas vous ennuyer.
Mireille: Vous ne m'ennuyez pas du tout! [**pause**] En fait, [**pause**] pour être franche, [**pause**] je vous trouve assez sympa.

Each segment lasts about one second. The words may be spoken slowly or fast, but they are all contained in the one-second bursts of speech between pauses. This is part of the **rhythm** of French.

These rhythmic bursts are not limited to speech. In fact, all behavior is segmented into such bursts of energy. In communication, the more synchronized people's rhythms are, the closer the sympathy they feel for each other. Look at Robert and Mireille walking together: they are absolutely in step, and each step takes about a second. Their instantaneous attraction is reflected in the highly synchronized dance of speech and movement they perform when they meet.

Content and learning objectives of lesson 14

This lesson illustrates ways of expressing agreement or disagreement with what people say and approval or disapproval of what they do. It will familiarize you with ways of talking about routine activities and referring to the past. Lesson 14 also shows how to respond to a compliment and how to identify different degrees of politeness.

The following points are highlighted in lesson 14 (you should concentrate on the sections that are marked with a √):

- *Avoir raison, avoir tort*
- √ *Dire*, present tense; *parler* and *dire* (14.8-14.11)
- *C'est* and *il est* with expressions of time
- *Vivre*, present tense
- Verb patterns, present tense
- √ Imperfect tense (14.23-14.27)
- √ Masculine and feminine forms, review and extension (14.28-14.29)

ASSIMILATION OF THE TEXT

14.1-14.3 Text work-up, aural comprehension, and oral production

Proceed as usual in these sections. (Refer to lessons 3.1, 3.2, and 4.3 for directions, if necessary.) Work with the text and illustrations in the textbook, as in previous lessons.

TOWARD COMMUNICATION

14.4, 14.5 Observation and activation: Pronunciation; the sound /i/

The sound /i/ is made with the lips stretched and close together, and the tongue just behind the front teeth. In writing, /i/ is represented by the letters *i* and *y:* **il**, **Y***vonne*. There is no difference in pronunciation between the two.

• Listen to the examples in 14.4 and repeat the words and phrases you hear in 14.5, imitating the voices on the audio recording as exactly as you can. Be alert to the fact that the mouth is more open for the sound /e/ than for /i/, and more open still for /ɛ/ than for /e/.

14.6, 14.7 Observation and activation: Good and bad; agreement and disagreement; *avoir raison, avoir tort*

The expressions *avoir raison* and *avoir tort* are used to express agreement and disagreement, to give your opinion of what people say in terms of what you think is true: "Robert est bête comme ses pieds." "—Oui, **tu as** peut-être **raison**!"

Avoir raison and *avoir tort* are also used to express approval or disapproval, to make value judgements about behavior in terms of what you feel is wise or proper. Suppose you are a nonsmoker. If someone says "Je fume," and you respond "**Tu as tort!**", you are not saying that what the person has told you isn't true, but rather that it's not a good idea to smoke.

Notice that in either case the degree of agreement or approval may be made stronger or weaker by using adverbs like *bien*, *peut-être*, *toujours*, *sûrement*. When Mireille says of the student demonstrators, "Ils ont **sûrement** raison," she is expressing her conviction that their cause is right (although her words are a little ironic, since she has no idea why they're there).

• Study the charts in 14.6 and complete exercise 14.7. You will hear a series of statements on the audio recording. Each one is confirmed or contradicted by a phrase printed in your workbook. Say whether the subject of the statement you heard is right or wrong.

Audio cues (for reference):
14.7 Activation orale: Approbation ou désapprobation

1. Robert pense que Mireille est sympathique.
2. Mireille pense que Robert est étudiant.
3. Mes amis pensent que le français est difficile.
4. Robert pense que Mireille est étudiante en psychologie.
5. Je crois que Robert est assez intelligent.
6. Robert et moi, nous trouvons Mireille gentille.

14.8, 14.9 Observation and activation: *Dire*

Walking with Robert, Mireille suddenly realizes she has forgotten to take her younger sister to a dance class, and she wonders what her mother's reaction will be: "Qu'est-ce que Maman va **dire**!" Chart 14.8 presents the forms of the verb *dire* in the present tense. Note the similarity in the *vous* forms of *dire*, *faire*, and *être*. (These are the three sole exceptions in French to the general pattern of *-ez* as the ending of the second person plural.)

• The sentences you will hear in exercise 14.9 suggest that various people are talkative. Agree, but point out that they have interesting things to say as well, using the verb *dire*.

Audio cues (for reference):
14.9 Activation orale: Parler, dire

1. Elle parle beaucoup!
2. Je parle beaucoup!
3. Robert parle beaucoup.
4. Nous parlons beaucoup, mon frère et moi.
5. Les soeurs de Mireille parlent beaucoup.
6. Et toi, tu parles beaucoup.
7. Mireille parle beaucoup?

14.10, 14.11 Observation and activation: Speaking versus saying

Chart 14.10 contrasts two verbs that both refer to talking, although from different points of view. *Parler* designates the activity, the **how** of talking. *Dire* refers to the contents of speech—to **what** is said. As you would expect, and as the examples show, *parler* is used with adverbs that characterize various ways of speaking, and with the names of languages: "Il parle **bien**," "Elle parle **russe**." *Dire* is used with direct object words that specify what is being said: "Dites **quelque chose**."

• In exercise 14.11, decide whether the sentences you see refer to speaking or to saying, and write the appropriate forms of *parler* or *dire*. Remember to read through each numbered section before you begin work on it; once you understand the context, the choice of *dire* or *parler* becomes much easier.

√ Check your answers in key 14.11 at the back of the workbook.

14.12 Observation: Time; *c'est/il est*

Chart 14.12 shows how *c'est* and *il est* introduce expressions of time. Note that *il est* is used with precise times of day (*7h*, *10h50*, *midi*), while *c'est* is used to identify larger, more inclusive units of time (*lundi*, *le matin*, *le 29 mai*).

14.13-14.15 Observation and activation: As time goes by; morning, noon, and night

In French, as in English, any point in the twenty-four-hour day can be referred to in terms of clock-time (*7h*, *10h50*, and so forth). But most people do not actually experience the day as a succession of hours, minutes, and seconds. They feel and refer to moments of the day in longer units of time: morning, afternoon, evening. The relationship between these two ways of reckoning time, and the terms that are used in French, are presented in chart 14.13

You can observe this distinction between chronological time and lived time even more clearly in chart 14.14. Words like *jour*, *matin*, and *soir* are labels for the periods that make up a day. They indicate **at what point** in the day a given activity took place. *Journée*, *matinée*, and *soirée*, on the other hand, are used when it is important to stress the **duration** of the activity. *Un jour* is a fact, a unit; there are 365 *jours* in the calendar year. *Une journée*, however, is a lived experience, an event: "Quelle journée!"

• In exercise 14.15, you will be asked what people do at various points in the day. Answer in terms of experienced time.

Audio cues (for reference):
14.15 Activation orale: Le temps qui passe

1. Mireille va à la fac le jour?
2. Robert va au cinéma le soir?
3. Les amis de Mireille vont au Luxembourg l'après-midi?
4. Ousmane va à la bibli le matin?
5. Robert va au Quartier Latin la nuit?

14.16-14.18 Observation and activation: *Vivre*

Sections 14.16 and 14.17 present the verb *vivre*, which is used in two separate situations illustrated by the examples in 14.16. *Vivre* refers to the fact of being alive; in this sense, it is the opposite of *mourir*. It can also be used to describe a living situation. The verb *habiter*, which refers to the place where you hang your hat, may also be used to talk about living situations. Notice that *habiter*, not *vivre*, is used with an address or a specific place-name.

• In exercise 14.18, you will be asked whether various people are from Paris. Confirm that they are, using the appropriate forms of *vivre*.

Audio cues (for reference):
14.18 Activation orale: Vivre

1. Mireille est parisienne?
2. Les parents de Mireille sont parisiens?
3. Vous êtes parisiens, vous deux?
4. Tu es parisien?
5. Mme Belleau est parisienne?

14.19, 14.20 Observation and activation: Habitual behavior

Robert tells Mireille where he and his family used to vacation when he was younger: "Nous **avions l'habitude de** passer nos vacances aux Bermudes." Chart 14.19 presents *avoir l'habitude de*, used with verbs in the infinitive to refer to habitual or routine patterns of behavior.

• The questions you will hear in exercise 14.20 suggest that various people's activities are routine. Confirm that they are, using *avoir l'habitude de* and the infinitive of the verb you heard in the question.

Audio cues (for reference):
14.20 Activation orale: Habitude

1. Tu travailles souvent à la bibliothèque?
2. Mireille va au cinéma le soir?
3. Robert prend souvent l'autobus?
4. Mireille rencontre souvent ses amis à la Sorbonne?
5. Vous étudiez le soir, vous deux?

14.21, 14.22 Observation and activation: Verb forms; present tense, singular and plural

You saw in lesson 12 that the singular forms of almost any verb in French are pronounced the same way—with the important exceptions of *avoir*, *être*, and *aller*.

Chart 14.21 extends this pattern to the plural forms. In *travailler*, the three singular forms and the *ils/elles* form of the plural are identical in pronunciation. Remember that the four forms may be **written** differently but that they are all **pronounced** the same way.

Furthermore, the sounds of the first and second persons of the plural consist of this basic form plus the sound /ɔ̃/ for *nous* and /e/ for *vous*.

As a result, if you know or hear one of the six forms of *travailler* in the present, you can predict all the remaining forms. This is true of a great many verbs in French—the majority of verbs in *-er* (which constitute eighty percent of the verbs in the language), and a number of others.

• In exercise 14.22, you will be asked who is involved in a variety of activities. Those responsible are identified in the workbook. Complete the answer using the corresponding form of the verb you hear.

Audio cues (for reference):
14.22 Activation orale: Formes verbales

1. Qui est-ce qui travaille ici?
2. Qui est-ce qui crie comme ça?
3. Qui est-ce qui parle français ici?
4. Qui est-ce qui parle français avec le professeur?
5. Qui est-ce qui passe la nuit à travailler ici?
6. Qui est-ce qui invente l'histoire?
7. Qui est-ce qui discute l'histoire avec le professeur?
8. Qui est-ce qui habite à Paris?
9. Qui est-ce qui habite près du Luxembourg, dans l'histoire?
10. Qui est-ce qui adore les histoires de crime ici?
11. Qui est-ce qui aime le cinéma ici?

14.23–14.27 Observation and activation: Time gone by; the imperfect tense

Chart 14.23 contrasts a series of verbs in the present tense with verbs in the imperfect tense. The imperfect is used to describe actions that took place in the past, as the examples demonstrate. The imperfect is one of two principal past tenses in French. Its use will be discussed in lesson 17.

Charts 14.24 and 14.25 show how to form the imperfect of any verb in French. The imperfect is made up of two elements: a basic or **stem** form, and an **ending** that is added to it. To find the stem form of the imperfect, take the first person plural of the present, the *nous* form, and eliminate the -*ons* ending. The result is the stem of the imperfect. This works with all verbs in the language . . . except *être*, whose imperfect stem, *ét*-, does not come from the first person plural of the present, *sommes*.

In sum, if you know the *nous* form of any verb in the present, you can predict all of its forms in the imperfect—provided, of course, that you know the endings of the imperfect. These endings are presented in 14.25. They are the same for all verbs—even *être*, despite its unconventional stem in the imperfect. Notice that the imperfect endings for the *nous* and *vous* forms (-**ions**, -**iez**) contain the -*ons* and -*ez* you saw in the present. These are the hallmarks of the first and second person plural endings in all tenses.

Read the charts and explanations carefully. Following the examples in 14.25, test your understanding of how to form the imperfect by predicting the imperfect forms of *faire*, *venir*, *connaître*, *suivre*, and *pouvoir*. Then complete exercises 14.26 and 14.27.

• In 14.26, the challenge is to listen for differences between forms of the present and forms of the imperfect. Decide whether each of the phrases you hear contains a verb in the present or a verb in the imperfect, and check the appropriate box on the grid in your workbook.

• In 14.27, listen to the sentences on the audio recording and write the missing forms of *avoir* and *être* in your workbook.

√ Check your answers in keys 14.26 and 14.27 at the back of the workbook.

14.28, 14.29 Observation and activation: Masculine and feminine forms (review and extension)

Chart 14.28 presents masculine and feminine forms you have encountered for the first time in this lesson, grouping them according to categories that are familiar from the examination of masculine and feminine forms in lessons 12 and 13.

As you study the chart, you will see patterns emerging that help you predict the masculine or feminine form of adjectives (and nouns formed from adjectives) that you hear for the first time.

For example, you saw the masculine form *dangereux* in lesson 13. You know from that lesson that in the feminine forms of words like *dangereux*, *ennuyeux*, and *généreux* there is an extra consonant sound, /z/ (written **-se**), at the end: *dangereu***se**. In this lesson, you see that words like *luxueux* and *cérémonieux* follow this pattern: their feminine forms end in a /z/ that is absent in the masculine. As a result, when you come across "un homme chaleureux" in lesson 18 you can be sure you would say of a warm-hearted woman that she is *chaleureuse*. And when a leg of lamb is called "délicieux" at dinner in lesson 24, you can confidently predict that *une crème renversée* brought out for dessert will be *délicieuse*.

• Study the chart, saying each pair of words out loud to get the feel of the difference in pronunciation—or, as in the case of words like *propre*, *sale*, and *sympathique*, the lack of difference. Then complete exercise 14.29, making the statements you hear about various males apply to their female counterparts.

Audio cues (for reference):
14.29 Activation orale: Formes masculines et féminines

1. Robert est un garçon cérémonieux.
2. Son père est gardien.
3. Son frère est parisien.
4. Il est plutôt silencieux.
5. Mon oncle est caissier.
6. Il est président d'une banque.
7. Robert est un garçon très vivant.
8. Il est aussi très sympathique.
9. Il est franc.
10. Son cousin est italien.

14.30 Observation: Events

Chart 14.30 groups together three expressions that are used to ask what is going on, or, in the negative, to say you don't know what is going on. *Qu'est-ce qui se passe?* asks for information about events, about what is happening. *Qu'est-ce qu'il y a?* and *de quoi s'agit-il?* focus more on the underlying cause or reason.

14.31 Observation: Reacting to a compliment

Chart 14.31 illustrates a number of ways of responding to a compliment. Note the various ways of using *gentil* to suggest that the compliment is appreciated, even though it is being turned aside. Note, too, that a response will tend to be longer and less direct—more "polite"—the less well you know the complimenter and his or her reasons for the compliment. (Compare the straightforward "tu es gentille, mais je ne te crois pas!" to the more flirtatious "vous êtes bien gentil de me dire ça, mais je ne sais pas si je dois vous croire.") We might call this the Politeness Factor.

14.32 Observation: Degrees of politeness

As you saw in 14.31, the politeness of a response will vary according to how familiar the speakers are with each other and whether they share certain assumptions about the exchange. Chart 14.32 illustrates how the gist of Robert's request to walk Mireille home may be communicated with varying degrees of politeness, ranging from degree 0 (casual or even brusque, depending on circumstance and tone of voice) to degree 5 (most polite). Notice the Politeness Factor at work here, too: the more polite the statement is, the longer it will tend to be.

When Robert asks Mireille if he can walk her home, he uses the longest and most roundabout formula he can find. This amuses Mireille. But apart from the fact that Robert does seem a bit ceremonious, he probably has good reasons for asking her in the way he does. First, he does not know Mireille; there is a respectful distance to begin with. Second, and more important, having never been to France, he does not know what behavior is culturally appropriate in this situation, and he very likely does not want to risk rejection by being too forward. So, prudent lad that he is, he takes no chances and opts immediately for degree 5.

14.33 Activation: Dialogue between Robert and Mireille

Listen to the conversation between Robert and Mireille and memorize Mireille's lines, imitating and repeating as usual.

TOWARD FREE EXPRESSION

14.34 Words at large

Proceed as usual. (If necessary, refer to lesson 3 for directions.)

14.35, 14.36 Role-playing and reinvention of the story

In 14.35, imagine you are Robert talking to Mireille in the courtyard of the Sorbonne. The hardest part—striking up a conversation—is over. Now keep the discussion going.

In 14.36, Jean-Pierre has gone to see a psychiatrist. Imagine the encounter.

Use the alternatives suggested in the workbook as a point of departure. If you work with a partner, take parts and complete each scene, then switch roles and do it again.

• **Suggested oral assignment.** Record a version of the dialogue between Jean-Pierre and the psychiatrist, choosing among the possibilities given in the workbook. You may dramatize the scene as much as you like. Send this assignment to your instructor on the cassette you use for summary quiz 14.

Your instructor may also ask you to record a second version of the dialogue, one that you make up on your own. See the course syllabus for details.

DOCUMENT

At the end of the textbook chapter for lesson 14 you will find a text for reading practice. This *devinette* is a little like the game of portraits you saw in lessons 9 and 10. (Remember Mireille: "Quelqu'un décrit une personne . . . et les autres **devinent** qui c'est.") Read the poem and guess who is its subject.

SELF-TESTING EXERCISES

- Complete and check exercises 14.37-14.40 as usual.

SUMMARY QUIZ

Consult the course syllabus or check with your instructor for information about completing and handing in summary quiz 14.

LESSON 15
Getting underway II

The story

The next morning, Robert gets stamps from a tobacconist and mails the postcard to his mother. Then he proceeds to wander around the Sorbonne as though he were looking for somebody. The teacher seems not to understand why Robert stays in that area when there are so many other important things to see in Paris.

At last Robert sees Mireille, but before he can speak to her she is greeted by her friend Hubert and walks off with him. Our hero goes to a café to lick this new wound. It heals very quickly when Mireille, sans Hubert, walks up to his table, says hello, apologizes for her hasty departure of yesterday, and suggests a walk in the Luxembourg Garden.

From their conversation we learn that Robert tries to be independent of his wealthy father, and that he is helped by cash gifts from his grandparents. Robert has a letter of introduction to an old friend of his mother, Mme Courtois. By an amazing coincidence, Mme Courtois turns out to be Mireille's godmother. Mireille tells Robert a little more about her family. Everything is going just fine when Mireille's little sister Marie-Laure butts in to announce that their mother, who is at home, is looking for Mireille. Mireille can't imagine why her mother is not at work, and rushes off, asking Robert to wait. We think he will.

Marie-Laure immediately takes over. She impresses Robert by guessing his nationality. Then, with the characteristic tact of a ten-year-old, she asks a question which, when you put the facial expression and the words together, amounts to: "What in the world can you possibly see in my sister?"

Notes on culture and communication

• **Le Mercredi.** In France there is no school on Wednesday for children in grade school and junior high school. But children do go to school on Saturday morning.

• **Public versus private selves.** In the space of two brief conversations, Robert has revealed a great deal of his personal and family history to Mireille. Even though she is a perfect stranger, he has volunteered information about such intimate family matters as his father's financial status, his parents' divorce, and his mother's remarriage. He even tells her how much money his grandparents used to give him at Christmas. Mireille is much less autobiographical. She shares certain facts about herself and her life, but she feels no compulsion to tell Robert about her family's finances or interpersonal relationships. Americans, with their open attitude toward strangers and their eagerness to make friends, tend to let their private selves spill into their public selves. The French, who as a rule are more formal (though no less friendly), prefer to keep their public and private lives distinct. Not until Robert gets to know Mireille much better—until he becomes a part of her personal life—will he learn as much about her as she has already learned about him.

Content and learning objectives of lesson 15

This lesson shows ways in which French speakers express certainty, uncertainty, and different degrees of agreement. It also reviews the days of the week, the months of the year, the French monetary system, and useful expressions for making everyday purchases.

The following points are highlighted in lesson 15 (you should concentrate on sections marked with a √):

√• Use of prepositions with place-names (15.17-15.18)
√• Contraction of *à* and *de* with *le* and *les*, review and extension (15.19-15.23)
• *En*, review and extension
• *Mener, amener, emmener, promener*
• Verb forms, review and extension

ASSIMILATION OF THE TEXT

15.1-15.4 Text work-up, aural comprehension, and oral production

• Proceed as usual in sections 15.1-15.4. (Refer to lesson 3.1-3.3 and lesson 4.3 for directions, if necessary.) Work with the text and illustrations in the textbook, as in previous lessons.

TOWARD COMMUNICATION

15.5 Activation: Pronunciation of /r/ (review)

The examples in 15.5 will help you brush up your /r/, first presented in lesson 5. Some of these examples, like *mystère*, contain only one /r/ sound;

others, like *leur chirurgien*, have several /r/ sounds in quick succession, which may make them seem like tongue-twisters.

• Listen, then repeat the words and expressions you hear, mimicking the voices as closely as you can. (Give yourself plenty of time with *leur chirurgien.*)

15.6-15.8 Observation and activation: Degrees of assent; certainty and uncertainty

Not all questions or statements require a simple yes-or-no response. Very often the most appropriate answer is somewhere between yes and no. Charts 15.6 and 15.7 present a number of conversationally useful phrases that enable you to react to what is said with gradations of assent.

The phrases in chart 15.6 show how to answer the same question in various ways, from noncommittal to emphatically positive.

In chart 15.7, you will find two lists of expressions that allow you to express certainty or uncertainty.

• In exercise 15.8, you will hear a series of questions that refer to the story of Robert and Mireille. For each question, three alternative answers are printed in your workbook. Choose the answer that makes the most sense in the context of the story, and circle the corresponding letter.

√ Check your answers in key 15.8 at the back of the workbook.

Audio cues (for reference):
15.8 Activation: Compréhension auditive; degrés d'assentiment; certitude, incertitude.

1. Mireille fait des études?
2. Est-ce que Jean-Pierre Bourdon va faire du droit?
3. Mireille connaît-elle les Courtois?
4. Est-ce que Marie-Laure va à l'école le mercredi?
5. Est-ce que Marie-Laure connaît Robert?

15.9, 15.10 Observation and activation: Calendar (review and extension)

Chart 15.9 extends the discussion of months and seasons you saw in lesson 11. Note the characteristic patterns:

En is used with the names of months.

Au is used with the expression *mois de* and the name of the month.

A is used with the names of holidays and other significant dates, such as birthdays.

• In exercise 15.10, you will be asked when various important events occur. Answer each question using the date you see in the workbook.

Audio cues (for reference):
15.10 Activation orale: Calendrier

1. C'est quand, l'anniversaire de Robert?
2. C'est quand, l'anniversaire de Mireille?
3. C'est quand, l'anniversaire de Marie-Laure?
4. Et Noël, vous savez quand c'est?
5. Et votre anniversaire, c'est quand?

15.11-15.14 Observation and activation: Accounts and expenses; buying; French money

This section presents vocabulary useful for making purchases in French. It also gives you a quick review of numbers.

Chart 15.11 lists the denominations of coins and bills that are in use in France.

Section 15.12 lists expressions used in a typical transaction: buying stamps at a tobacconist's. Notice the variety of expressions for requesting a stamp and asking how much one owes.

You saw in lesson 14 that the longer an expression is, the more polite it will usually be. The same is true of the statements and questions in 15.12. "Est-ce que je pourrais avoir un timbre, s'il vous plaît?" is somewhere in the neighborhood of Degree 4 on the politeness scale, compared to Degree 2 or 3 for "Un timbre, s'il vous plaît." (Degree 0 would be: "Un timbre.")

• Exercises 15.13 and 15.14 review the use of numbers in making purchases. In 15.13, you will hear the prices of a number of different items; write each price in figures in the corresponding space in your workbook.

√ Check your answers in key 15.13 at the back of the workbook.

• In 15.14, give the correct combination of banknotes and coins you would give the seller for each of the purchases in 15.13 (presuming that you have exact change). You may want to review the available denominations in chart 15.11 before you begin 15.14. Try not to look at the chart as you complete the exercise.

15.15, 15.16 Observation and activation: Approximation

Chart 15.15 shows the expressions that are used to indicate round numbers. While *dix* is exactly 10 and *quinze* is exactly 15, anything from 9 to 11 may be lumped into *une dizaine;* an amount around 15 is *une quinzaine;* 50, more or less, is *une cinquantaine;* and so forth.

• In exercise 15.16, you will hear a series of questions about quantities. For each question, an exact number is given in your workbook. Answer with the nearest round number.

Audio cues (for reference):
15.16 Activation orale: Approximation

1. Ça fait combien?
2. Il y avait beaucoup de monde à votre anniversaire?
3. Je vous dois combien?
4. Ça fait combien?
5. C'est combien?
6. Combien de personnes y avait-il à votre anniversaire?
7. Il y avait du monde à votre anniversaire?
8. Et à Noël, il y avait beaucoup de monde chez vous?

15.17, 15.18 Observation and activation: Where? whereabouts?

The expressions in 15.17 show ways of referring to various places and locations. As you study the list, notice that the expressions are different for different categories of places:

You would say "**à la** fac" but "**à** Paris," since *Paris* is the name of a city and is not preceded by a definite article.

You would say that people are "**à la** Sorbonne" or "**au** bureau" to indicate a general location, but "**dans la** cour de la Sorbonne" to specify that they are inside a more or less enclosed space.

Note that *la place* is considered a space upon which people walk ("**sur** la place"), and *la rue* a space that is closed in by the houses on either side ("**dans** la rue").

Notice that articles are generally not used with addresses: "les Courtois habitent **Quai de Grenelle.**" Note the **comma** after street numbers: "Mireille habite **18,** rue de Vaugirard."

• In exercise 15.18, you will be asked about activities that happen or things that can be found in certain places. For each question, the workbook contains an incomplete answer with a place-name. Complete the answers.

√ Check your answers in key 15.18 at the back of the workbook.

Audio cues (for reference):
15.18 Activation orale et écrite: Où? A quel endroit?

1. Est-ce qu'il y a un bureau de tabac près d'ici?
2. Y a-t-il une boîte aux lettres près d'ici?
3. Vous cherchez un Prisunic?
4. Vous avez rendez-vous avec Robert? Où ça?
5. Mireille fait-elle des études?
6. Tu connais le jardin du Luxembourg?
7. Où est l'hôtel de Robert?
8. Où est-ce que Mireille rencontre Hubert?

15.19–15.23 Observation and activation: Contractions of *de* and *à* with *le* and *les* (review and extension)

You have seen in a number of earlier lessons how *de* and *à* combine with the articles *le* and *les* to produce *du, des, au,* and *aux.* Charts 15.19 and 15.20 review these contractions, and show that they occur no matter what the function of *à* or *de* may be (indicating destination, indicating origin, expressing a partitive, and so on).

Chart 15.21 summarizes the use of *de* and *à* with all the definite articles: *le*, *la*, *l'*, and *les*. It shows that only *le* and *les* produce contracted forms with *à* and *de*.

• In exercise 15.22, you will hear various suggestions for where Robert and Mireille might meet. Go along with each suggestion and say that that's where they will meet. Use *à* and the definite article you hear, remembering to produce combined forms where appropriate.

Audio cues (for reference):
15.22 Activation orale: Contractions avec à

1. Je préfère la bibliothèque.
2. Je préfère le Luxembourg.
3. Je préfère le Quartier Latin.
4. Je préfère la Sorbonne.
5. Je préfère le restaurant universitaire.
6. Je préfère la maison de Mireille.
7. Je préfère le cinéma.
8. Je préfère la terrasse d'un café.
9. Je préfère les Etats-Unis.

• In 15.23, you will be asked whether you were in various places. Respond to each query, saying yes, you have just come from there. Use *de* and the definite article you hear, producing combinined forms where appropriate.

Audio cues (for reference):
15.23 Activation orale: Contractions avec de

1. Mais où étais-tu? Tu étais à l'hôtel?
2. Tu étais au restaurant?
3. Tu étais au Quartier Latin?
4. Tu étais à la Cité Universitaire?
5. Tu étais au cinéma?
6. Tu étais à la banque?
7. Tu étais au bureau?
8. Tu étais à la maison?
9. Tu étais à la douane?
10. Tu étais aux Etats-Unis?

15.24, 15.25 Observation and activation: *En* (review and extension)

The charts in 15.24 extend the presentation of the **partitive** use of *en*, first described in lesson 9. In a partitive phrase, you remember, a noun is used with *du*, *de la*, *de l'*, or *des* to indicate an unspecified number or amount. As you see from the chart, *en* can replace the noun that is being talked about: "Je voudrais **des timbres.**" "—Combien **en** voulez-vous?" *En* represents both the noun and the partitive notion expressed by *du*, *de la*, and *des*.

En is used, along with expressions of quantity, to indicate how much or how many of the item in question you are referring to: "**J'en** voudrais **deux.**" The quantity may be given in numbers—*deux, quatre*—or by using less precise expressions of quantity—*une dizaine, beaucoup*—or, in the negative, with *pas*.

• In exercise 15.25, you will be asked about the availability of certain items. Answer each question using *en* and the expression of quantity you see printed in the workbook.

Audio cues (for reference):
15.25 Activation orale: En

1. Y a-t-il un bureau de poste dans le quartier?
2. Il reste des boules de gomme?
3. Y a-t-il un bon hôtel dans le quartier?
4. Y a-t-il des manifestants dans la rue?
5. Combien de bancs y a-t-il dans le jardin de Luxembourg?
6. Combien est-ce qu'il y a de cinémas dans le quartier?
7. Y a-t-il une boîte aux lettres dans cette rue?
8. Est-ce qu'il vous reste de l'argent?
9. Il reste des timbres?
10. Il vous reste des boules de gomme?

15.26, 15.27 Observation and activation: Promenades; *mener, amener, emmener, promener*

The chart in 15.26 presents four verbs that are related in meaning and that are formed from the same root, *mener*, preceded by various prefixes: *a-*, *-em-*, and *pro-*.

Examples 1-5 illustrate the uses of these four verbs. Note particularly the distinction between *amener* and *emmener*. *Amener* refers to movement from elsewhere to the "here" of the speaker. *Emmener* refers to the opposite movement: from the "here" of the speaker to somewhere else. Inviting her children and grandchildren to Sunday dinner, Grandma Belleau might say, "**Amenez** Marie-Laure!" After Marie-Laure has created havoc in her house, Grandma might say, "**Emmenez**-la!"

Remember that these verbs show a shift in vowel sounds in the stem.

When the syllable is open (that is, when it ends in a vowel sound), the stem vowel is /ə/, as in *le*: *pro-me-ner*.

When the syllable is closed (when it ends in a consonant sound), the stem vowel is /ɛ/, as in *elle: pro-mène*.

• In the dictation exercise in 15.27, listen to the sentences on the audio recording and write the verb forms in your workbook.

√ Check your answers in key 15.27 at the back of the workbook.

15.28, 15.29 Observation and activation: Verb forms; present tense (review and extension)

In lesson 14 you saw that for the majority of verbs ending in *-er*, as well as a number of others, the three singular forms and the third person plural form are all pronounced the same way. The *nous* and *vous* forms are made by adding /ɔ̃/ (written *-ons*) and /e/ (written *-ez*) to this basic form.

These rules apply to the verbs listed in chart 15.28, except that there is an added semivowel sound, /j/, heard before the endings of the *nous* and *vous* forms. This semivowel sound is written *-i-* after consonants (*sourions) and* *-y-* after vowels (croy*ons*).

• In exercise 15.29, complete the sentences you see in your workbook with the appropriate form of the verb you hear.

√ Check your answers in key 15.29 at the back of the workbook.

Audio cues (for reference):

15.29 Activation orale et écrite: Formes verbales

1. -Mireille sourit.
   -Ah? A qui?
2. Mireille sourit. Et Robert?
3. Et vous, vous souriez souvent?
4. Mireille étudie à la Sorbonne. Vous aussi?
5. Ousmane et Colette aussi?
6. - Je vois quelqu'un.
   - Ah oui...?
7. Je crois que c'est Mireille.
8. Oui, c'est elle. Elle s'ennuie.
9. Ah, oui? Moi je ne m'ennuie pas.

15.30, 15.31 Observation and activation: Verb forms; additional consonant in the plural

Chart 15.30 presents a category of verbs in which the three singular forms are pronounced the same way, but the plural forms have a consonant sound that is not heard in the singular.

• In exercise 15.31, you will hear four questions or statements on the audio program. Each one corresponds to a paragraph in the workbook. Complete each paragraph in the workbook with the appropriate forms of the verb you hear.

√ Check your answers in key 15.31 at the back of the workbook.

Audio cues (for reference):

15.31 Activation orale et écrite: Formes verbales; consonne supplémentaire aux personnes du pluriel

1. Vous savez où est la place Saint-Michel?
2. Vous ne connaissez pas Mireille Belleau?
3. Moi, je sors de la fac à 4h.
4. Vous partez?

15.32 Activation: Dialogue between Marie-Laure and Robert

Listen to the conversation between Marie-Laure and Robert and memorize Robert's lines, imitating and repeating as usual.

TOWARD FREE EXPRESSION

15.33 Words at large

Proceed as usual. (If necessary, refer to lesson 3 for directions.)

15.34, 15.35 Role-playing and reinvention of the story

In 15.34, describe a birthday party to which you have been invited, using the suggestions in the workbook to get started and inventing others if you like. If you work with a partner, pretend you have both been invited to different birthday parties, and compare notes.

In 15.35, Robert's mother has arrived in Paris and is walking in the Luxembourg Garden with her childhood friend, Mme Courtois. They run into Robert and Mireille. Imagine the scene, supplementing the suggestions you see in the workbook with others you invent. If you work with a partner, take parts and complete the exercise, then switch roles and do it again.

• **Suggested written assignment.** Write out a version of the surprise encounter in 15.35. You may begin your version by combining the suggestions given in the workbook, but try to invent an ending of your own. Write ten to fifteen sentences. Send this assignment to your instructor along with summary quiz 15. (See the course syllabus for details.)

DOCUMENT

At the end of the textbook chapter for lesson 15 you will find a passage for reading practice, disguised as a tourguide's introduction to the *Quartier Latin* in Paris. The imaginary guide locates the *Quartier Latin* on the Left Bank, points out the places of interest to tourists and students (the ethnic restaurants, the movie houses, the cafés), and reminds us that the *Quartier Latin* is also a center of learning, with three branches of the University of Paris.

SELF-TESTING EXERCISES

• Complete and check exercises 15.36-15.39 as usual.

SUMMARY QUIZ

Consult the course syllabus or check with your instructor for information about completing and handing in summary quiz 15.

LESSON 16
Getting underway III

The story

Marie-Laure sees her sister coming back and decides to go sail her boat while the wind lasts. The real reason she wants to cast off is that she has sent Mireille on a wild-goose chase. She asks Robert not to tell, gives him a gumdrop, and leaves. Smart move. Mireille is furious.

Robert adroitly changes the subject from Marie-Laure to the Basque country, which Mireille knows slightly and which he wants to visit because his mother used to talk about it. She spent most of her childhood there, and it was there that she met Mme Courtois. By the way, couldn't Mireille get herself invited to the Courtois's tomorrow, too? No, tomorrow she must go to Chartres, to a little museum near the great cathedral. In that case, might he join her? Well, what about the Courtois? Oh, that can wait a day.

Marie-Laure returns to ask for help with her becalmed vessel. Mireille has no patience with her, but Robert responds to the S.O.S. and, graciously, straightens out the rigging. Both sisters are impressed by his kindness. At last, there are introductions between Robert Taylor (no relation to the actor) and Mireille Belleau (no relation to the rather obscure sixteenth-century poet Rémy Belleau).

Notes on culture and communication

• **Le Pays basque.** The French Basque Country is situated along the southwestern edge of France, on the border between France and Spain. It comprises the Atlantic end of the Pyrenees and the coastal area surrounding it. A strong cultural and political regionalism pervades the Basque Country. Local crafts include the production of table and bed linens (*toile basque*). Folk traditions have remained vital, among them the game of jai-alai. Tourism is a major source of income, especially along the coast, in such well-known resorts as Biarritz and St. Jean de Luz.

• **Mon grand-père était juge.** In France, judges are civil servants, appointed to their positions by the government Ministry of Justice. French judges are regularly transferred from circuit to circuit throughout their careers.

• **Facial expression, words, and communication.** In the Luxembourg Garden, Robert and Mireille appear to be discussing their family backgrounds. Their faces reveal, however, that the progression of their relationship is more important here than the subject of conversation. Facial expressions often reveal more about communication than do the words that are spoken. (The psychologist Albert Mehrabian discovered that in normal conversation the dictionary meaning of words carries only 7% of the communication. A further 38% comes from the way the words are pronounced. Fully 55% comes from facial expression. And the eyes are by far the biggest factor.) If you time the duration of Robert's and Mireille's gaze, you will see that it is much longer than in a normal conversation. Humans (and animals) can maintain a long gaze only in a situation of love or hate, and it is clear that what is happening between these two is not hate. Notice how Mireille averts her gaze, closes her eyes, slowly turns her head toward Robert and then flashes a wide open gaze and a smile and holds the gaze. No wonder Mireille is annoyed when Marie-Laure interrupts her conversation!

Content and learning objectives of lesson 16

This lesson illustrates ways in which French speakers express agreement, disagreement, and obligation, how they talk about going places, and how they refer to the past.

The following points are highlighted in lesson 16 (you should concentrate on sections marked with a √):

- • *Ne . . . aucun*
- √• *Y* and place names (16.8, 16.9)
- • *Devoir*
- • The *passé composé*
- √• *Vouloir* and *pouvoir*, review and extension (16.17-16.21)
- √• *Connaître* and *savoir*, review (16.28-16.30)
- √• Verb forms (16.31-16.33)

ASSIMILATION OF THE TEXT

16.1-16.3 Text work-up and aural comprehension

• Proceed as usual in sections 16.1-16.3. (Refer to lesson 3.1-3.3 for directions, if necessary.) Work with the text and illustrations in the textbook, as in previous lessons.

TOWARD COMMUNICATION

16.4 Observation and activation: Pronunciation; /s/ and /z/

Section 16.4 stresses the distinction between two consonant sounds that can be written in several different ways.

In writing, /s/ can appear as *s, ss, sc, c, ç,* or even *t* when followed by *i.* The sound /z/ may be written *s, z,* or *x.* As the examples show, however, the presence of other consonant or vowel sounds next to these letters affects the way they are pronounced.

Double *ss* is always pronounced /s/ in French (*bassin*), as is *c* before *e* or *i* (*célèbre, ici*). But a single *s* sandwiched between vowels is pronounced /z/, whether it occurs inside a word (*oiseau*) or as a by-product of *liaison* between two words (*les enfants*).

The distinction between *s* pronounced /s/ and *s* pronounced /z/ is not merely a matter of correct pronunciation. The wrong sound can actually change the meaning. If you go into a restaurant to satisfy a craving for seafood, be sure to order *du poisson*, not *du poison.* Similarly, *ils sont deux garçons* refers to two boys who are brothers and have no other brother, while *ils ont deux garçons* refers to parents who have two young sons. In these two sentences, the enormous difference between the verb *être* (*ils sont*) and the verb *avoir (ils ont)* comes down to the difference between the sounds /s/ and /z/.

• Listen to the examples in 16.4 and repeat the expressions in 16.5, imitating what you hear as exactly as possible.

16.6 Observation: Agreement, disagreement

You saw the expressions *avoir raison* and *avoir tort* in lesson 14. Chart 16.6 adds other useful expressions for indicating agreement and disagreement.

16.7 Observation: Absence

In lesson 5 you saw how to use *pas de* as the negative of the indefinite articles *un, une, des.* As a negative expression, *pas de* expresses absence or lack: "J'ai un frère" ⇒ "Je **n'**ai **pas de** frère." Chart 16.7 presents a more emphatic negative expression than *pas de. Aucun* suggests complete absence, total lack. Notice that *aucun* functions as an adjective, becoming *aucune* when used with feminine nouns. Notice, too, that is is **always singular**.

16.8, 16.9 Observation and activation: Speaking about places; *on y va, on y est, y*

As the examples and the chart in 16.8 show, the expression *y* can be used to indicate both where you are going and where you are. *Y* stands in for the name of a place you have already referred to. It replaces nouns or place-names that are preceded by a preposition that indicates location: **à** *Chartres*, **sur** *la table*, **en** *France*, **chez** *les Courtois*. Note that *y* is placed **before** the verb.

• In exercise 16.9, you will be asked whether people are going various places. Say yes, substituting *y* for the the place-names you hear.

Audio cues (for reference):
16.9 Activation orale: Pour parler d'un endroit

1. Mireille va au Pays Basque?
2. Robert va en France?
3. Robert et Mireille vont au Luxembourg?
4. Et Marie-Laure elle va aussi au Luxembourg?
5. Vous allez à Chartres, vous deux?
6. Les parents de Robert vont en Amérique Latine?
7. Tu vas au cinéma quelquefois?
8. Robert va aller chez les Courtois?
9. Mireille doit aller au musée de Chartres?
10. Robert veut aller à Chartres aussi?

16.10, 16.11 Observation and activation: Obligations and assumptions; present tense of *devoir*

The verb *devoir* can be used to express **obligation** or **necessity**, as when Mireille tells Robert she has to go to Chartres: "Je **dois** aller à Chartres demain."

Devoir can also express an **assumption** you are making about a situation. When Mireille learns that Robert's father is a banker, she assumes Robert is well-off: "Vous **devez** être riche!"

(Note that a similar situation exists in English: compare the two meanings of *must* in "I must be going!" and "you must be kidding!")

• In exercise 16.11, you will be asked whether various people want to do various things. Say no, but point out that they must do them anyway, using *devoir* as in the example.

Audio cues (for reference):
16.11 Activation orale: Devoir

1. Tu crois que j'ai envie de rentrer?
2. Vous croyez que nous avons envie de rentrer?
3. Il a envie d'aller à la bibli?
4. Elle a envie y d'aller?
5. Ils ont envie d'aller au cours?
6. Tu as envie de travailler?
7. Vous avez envie de partir, vous deux?

16.12-16.14 Observation: As time goes by; *après-demain, avant-hier*

Charts 16.12 and 16.13 present useful expressions for talking about periods of time that precede and follow the immediate present.

The expressions in chart 16.12 are used in relation to the present moment. Notice that *tout à l'heure* may refer to either the past or the future, depending on the **tense** of the verb: "Je **vais sortir** tout à l'heure" (future); "il **est passé** tout à l'heure" (past).

The expressions in chart 16.13 refer to days on either side of today. You are familiar with *hier* and *demain* from lesson 11. Two new terms, applying to the day before *hier* and the day after *demain*, are given here.

• In the dictation exercise in 16.14, listen to the text of a postcard from Robert to his mother on the audio recording and complete the written text in the workbook.

√ Check what you have written in key 16.14 at the back of the workbook.

16.15 Observation: As time goes by; years and centuries

Chart 16.15 lists the names of centuries in French. Notice the characteristic use of Roman numerals followed by *-ème* to write the number of the century. When the names of centuries are spelled out, the ordinal form of the number is used: *le* **seizième** *siècle*.

16.16 Observation: As time goes by; the *passé composé*

The sentences in 16.16 are all in the past tense. As the examples show, however, the verbs in these sentences reflect two kinds of past tenses: the *imperfect*, which was presented in lesson 14, and the *passé composé*.

These two past tenses can refer to exactly the same time, but they describe it from two different points of view. The differences between the imperfect and the *passé composé* will be studied in later lessons. For the time being, you need only to be aware that both exist.

16.17-16.21 Observation and activation: Permission and will; *vouloir* and *pouvoir* (review and extension)

You saw the forms of *pouvoir* in lesson 12. Chart 16.17 reintroduces it with the verb *vouloir*, to illustrate the similarity of forms of the two verbs.

Chart 16.18 shows that *pouvoir* is used to talk about permission to do something, and also to refer to the ability to do it. (Here French uses one verb where two are used in English: "**May** I join you?"; "I **can't** get started!")

Exercises 16.19-16.21 give you practice using *vouloir* and *pouvoir* in the present tense.

• In 16.19, you will hear that certain people's parents have a lot of money. Agree, but point out that the children want to be independent, using appropriate forms of *vouloir*.

Audio cues (for reference):
16.19 Activation orale: Vouloir; présent de l'indicatif

1. Vos parents ont de l'argent!
2. Tes parents ont de l'argent!
3. Les parents de Robert ont de l'argent!
4. Les parents de Mireille ont de l'argent!

• In 16.20, say that various people are unable to come along, using *pouvoir*.

Audio cues (for reference):
16.20 Activation orale: Pouvoir; présent de l'indicatif

1. Vous m'accompagnez, tous les deux?
2. Tu m'accompagnes?
3. Robert t'accompagne?
4. Votre soeur vous accompagne?
5. Vos amis nous accompagnent?

• In 16.21, you will be asked whether various people may come along. Say they may if they want to, using *pouvoir* and *vouloir*.

Audio cues (for reference):
16.21 Activation orale: Vouloir, pouvoir

1. Nous pouvons vous accompagner?
2. Je peux t'accompagner?
3. Robert peut nous accompagner?
4. Nous pouvons venir à Chartres avec vous?
5. Mes amis peuvent venir, eux aussi?

16.22-16.24 Observation and activation: Wanting

Chart 16.22 illustrates two ways in which *avoir envie* is used to express desire: with *de* and a verb in the infinitive, and with *de* and a noun. In both cases the pronoun *en* may replace *de* and what follows it; *en* is placed **before** the verb *avoir*.

• In exercise 16.23, you will be asked whether various people are going to do various things. Say yes, they want to do them, using *avoir envie*.

Audio cues (for reference):
16.23 Activation orale: Avoir envie de

1. Tu viens avec nous?
2. Robert va à Chartres?
3. Tu pars?
4. Tu restes?
5. Les parents de Mireille vont au Pays Basque cet été?
6. Et vous deux, vous y allez aussi?
7. Et toi, tu restes à Paris?

• In 16.24, say the people involved have no desire to do the things mentioned, using *avoir envie de* in the negative.

Audio cues (for reference):
16.24 Activation orale: Avoir envie de

1. Tu viens?
2. Robert va au Louvre cet après-midi?
3. Vous jouez aux portraits, tous les trois?
4. Tes soeurs viennent avec nous?
5. Marie-Laure travaille?

16.25-16.27 Observation and activation: Taking advantage of the circumstances; *profiter de . . . pour, en profiter pour*

The examples in 16.25 show how the verb *profiter* is used with *de* and a noun to refer to taking advantage of something. Notice that *de* combines as usual with the definite articles *le* and *les* to produce *du* and *des*. Notice also that *de* and the noun that follows it may be replaced by *en* positioned directly in front of the verb.

• In exercise 16.26, you will hear that the conditions are right for various leisure activities. Urge everyone to take advantage of the situation, using *profiter de* + noun *pour* + verb. (Watch out for number 4, where the favorable condition is described by *il fait beau*. There is no noun in *il fait beau*, so you will need to supply one. Try *beau temps*.)

Audio cues (for reference):
16.26 Activation orale: Profiter de...pour

1. Il y a du vent. Allons faire du bateau.
2. Il y a du soleil. Allons faire du bateau.
3. Il y a de la neige. Allons faire du ski.
4. Il fait beau. Allons à Chartres.
5. Nous avons des vacances. Allons au Pays Basque.
6. Il y a du vent. Allons faire de la voile.

• In 16.27, weather conditions are influencing what various people are doing. Say how they're taking advantage of the conditions, using *en profiter pour* + verb, as in the example.

Audio cues (for reference):
16.27 Activation orale: En profiter pour...

1. Il fait beau. Robert va se promener.
2. Il fait beau. Mireille fait du bateau.
3. Il fait mauvais. Ils vont au cinéma.
4. Il fait mauvais. Je travaille.
5. Il y a de la neige. Mireille lit Tolstoy.

16.28-16.30 Observation and activation: Knowing; *connaître* and *savoir* (review)

You saw in lesson 10 how *connaître* is used to refer to acquaintanceship or familiarity, while *savoir* is used to refer to intellectual knowledge or certainty. Chart 16.28 contrasts these uses; chart 16.29 compares the forms of the two verbs in the present tense.

• In exercise 16.30, complete the dialogues printed in your workbook with the proper forms of *connaître* or *savoir*, according to the context.

√ Check your answers in key 16.30 at the back of the workbook.

16.31 Observation: *Voir, croire, essayer*, present tense

You saw in lesson 16 a group of verbs (*sourire, étudier, s'ennuyer, croire, voir*) whose *nous* and *vous* forms contain a semivowel sound, /j/, that is absent in the other forms. Chart 16.31 reviews this phenomenon, which can occur in verbs whose infinitives end in *-er*, *-ir*, or *-re*. Notice that even though *voir* and *croire* have different endings in the infinitive, they are conjugated identically in the present indicative (and in most other tenses as well).

16.32 Observation: *Venir, tenir, comprendre,* present tense; three different vowels in the stem

Chart 16.32 presents three very common verbs that have a common peculiarity: in the six forms of the present tense, the stem has three different vowel-sounds.

Take *venir*, for instance. The three singular forms, *je* **viens**, *tu* **viens**, *il/elle* **vient**, have the same nasal vowel in the stem. In *ils/elles* **viennent**, there is an oral vowel followed by an /n/ sound. And in *nous* **venons** and *vous* **venez**, there is yet another vowel sound, /ə/ (as in *je* and *le*), different from the first two.

This is also true of *tenir* and *comprendre*, and of the various compound verbs formed from these verbs.

16.33 Activation: Verb forms; present tense

Study charts 16.31 and 16.32, making sure you can identify the vowel changes that take place in the stems of the verbs you see. Then complete exercise 16.33.

• In 16.33, you will hear a series of sentences on the audio recording; each sentence contains one of the verbs you have just been studying. In the example given in the workbook, you will see three incomplete responses. Complete each response with the appropriate form of the verb you hear.

Audio cues (for reference):
16.33 Activation orale: Formes verbales; présent de l'indicatif

1. Vous me croyez?
2. Vous essayez?
3. Vous venez?
4. Vous comprenez?

16.34 Activation: Dialogue between Marie-Laure and Mireille

Listen to the conversation between Marie-Laure and Mireille and memorize Mireille's lines, imitating and repeating as usual.

TOWARD FREE EXPRESSION

16.35 Words at large

Proceed as usual. (If necessary, refer to lesson 3 for directions.)

16.36 Role-playing and reinvention of the story

In 16.36, you are Robert. You meet Marie-Laure in the Luxembourg Garden. Imagine your conversation, out loud, using the suggestions in the workbook to get started. If you work with a partner, take parts and complete the exercise, then switch roles and do it again.

• **Suggested oral assignment.** Record a version of the conversation between Robert and Marie-Laure in 16.36. Say at least eight sentences (four exchanges between them). Send this assignment to your instructor on the cassette you use for summary quiz 16. (See the course syllabus for details.)

SELF-TESTING EXERCISES

• Complete and check exercises 16.37, 16.38, and 16.39 as usual.

SUMMARY QUIZ

Consult the course syllabus or check with your instructor for information about completing and handing in summary quiz 16.

LESSON 17
In all labor there is profit I

The story

Mireille says that Robert's last name, Taylor, probably comes from the clothing biz. Robert isn't sure, and he mentions the difference in spelling between *tailor* and *Taylor*. This launches Mireille into a catalogue of family names that originated with occupations. Among others, she mentions Boucher, Charpentier, and Boulanger. Like their English equivalents Butcher, Baker, and Carpenter, they are relatively common names. Of course, the name is no longer a reflection of a person's occupation. Mireille knows of a pharmacist named Boucher and two composers named Charpentier and Messager. When she gets to Marin (sailor), the talk turns to childhood ambitions. Little Mireille wanted to be a nurse who moonlighted as an actress. Robert at eight or nine saw himself as a heroic fireman, braving infernos to save sleeping babies.

At this point Marie-Laure, having fallen into the boat-pond, shows up drenched. Fortunately, she knows how to swim. She loves water. Maybe one day she'll be an Olympic swimmer, or—who knows?—an undersea explorer with the Cousteau team. We end on a profoundly philosophical note: "You never know how things will turn out." Heavy!

Notes on culture and communication

• **Jacques-Yves Cousteau** (b. 1910), a well-known French oceanographer and filmmaker, invented an underwater respiratory device and a "floating island" designed for oceanographic exploration.

• **Infatuation and eye contact.** For two people to look fixedly into each other's eyes is painful unless they are furious at each other (the baseball player and the umpire) or in love. Many cultures have invented rituals to avoid such painful situations in everyday life. In most of the world's non-Western cultures it is simply forbidden to gaze into the eyes of someone who commands respect. In Western cultures, however, it is expected that a person listening to another person will look fixedly into the eyes of the speaker. It is the social duty of the speaker not to stare back but to look elsewhere, except for a brief glance now and then to record the reactions of the listener.

In this episode, Mireille speaks most of the time and Robert listens. This permits Robert to look constantly into Mireille's eyes. Mireille would like to look at him in the same way, but convention is too strong! She is obliged to look to the side after each fragment of speech, but then she blinks, turns toward him with her eyes closed, and flashes an intense smile that expresses her feelings—feelings that could be interpreted as infatuation.

<u>**Content and learning objectives of lesson 17**</u>

This lesson will introduce you to ways in which French speakers refer to occupations and professions practiced by women and men, and how they identify and describe people through their occupations.

The following points are highlighted in lesson 17 (you should concentrate on sections marked with a √):

- Tonic stress
- √ Masculine and feminine forms (17.6-17.11)
- √ *C'est* versus *il/elle est* (17.12-17.16)
- √ *Savoir* versus *connaître* (17.17-17.19)
- √ The imperfect, review (17.20-17.25)
- √ *Ne . . . plus* (17.26-17.29)

ASSIMILATION OF THE TEXT

17.1-17.4 Text work-up, aural comprehension, and oral production

Proceed as usual in these sections. (Refer to lesson 3.1-3.3 and lesson 4.3 for directions, if necessary.) Work with the text of lesson 17 in the textbook, as in previous lessons.

TOWARD COMMUNICATION

17.5 Observation and activation: Pronunciation; tonic stress (review)

Recall that syllables in the middle of French words are **not** stressed. There **is** a slight stress at the end of a rhythmic group, whether the group is made up of several words or a single word said by itself.

Repeat the words and phrases you hear in 17.5. When you have completed the section, go back to the beginning and repeat it, giving the syllables in each group a nonsense sound: *une pro-fe-ssion* ⇒ ta-ta-ta-TA. (Or use scat syllables if you prefer: *une pro-fe-ssion* ⇒ fwa-dat-n-DOO!). Tap the syllables out on the table as you say them. This kind of practice will help you feel the evenness of the syllables and the stress that occurs at the end of each group.

17.6-17.11 Observation and activation: Men's and women's occupations; *berger/bergère*

Nouns in French are masculine or feminine, incuding the names given to practitioners of various occupations and professions. Many occupations have traditionally been practiced by both men and women, and have names with separate masculine and feminine forms: for example, *ouvrier/ouvrière.* The same is true of the names of many new occupations in which both men and women are employed: *informaticien/informaticienne.* However, in the case of occupations that have historically been the province of men (*chirurgien, pompier*), the masculine form alone is used, even for women, despite the presence of active and successful women in those fields.

The three charts in this section of the lesson present three categories of occupational names. The exercises that follow each chart give you practice in using feminine and masculine forms.

Chart 17.6 lists masculine and feminine forms in *-er/-ère* and *-ier/-ière.* Notice that they function like the familiar adjectives *cher* and *premier.*

Several masculine names in this category that do not have feminine equivalents are also listed in 17.6. The supplemental note gives a good example of a profession—*couturier*—so traditionally dominated by men that the corresponding feminine word, *couturière*, refers only to the neighborhood dressmaker. The great women designers are all known as *couturiers.*

Chart 17.8 presents masculine and feminine forms in *-cien/-cienne* (compare *canadien/canadienne*).

Chart 17.10 lists occupational names for which there is no independent feminine form. Note that *médecine* is not the feminine equivalent of *médecin*, but the name of the profession itself.

• In exercises 7.7, 7.9 and 7.11, you will hear what various men do for a living. Replace men with women, substituting feminine forms for the masculine forms you hear, when a separate feminine form exists.

Audio cues (for reference):
17.7 Activation orale: Métiers au masculin et au féminin

1. Il est fermier.
2. Il est ouvrier.
3. Il est berger.
4. Il est boucher.
5. Il est infirmier.
6. Il est boulanger.
7. C'est un couturier.

Audio cues (for reference):

17.9 Activation orale: Métiers au masculin et au féminin

1. Il est technicien.
2. Il est acteur.
3. Il est musicien.
4. Il est informaticien.
5. Il est pharmacien.
6. Il est conducteur de tracteurs.
7. C'est un aviateur.
8. C'est un grand explorateur.

17.11 Activation orale: Métiers au masculin et au féminin

1. Il est pompier.
2. Il est ingenieur (chez Renault).
3. Il est chef de service (au Ministère).
4. Il est médecin.
5. Il est agent de police.

17.12-17.16 Observation and activation: Identification and description

Charts 17.12 and 17.13 show ways of referring to people for two different purposes.

The first is to **identify** them for the benefit of others who know nothing about them: "Qui est-ce?" "—C'est un ingénieur." Note that the word *ce* occurs in both the question (*qui est-***ce***?*) and the answer (**c'***est*).

The second is to **describe** them to others who may want more information: "Qu'est-ce qu'il fait?" "—Il est ingénieur." Note here that the word *il* occurs in both the question (**il** *fait*) and the answer (**il** *est*).

When *c'est* is used to identify somebody, it is followed by a noun that is preceded by an article or a possessive: *c'est* **un** *ingénieur*, *c'est* **ma** *tante*. Such articles and possessives are known as **determinants.**

When *il est* or *elle est* is used to describe somebody, it is followed by an adjective or noun with **no determinant** before it: *il est ingénieur*, *elle est médecin*.

• In exercise 17.14, listen to each statement and determine the question to which it provides the answer. Say the question and mark the appropriate box on the grid in your workbook.

Audio cues (for reference):

17.14 Activation orale: Identification et description; c'est/il est

1. Il est médecin.
2. Il est sympathique.
3. C'est un grand chirurgien.
4. C'est un ami de Mireille.
5. C'est un ingénieur.
6. Il est employé chez Renault.
7. Il est ingénieur.
8. Il est très grand.
9. C'est un gros banquier.
10. C'est un grand couturier.
11. Il est acteur.
12. Il est douanier.
13. C'est un professeur américain.
14. Il est très intelligent.

• In 17.15, you will hear a series of questions about who people are and what their circumstances are (what do they do, are they married, and so forth). Decide whether each question asks for an identification or a description, then choose between *c'est un/une* or *il/elle est* and answer, writing the appropriate expression in your workbook.

Audio cues (for reference):

17.15 Activation orale et écrite: Identification et description

1. Qui est-ce, ce Monsieur?
2. Qu'est-ce qu'il fait (dans la vie)?
3. Est-ce qu'il est marié?
4. Et la dame avec lui, qui c'est?
5. Qu'est-ce qu'elle fait? Elle travaille?
6. Est-ce qu'elle est mariée?

• In 17.16, you will see a series of incomplete sentences. Decide whether each sentence identifies a character or describes that character. Then complete the sentence, writing *c'* or *elle* before *est*, as appropriate.

√ Check your answers in keys 17.14, 17.15, and 17.16 at the back of the workbook.

17.17–17.19 Observation and activation: Knowledge and acquaintanceship (review and extension)

You saw in lesson 10 that two different verbs are used to indicate two distinct kinds of knowing. *Connaître* refers to familiarity or acquaintanceship; *savoir* implies the certain knowledge about things that comes from experience or learning.

Charts 17.17 and 17.18 reintroduce this distinction. Notice that the objects of *connaître* are generally nouns, and that the objects of *savoir* are often phrases that contain a verb. (An important exception in the case of *savoir* is the names of languages: "Elle ne **sait** pas **l'espagnol**." When the object of *savoir* is a noun, that noun will refer to something that can be learned.)

• In exercise 17.19, decide whether each incomplete sentence you see refers to acquaintanceship or to knowledge acquired through experience or learning, and write the appropriate forms of *connaître* or *savoir*.

√ Check your answers in key 17.19 at the back of the workbook.

17.20-17.25 Observation and activation: Then and now; imperfect (review)

In lesson 14 you saw how the imperfect is formed. Charts 17.20-17.22 review this tense in detail.

You can confidently produce a form of the imperfect by starting from the *nous* form of the present and adding the imperfect endings, as chart 17.20 shows.

Chart 17.21 reviews the one exception to this rule: the verb *être*, which has an unconventional stem in the imperfect. Notice the spelling change from the infinitive and the *vous* form of the present to the stem of the imperfect: **ê***tre*, **ê***tes* ⇒ **é***tions*, **é***tiez*, and so on. Fortunately, the imperfect **endings** are the same for **all** verbs in the language, including *être*.

Chart 17.22 highlights differences in pronunciation between forms of the present and forms of the imperfect. In the *nous* and *vous* forms, there is a semi-vowel sound, /j/, in the imperfect that is lacking in the present.

Note. Don't be startled by the fact that a verb like *étudier* whose imperfect stem ends in an *-i* (*étud***i***-ons*) will have two *i*s in the *nous* and *vous* forms of the imperfect: *étud***ii***ons*, *étud***ii***ez*.

• Exercise 17.23 will give you practice in producing imperfect forms by adding the appropriate endings to the imperfect stem, which is identical to the stem of the *nous* form of the present. You will hear a series of statements about us. Say that what **is** true of us **was** true of him. (It boils down to replacing the *-ons* of the present with the *-ait* of the imperfect.)

Audio cues (for reference):
17.23 Activation orale: Formes de l'imparfait

1. C'est ce que nous voulons.
2. C'est ce que nous attendons.
3. C'est ce que nous cherchons.
4. C'est ce que nous préférons.
5. C'est ce que nous croyons.
6. C'est ce que nous disons.
7. C'est ce que nous faisons.
8. C'est ce que nous voulons.

• In exercise 17.24, you will hear about things that are no longer true of various people. Point out that these things were true, however, when they were little, using the imperfect. This time you will have to figure out what the imperfect stem is, since not all the verbs you hear will be *nous* forms. Then add the appropriate imperfect ending.

Audio cues (for reference):
17.24 Activation orale: Formes de l'imparfait

1. Maintenant, je ne veux plus être pompier.
2. Maintenant, ça ne m'intéresse plus.
3. Maintenant, nous n'allons plus en Bretagne.
4. Maintenant, ce n'est plus à la mode.
5. Maintenant, je n'aime plus la Bretagne.
6. Maintenant, je n'ai plus envie d'y aller.
7. Maintenant, nous n'habitons plus à Paris.
8. Maintenant, mon père ne travaille plus à Paris.
9. Maintenant, on ne fait plus ça.
10. Maintenant, l'ami de Robert ne croit plus en Dieu.

• In 17.25, you will be asked whether various people were doing various things last year. Answer no, using the appropriate forms of the imperfect. (Since the verbs you hear will be in the imperfect, the imperfect stem will not be a problem; all you need to do is find the proper ending.)

Audio cues (for reference):
17.25 Activation orale: Formes de l'imparfait

1. Vous étiez à Saint-Tropez l'année dernière?
2. Est-ce que vous étiez en France l'année dernière?
3. Est-ce que Robert était en France l'année dernière?
4. Est-ce que vous connaissiez Mireille l'année dernière?
5. Est-ce que Robert connaissait Mireille l'année dernière?
6. Est-ce que Robert était à l'Université l'année dernière?
7. Est-ce que vous étudiiez le français l'année dernière?
8. Est-ce que vous saviez beaucoup de français l'année dernière?
9. Est-ce que vous faisiez du russe l'année dernière?
10. Est-ce que vous étiez marié l'année dernière?
11. Est-ce que nous étions en France l'année dernière?
12. Est-ce que nous connaissions Mireille l'année dernière?
13. Est-ce que Robert et Mireille étaient à Saint-Tropez l'année dernière?
14. Est-ce que Robert et Mireille se connaissaient l'année dernière?

17.26–17.29 Observation and activation: Say no more; negation with *ne . . . plus*

The examples and the chart in 17.26 introduce a negative expression that behaves like *ne . . . pas* but is used in different circumstances. *Ne . . . pas* indicates simple negation: X, instead of being, is not. *Ne . . . plus*, on the other hand, indicates a **change over time**: X was, but is no longer.

In the exercises that follow, note the use of the imperfect to establish a situation that existed in the past, and the use of the present with *ne . . . plus* to indicate that it no longer exists.

• In exercise 17.27, you will be asked whether or not you used to do various things. Say yes, you did indeed, but you don't do them any longer, using *ne . . . plus*.

Audio cues (for reference):
17.27 Activation orale: Négation; ne...plus

1. Vous n'alliez pas aux Bermudes autrefois?
2. Vous n'alliez pas en Bretagne autrefois?
3. Vous n'habitiez pas à Chartres autrefois?
4. Vous n'étiez pas à la fac autrefois?
5. Vous n'étiez pas à la Cité Universitaire autrefois?
6. Vous ne mangiez pas au restau-U autrefois?
7. Vous ne descendiez pas au Home Latin autrefois?

• In 17.28, you will again be asked whether various actions and situations occurred in the past; say they did, but do no longer.

Audio cues (for reference):
17.28 Activation orale: Négation; ne...plus

1. Elle faisait du karaté autrefois?
2. Il y avait un boulanger ici autrefois?
3. Il y avait un boucher ici autrefois?
4. Il y avait un charbonnier ici autrefois?
5. Il y avait un pharmacien ici autrefois?
6. Il y avait un tailleur ici autrefois?

• In 17.29, you will hear what a number of people wanted to be when they were little. Point out that they no longer have these ambitions.

Audio cues (for reference):
17.29 Activation orale: Négation; ne...plus

1. Quand il était petit, il voulait être pompier.
2. Quand elle était petite, elle voulait être infirmière.
3. Quand elle était petite, elle voulait être actrice.
4. Quand il était petit, il voulait être marin.
5. Quand nous étions petits, nous voulions être peintres (comme Boucher!).
6. Quand elles étaient petites, elles voulaient être aviatrices (comme Hélène Boucher).

17.30 Activation: Dialogue between Mireille and Robert

Listen to the conversation between Robert and Mireille and memorize Mireille's lines, imitating and repeating as usual.

TOWARD FREE EXPRESSION

17.31 Words at large

Proceed as usual. (If necessary, refer to lesson 3 for directions.)

17.32 Role-playing and reinvention of the story

Imagine a conversation between Robert and Mireille in which they speak about what they wanted to do when they were little, and in which they find out each other's names. The dialogue—and the names—are up to you. You may want to use the suggestions in the workbook to get started. If you work with a partner, take parts and complete the scene, then switch roles and do it again. If you work by yourself, take both parts.

• **Suggested written assignment.** Write a short paragraph about what you liked to do when you were little, and what you wanted to be. Thirty to forty words is about right. Send your paragraph to your instructor along with summary quiz 17. (See the course syllabus for details.)

DOCUMENT

At the end of the textbook chapter for lesson 17 you will find a poem for reading practice: "Mon ministre des finances," by Boris Vian, author of the poem about blondes, brunettes, and redheads in lesson 6.

Here Vian imagines a kind of Rube Goldberg contraption for committing thievery undetected—a fire engine (stolen), equipped with an extension ladder and a small monkey. It's an idea of genius, he says with tongue in cheek, and such an unexpected combination that no one ever guesses what its real purpose is. The poet and his monkey go from window to window, taking what they find. Now they are well-off. They live discreetly, too, as gentlemen should—except for the noise of the motor when the ladder goes up.

SELF-TESTING EXERCISES

• Complete and check exercises 17.33-17.36 as usual.

SUMMARY QUIZ

Consult the course syllabus or check with your instructor for information about completing and handing in summary quiz 17.

LESSON 18
In all labor there is profit II

The story

The subject is still the unpredictability of fate. Robert tells of a gifted violinist friend who ultimately became a sausage-maker, and Mireille adds the example of Ghislaine's sister, once an aspiring pianist, now a typist in her father's office.

Then Marie-Laure returns and, in response to Mireille's impatience, eloquently defends public ownership of park benches, which prompts Robert to predict a legal career for her. But no, she likes neither law nor politics. What, then? Maybe plumbing. She likes playing with water and there are other advantages, but life is perverse. Papa wanted to be a masseur, but he has cold hands, so now he makes cars. No matter. As Aunt Georgette says, "Cold hands, warm heart."

A few more cases of thwarted ambition culminate in the story of Robert's friend who wanted to be a priest but lost his faith. Now that he no longer believes in Providence, he works for an insurance company, the Provident.

All Mireille's friends want to go into films, but the world needs more than actors and directors. Anyway, no one knows for sure what the future will bring. Mireille wants to know what Robert is going to do. Well, he is going to invite her to a café, the Closerie des Lilas. And what will she do? She will accept. Marie-Laure is sent home to finish her homework, but first she makes a date with Robert to help her with her English later in the afternoon. It looks as if Mireille may have some serious competition!

Notes on culture and communication

• **Le Conseil d'Etat** is the highest jurisdictional council of the French state. It acts as the supreme administrative court of justice and protects fundamental civil rights and liberties under the Constitution.

• **Devoirs et leçons.** The assignments Marie-Laure refers to are the written and oral preparations that are the bane of French schoolchildren's existence from grade school through high school. Intensive homework is a hallmark of the French school system.

• **Verbal aggression.** Mireille is furious at Marie-Laure for interrupting her *tête-à-tête* with Robert, and she lashes out verbally at her little sister. Marie-Laure reacts with a long diatribe against Mireille. The words they exchange are harsh, and their tone is aggressive, but this does not mean there is any real hostility between the two sisters. Each is merely playing the game by giving the other a piece of her mind. In French culture, verbal aggression is not only accepted but encouraged. One French grandmother says that when her grandchildren start hitting each other her reprimand is always: "Don't fight! What do you have a tongue for?"

Content and learning objectives of lesson 18

This lesson will introduce you to ways in which French speakers talk about work and people who work. It also shows how they talk about things that are commonly done, and how they react to others who are bothersome.

The following points are highlighted in lesson 18 (you should concentrate on sections marked with a √):

√• *On*, review and extension (18.6, 18.7)
• Masculine and feminine forms
√• Stressed pronouns, review (18.17, 18.18)
√• Imperative and direct object pronouns (18.19-18.24)
• Possessives, review
√• Indirect object pronouns (18.27-18.31)
√• *Toujours, quelquefois, ne . . . jamais* (18.32, 18.33)

ASSIMILATION OF THE TEXT

18.1-18.3 Text work-up, aural comprehension, and oral production

Proceed as usual in these sections. (Refer to lesson 3.1-3.3 for directions, if necessary.) Work with the text and illustrations in the textbook, as in previous lessons.

TOWARD COMMUNICATION

18.4 Observation and activation: Pronunciation; non-diphthongized vowels

In the one-syllable English word *day*, the sound *-ay* is actually two sounds: it begins as /e/, then the tongue moves toward the position for the sound /i/ without quite getting there. This shift—in which the lips and tongue slip from one vowel sound to another in the same syllable—is called a **diphthong**. Most vowels in American English **slide** in this way from one sound to another; diphthongization is an important feature of the sound of American English.

In French, vowels are not diphthongized at all. Lips and tongue do not slip and slide during vowel sounds. The quality of each vowel sound remains **constant** for the duration of the syllable.

• Listen to the examples in 18.15 and repeat them, looking at their written forms in the workbook as you repeat. Do not move your tongue or lips while saying the vowel sounds. Concentrate on making short, clear, constant sounds for the vowels printed in italics.

18.6, 18.7 Observation and activation: People in general; *on* (review and extension)

On is a third person singular pronoun. You saw in lesson 10 how *on* is used to refer to people in general. In informal speech, *on* is also used as a substitute for *nous*.

• In exercise 18.7, you will hear about what French people do or don't do. Change each sentence to say what people do or don't do in France, replacing *les Français* with *on*, as in the example.

Audio cues (for reference):
18.7 Activation orale: On

1. Les Français aiment bien manger.
2. Les Français voyagent beaucoup en train.
3. Les Français ont mauvais caractère.
4. Les Français vont souvent en vacances.
5. Les Français font beaucoup de ski.
6. Les Français sont moqueurs.
7. Les Français ne travaillent pas le samedi.

18.8, 18.9 Observation and activation: *Ce qui se dit, ce qui se fait*

As you saw in the preceding section, *on* is used to talk about people in general. In the expressions *on dit ça* and *on fait ça*, *on* refers to more or less everyone.

Chart 18.8 presents an equivalent way of expressing things that are commonly done. Notice that in *ça se dit* and *ça se fait*, and expressions like them, the verb is used reflexively.

• In exercise 18.9, you will be asked whether certain things are commonly done. Answer yes, replacing *on* with *ça* and the reflexive form of the verb.

Audio cues (for reference):
18.9 Activation orale: Ce qui se dit, ce qui se fait

1. On appelle ça un vingt-tonnes?
2. On dit ça?
3. On ne dit pas ça?
4. On fait ça?
5. On écrit ça avec un "y"?
6. On écrit Taylor avec un "y"?
7. On écrit tailleur avec deux "l"?
8. On voit ça?

18.10-18.14 Observation and activation: People and their occupations

This section of the lesson presents ways of talking about work and about people who work.

Chart 18.10 lists the names given to various occupations and to the people in them. Notice the use of the **definite article** with the names of occupations.

Chart 18.12 illustrates the use of *faire de* with occupations. (You saw *faire de* used with names of sports in lesson 6.) Again, the **definite article**, in combination with *de*, precedes the name of the occupation. Note that *faire de* cannot be used with every occupation.

Chart 18.13 shows how to express the distinction between professionals and nonprofessionals in sports, music, and the arts, where there can be both amateurs and professionals. *Etre* and the occupational title indicate professional status. *Faire de* and the name of the activity, or *jouer de* and the name of the musical instrument, refer to amateur status.

• Exercise 18.11 will give you practice in using names of occupations with the definite article. Give the name of the occupation that corresponds to the occupational title you hear, as in the example.

Audio cues (for reference):
18.11 Activation orale: Les personnes et leurs professions

1. Quand on est marin...
2. Quand on est cinéaste...
3. Quand on est militaire...
4. Quand on est enseignant...
5. Quand on est ambassadeur...
6. Quand on est magistrat...

• In exercise 18.14, listen to the sentences on the audio recording and decide which refer to professionals and which refer to amateurs. Mark the appropriate box on the grid in your workbook.

√ Check your answers in key 18.14 at the back of the workbook.

18.15, 18.16 Observation and activation: Professions; masculine and feminine

Chart 18.15 shows how occupational titles are used for men and women. Two equivalent expressions may be used with the title: *il/elle est* or *c'est un/une*.

The chart shows a number of occupations for which there is a separate feminine form. In many others, however, there is no separate feminine form. Note that *elle est* may be used with any occupational title, feminine or masculine. The situation is more complicated with *c'est une*, as the chart shows. In a situation where you are not sure whether there is a separate feminine form, the simplest course of action is to use *elle est*.

• In exercise 18.16, you will hear a series of sentences referring to men or women in various occupations. Change the masculine forms to feminine, and vice versa.

Audio cues (for reference):

18.16 Activation orale: Professions; masculin et féminin

1. Elle est masseuse.
2. Il est enseignant.
3. Il est magistrat.
4. Il est commerçant.
5. Il est cinéaste.
6. Il est avocat.
7. Elle est violoniste.
8. Elle est enseignante.
9. Elle est femme d'affaires.

18.17, 18.18 Observation and activation: At home; stressed pronouns

You saw the use of stressed pronouns in lessons 9 and 10. Chart 18.17 shows how they are used after the expression *chez* as an equivalent of *à la maison*. Note that *à la maison* is usually interpreted to mean at the home of the person speaking.

• In exercise 18.18, you will be asked where various people are going. Say they're going home, using *chez* and the appropriate stressed pronoun.

Audio cues (for reference):

18.18 Activation orale: Pronoms accentués (révision)

1. Où vas-tu?
2. Où va Jean-Pierre?
3. Où vont-elles?
4. Où allez-vous, toutes les deux?
5. Où vont-ils?
6. Et nous, où est-ce que nous allons?

18.19-18.24 Observation and activation: Dealing with bothersome people; imperatives

You saw the imperative or command form of the verb in lesson 12. The four charts in 18.19-18.22 review the imperative and the use of pronouns in imperative expressions.

Chart 18.19 features ways of expressing impatience with someone who is bothering you, as a means of illustrating the use of pronouns with imperatives.

Chart 18.20 reviews positive and negative forms of the imperative.

Chart 18.21 compares the position of object pronouns in the indicative with their position in the imperative. In the indicative (*tu l'embêtes*) and the **negative** imperative (*ne l'embête pas!*), the object pronoun comes **before** the verb. In the **positive** imperative, however (*laisse-la tranquille!*), it comes **after** the verb.

Chart 18.22 illustrates the use of the positive and negative imperative with all of the personal pronouns. Note that, in the positive imperative, *me* and *te* are replaced by *moi* and *toi*. (In the case of *dérange-toi* and *dérangez-vous* the pronouns have become reflexive, since the subject and object of the verb are the same. This changes slightly the meaning of the verb.)

• In exercise 18.23, tell a bothersome person not to pester you and various other people, using the negative imperative and appropriate direct object pronouns.

Audio cues (for reference):
18.23 Activation orale: Impératif négatif et pronoms

1. Tu me déranges!
2. Tu ennuies Mireille!
3. Tu ennuies tes soeurs!
4. Tu nous embêtes!
5. Tu m'embêtes!
6. Tu déranges ton père.

• In 18.24, tell this bothersome person to leave you and others alone, using the positive imperative of *laisser tranquille* and the appropriate pronoun.

Audio cues (for reference):
18.24 Activation orale: Impératif positif et pronoms

1. Ne la dérange pas!
2. Ne dérange pas tes soeurs!
3. Ne dérange pas Robert!
4. Ne me dérange pas!
5. Ne nous dérange pas!
6. Ne dérange pas Mireille!

18.25, 18.26 Observation and activation: Expressing ownership; *être à*, *appartenir à*, possessives

Chart 18.25 contrasts three different ways of expressing ownership. You have seen the expression *être à* (used with stressed pronouns) and possessive adjectives in lessons 8 and 9. The chart introduces a new verb, *appartenir à*, and a new kind of object pronoun—the indirect object pronoun—that will be described in detail in 18.27, 18.28, and 18.29.

• Exercise 18.26 will give you practice in using possessive adjectives. You will be asked whether various things belong to various people. Say yes, the items in question are theirs, using the appropriate possessive.

Audio cues (for reference):
18.26 Activation orale: Possessifs (révision)

1. Ce bateau est à vous?
2. Ce bateau est à Marie-Laure?
3. Ce banc est à Robert et Mireille?
4. Ce livre est à Robert?
5. Ce briquet est à toi?
6. Ces cigarettes sont à toi?
7. Ces cigarettes sont à Jean-Pierre?
8. Ces bateaux sont aux enfants?

18.27-18.31 Observation and activation: Indirect object pronouns

You saw in lesson 11 that objects are the targets or recipients of the action of a verb.

In "Le jeune homme remarque **Mireille**," there is no preposition between the verb and the object; such objects are called **direct objects**.

In "Il parle à la jeune fille" (chart 18.27), there is an object, *la jeune fille*, but it is not a direct object. There is a preposition, *à*, between the verb and the object, creating a different kind of relationship between them. This relationship is called an **indirect object** relationship, and *la jeune fille* is called an **indirect object**.

You saw in lesson 11 how direct object nouns can be replaced by pronouns: "Il remarque **Mireille**" ⇒ "Il **la** remarque." As chart 18.28 demonstrates, indirect object nouns can also be replaced by pronouns: "Il parle **à la jeune fille**" ⇒ "Il **lui** parle." Notice that the indirect object pronoun comes before the verb, as does the direct object pronoun.

Note that many verbs can take both a direct and indirect object. Four of the verbs listed in chart 18.28 (*appartenir*, *sourire*, *ressembler*, and *téléphoner*) can take only indirect objects, but one (*demander*) can take both direct and indirect objects. In "Il demande du feu à la jeune fille," *du feu* is a direct object and *à la jeune fille* is an indirect object.

Chart 18.29 allows a systematic comparison of direct and indirect object pronouns. Notice that the direct and indirect object pronouns are **different** in the **third person**; in the first and second persons they are identical.

• In exercise 18.30, the question is whether a certain bench and a certain boat belong to various people. Say no, using the indirect object pronouns that correspond to each person or group of people.

Audio cues (for reference):
18.30 Activation orale: Pronoms objets indirects

1. C'est votre banc?
2. C'est le banc de Mireille?
3. C'est le banc de Robert?
4. C'est ton bateau?
5. C'est mon banc!
6. C'est notre banc!

• In 18.31, complete the sentences with the appropriate direct or indirect object pronoun. To decide whether the object pronoun should be direct or indirect, examine the question and determine whether the object used is direct (with no preposition) or indirect (with a preposition).

√ Check your answers in key 18.31 at the back of the workbook.

18.32, 18.33 Observation and activation: *Toujours, quelquefois, jamais*; negatives

Toujours and *quelquefois* tell you how often an action or situation occur.

Publicly, Jean-Pierre Bourdon would maintain that his technique of meeting women by asking them for a light has a 100% rate of success: "Ça marche **toujours!**" Privately, he might concede only occasional success: "Ça marche **quelquefois.**" As far as we can tell, however, it never works: "Ça **ne** marche **jamais.**"

Jamais is thus the opposite of both *toujours* and *quelquefois*. Note that the position of *jamais* in a negative sentence is the same as that of *pas* and *plus*.

• The challenge in exercise 18.33 is to choose whether to use *pas*, *plus* or *jamais* in negative situations.

(Recall that *ne . . . plus* is used to refer to a situation that occurred in the past but is occurring no longer. It is the opposite of *encore*.)

You will be asked whether various situations are occurring, are still occurring, or occasionally occur. Answer no in every case, using *plus* if you hear *encore*, *jamais* if you hear *quelquefois*, and *pas* if you hear no expression of duration or frequency.

Audio cues (for reference):
18.33 Activation orale: Négation; pas, plus, jamais

1. Marie-Laure est là?
2. Marie-Laure est encore là?
3. Marie-Laure est là, quelquefois?
4. Vous sortez quelquefois?
5. Ça marche encore?
6. Tu travailles encore?
7. Vous acceptez?
8. Tu comprends?
9. Elle comprend quelquefois?
10. Tu sors encore?
11. Tu viens?
12. Vous allez à la Closerie des Lilas, quelquefois?

18.34 Activation: Dialogue between Mireille and Marie-Laure

Listen to the conversation between Mireille and Marie-Laure and memorize Marie-Laure's lines, imitating and repeating as usual.

• **Suggested oral assignment.** Do a dramatic reading of the dialogue between Mireille and Marie-Laure, and send it to your instructor on the cassette you use for summary quiz 18. (See the course syllabus for details.)

TOWARD FREE EXPRESSION

18.35 Words at large

Proceed as usual. (If necessary, refer to lesson 3 for directions.)

18.36, 18.37 Role-playing and reinvention of the story

In 18.36, make up a conversation in which Marie-Laure explains to Robert what she wants to be when she grows up. Use the outline in the workbook as a point of departure. If you work with a partner, take parts and complete the dialogue, then switch roles and do it again. If you work by yourself, take both parts.

In 18.37, Robert and Mireille are on their way to the Closerie des Lilas, blissfully unaware that a gangster is waiting for them. Imagine what this new character is doing, and why.

DOCUMENT

At the end of the textbook chapter for lesson 18 you will find a brief poem for reading practice, "Nationale Sept; poids-lourd" by Norge (Georges Mogin, b. 1898).

The trucker who is the subject of this poem is proud of his image as a man in charge. He doesn't give a damn about the chickens—or the cops—on the road (*les poulets* are barnyard fowl but also, in French slang, policemen). He is happiest when he catches a woman's eye as he speeds down the road in a cloud of diesel smoke. Changing a tire, oil in his hair, he flexes his brawny forearms and spits out his cigarette butt to let everyone know he's in command.

SELF-TESTING EXERCISES

- Complete and check exercises 18.38, 18.39, and 18.40 as usual.

SUMMARY QUIZ

Consult the course syllabus or check with your instructor for information about completing and handing in summary quiz 18.

LESSON 19
Entering school zone I

The story

Mireille and Robert cross the Luxembourg Garden. They pass in front of the Art Institute, where Mireille has a class, and arrive at the terrace of the Closerie des Lilas. Robert sets his watch, which was still showing New York time, and then explains that he chose this café because it is mentioned in books he's read by American authors. Mireille has never been here, but that's only because it's a bit expensive.

They get the waiter to recite a long list of typically French apéritifs. Both decide on a kir. Robert's question about her studies sends Mireille into a story about her love of fingerpaints in nursery school and her discovery of Matisse in elementary school. She wasn't able to pursue her passion for art on the secondary level; there were just too many required courses. There was Latin, French, math (not her favorite), several sciences, philosophy, German, and English. Nothing in great depth, but still an enormous amount of work, with the menacing baccalaureate exam waiting at the end. Mireille is happy to have gotten through it all. Now, at the university, she has much more freedom of choice. She likes all her courses, particularly Greek Art, where she has what sounds like a crush on the professor. Robert is less than delighted.

Notes on culture and communication

• **L'éducation nationale.** In the French educational system, as in the American, private schools coexist with public schools, which constitute the majority. Some private schools are religious, others are nondenominational. Ever since the reforms of Napoleon, public schools have been run by the state in a highly centralized fashion. Teachers in the public-school system are civil servants appointed by the state. The Ministry of Education defines the curriculum of studies up to the *Baccalauréat*, the national examination that takes place at the end of senior year in high school and that serves as an entrance examination for French universities.

• **Je vais prendre un kir.** Mireille and Robert sit at a café table and order a kir. Eventually they will each have three glasses of this very French drink, which is considerably lower in alcohol than the other common apéritifs the waiter lists. *Le kir* was named rather recently after a priest named Félix Kir, a canon in the church hierarchy who went into politics and became mayor of Dijon, in Burgundy, and a member of the French legislature, the Chambre des Députés. He was particularly fond of this traditional drink, made of two products from his region: white wine and blackcurrant liqueur. In recent times it has caught on and become a favorite apéritif in France, and it is rapidly making its way in this country. For that we have to thank Monsieur le Chanoine-Député-Maire Kir, as he liked to be called.

Content and learning objectives of lesson 19

This lesson shows how French speakers express various degrees of agreement and disagreement. It will also familiarize you with ways of saying what time it is.

The following points are highlighted in lesson 19 (you should concentrate on sections marked with a √):

√ • The *passé composé* (19.16-19.22)
 • Compounds of *prendre*
√ • *Plaire* (19.24-19.30)
 • Adverbs

ASSIMILATION OF THE TEXT

19.1-19.3 Text work-up, aural comprehension, and oral production

Proceed as usual in these sections. (Refer to lesson 3.1-3.3 for directions, if necessary.) Work with the text and illustrations in the textbook, as in previous lessons.

TOWARD COMMUNICATION

19.4-19.6 Observation and activation: Pronunciation; the sound /r/ (review)

Recall that to produce /r/, the back of the tongue is raised as if to produce a /k/ or /g/ sound (or the sound at the end of *yuchhh!*), and a slight friction or dry gargle is produced; the tip of the tongue lies lightly against the lower teeth.

• In 19.5, identify which words or phrases contain /r/, marking your choices on the grid in your workbook.

√ Check your answers in key 19.5 at the back of the workbook.

• In 19.6, repeat the words and phrases you hear.

19.7, 19.8 Observation and activation: A question of identification

In the story, Mireille asks the waiter at the Closerie des Lilas what they have in the way of typically French apéritifs. She uses the expression *comme* with a noun: "Qu'est-ce qu'il y a **comme** apéritifs bien français?"

Chart 19.7 illustrates the uses of *comme* to present items as belonging to a general category. Notice that there is no article between *comme* and the noun.

• In exercise 19.8, you will hear a series of questions about categories; modify each question to ask about specific items belonging to those categories. Use *comme* and the name of the category, without an article.

Audio cues (for reference):
19.8 Activation orale: Question d'identification

1. Il y a des apéritifs français?
2. Vous connaissez des peintres d'avant-garde?
3. Vous connaissez des rois de France?
4. Vous avez fait des sciences naturelles?
5. Vous faites des études?
6. Vous faites une langue étrangère?
7. Vous faites du sport?

19.9 Observation: Different degrees of agreement and disagreement

Chart 19.9 presents a number of useful phrases that enable you to express degrees of agreement or disagreement. These expressions cover the spectrum from emphatic disagreement (degree -1) to enthusiastic agreement (degree +1).

19.10-19.15 Observation and activation: As time goes by; times of day

In the left-hand column of chart 19.10 you will see a number of expressions French speakers use to ask what time it is. They are all roughly equivalent, but they reflect the politeness factor: the last three are more polite—and therefore longer—than the first three.

The right-hand column contains a number of possible answers to give when you know the time (the first two items), and when you don't know the time, or don't want to get involved (the last five).

Chart 19.11 shows how to refer to differences in local time between cities in different time zones around the globe.

Chart 19.12 shows two different systems of reckoning time. System 1, in the left-hand column, is used in everyday speech; it is based on a twelve-hour day. System 2, used for rail and air and other official and technical schedules where there is activity day and night, is based on a 24-hour day. Thus, 12 noon is *midi* in everyday speech but *douze heures* in official speech; 1:00 in the afternoon is *une heure* in system 1 but *treize heures* in system 2; 12 midnight is, respectively, *minuit* and *vingt-quatre heures.*

• In exercise 19.13, determine what time it is on each of the clocks you see in the workbook and say the time in everyday terms.

• In 19.14, you will see a railroad schedule of trains from Paris (Gare Montparnasse) to Chartres. Using system 2 (official terminology), say at what times there are trains leaving for Chartres.

• Finally, for Robert's benefit, translate the official times you see in exercise 19.15 into everyday terms.

19.16-19.22 Observation and activation: As time goes by; the *passé composé*

You saw how to recognize the *passé composé* in lesson 16. In this lesson you will learn how to form this past tense.

The verbs contained in the examples in chart 19.16 are in the past—not the imperfect, but the *passé composé.* The *passé composé* gets its name from the fact that it is a compound tense, **composed** of two parts. These parts are a helping verb, or **auxiliary**, and the **past participle** of the main verb.

As chart 19.16 shows, there are **two auxiliary verbs** that do service in the *passé composé:* **avoir** and **être**. The auxiliary verbs are used in the present tense.

Chart 19.17 shows the full range of forms for two verbs in the *passé composé:* one conjugated with *avoir* and one conjugated with *être*. Note that despite one or two differences of spelling in the case of *arriver*, the past participle of each verb is pronounced in exactly the same way from form to form.

Exercises 19.18 through 19.22 will give you practice in using the forms of the *passé composé*. The challenges you face are to decide whether *être* or *avoir* is the proper auxiliary and to come up with the past participle of the verb in the question.

Carefully review the forms of *avoir* and *être* in chart 19.17 before you begin. The exercises will go very rapidly if you know these verbs inside out.

• In 19.18, give positive answers to the questions you hear, using the appropriate form of *avoir* or *être* and the past participle you heard in the question.

• In 19.19, note the auxiliary and past participle used in the first part of each numbered section in your workbook. Then complete the second part with appropriate forms of the same verbs.

√ Check your answers in key 19.19 at the back of the workbook.

• In 19.20, you will be asked whether various people know certain languages. Say they don't, although they've taken courses in those languages.

Audio cues (for reference):
19.20 Activation orale: Le passé composé

1. Tu sais le latin?
2. Tu sais le français?
3. Il sait l'allemand?
4. Vous savez le latin, vous deux?
5. Vos parents savent le japonais?

• 19.21 will give you practice using the *passé composé* of the verb *choisir*. You will be asked whether people are majoring in various scientific subjects. Say no, they've chosen humanities.

Audio cues (for reference):
19.21 Activation orale: Le passé composé

1. Vous allez vous spécialiser en physique nucléaire?
2. Tu vas te spécialiser en chimie?
3. Il va faire de la biologie?
4. Ils vont faire des sciences?
5. Vous allez vous spécialiser en astrophysique, vous deux?

• In 19.22, answer by saying the people referred to have ordered a kir.

Audio cues (for reference):
19.22 Activation orale: Le passé composé

1. Qu'est-ce que vous prenez, vous deux?
2. Qu'est-ce que tu prends, toi?
3. Qu'est-ce que Mireille prend?
4. Qu'est-ce que Mireille et Robert prennent?
5. Qu'est-ce que vous prenez, vous deux?

19.23 Observation: Verbs derived from *prendre*

Chart 19.23 gathers together a number of verbs familiar from this lesson and earlier lessons that are formed from the verb *prendre*.

Note that the past participle of *prendre* is *pris*. *Incomprise* is an adjective formed from the past participle of *comprendre*.

19.24-19.30 Observation and activation: *Plaire*, present and *passé composé*

Plaire is a verb that French speakers frequently use to say they like something. Charts 19.24, 19.25, and 19.26 present the forms of *plaire* in the present and the *passé composé*, and show how it functions with indirect object pronouns.

Chart 19.24 illustrates forms of *plaire* in the present tense. Note the circumflex accent (^) over the *î* (*i accent circonflexe*) in the third person singular *plaît*.

In chart 19.25, notice that *plaire* is conjugated with the auxiliary verb *avoir*.

Chart 19.26 shows that *plaire* is used with *à* ("Robert **plaît à** Mireille"), and that its objects are therefore **indirect objects** (see lesson 18).

Note that "Mireille trouve Robert sympa" describes Mireille's impression of Robert; Mireille is the subject. "Robert plaît à Mireille," on the other hand, describes the impression Robert makes on Mireille; Robert is the subject. The two sentences refer to the same situation (Mireille likes Robert), but from different points of view.

The two sentences use different verbs that govern different objects. The object of *trouve* is a direct object, and can be replaced by a direct object pronoun: "Elle **le** trouve sympa." But the object of *plaît à* is an indirect object, and must be replaced by the corresponding indirect object pronoun: "Il **lui** plaît."

In the exercises on *plaire*, you are asked for reactions to people and things. In the questions you will hear, these people and things are the direct object of various verbs. In giving answers with *plaire*, remember that the **direct object** of the question will become the **subject** of your answer, and the **subject** of the question will become an **indirect object** pronoun in your answer.

• In 19.27 and 19.28, you will be asked various people's reactions to various things. Answer using *plaire* in the present (19.27) or the *passé composé* (19.28). The thing that is the subject of *plaire* in each case will be expressed by *ça*, and so the verb form will stay the same (*plaît* or *a plu*). Your task is to decide which **indirect object pronoun** to use for the person being pleased.

Audio cues (for reference):
19.28 Activation orale: Plaire; passé composé

1. Vous avez fait des maths? Vous avez aimé ça?
2. Tu as aimé les maths, toi?
3. Et vous deux, vous avez aimé ça?
4. Vos enfants ont aimé la chimie?
5. Votre fils a aimé le latin?
6. Votre fille a aimé la physique?

• In 19.29 and 19.30, you will be asked for your reaction to other people; answer with *plaire* in the present or *passé composé*. In each sentence, the indirect object of *plaire* will be *me*, since the questions are directed to *tu*. The challenges here are to choose the appropriate **subject pronoun** and the **form** of *plaire* that matches it.

Audio cues (for reference):
19.29 Activation orale: Plaire; présent de l'indicatif

1. Comment trouves-tu le nouveau prof de maths?
2. Comment trouves-tu les Parisiennes?
3. Comment trouves-tu Robert?
4. Comment trouves-tu Mireille?
5. Comment trouves-tu les parents de Mireille?
6. Comment trouves-tu ses soeurs?
7. Et moi, comment me trouves-tu?

19.30 Activation orale: Plaire; passé composé

1. Tu as rencontré le nouvel ami de Mireille?
2. Tu as rencontré la cousine de Mireille?
3. Tu as rencontré ses parents?
4. Tu as vu ses soeurs?
5. Tu as vu son oncle?
6. Tu as rencontré ses cousines?

19.31-19.34 Observation and activation: One way or another; adverbs

Charts 19.31 and 19.32 contrast adjectives, which qualify nouns, and adverbs, which qualify verbs. Notice that all the adverbs in the charts end in *-ment*. This is the ending of a large number of adverbs in French.

Very often, an adverb can be formed by adding *-ment* to the feminine form of the corresponding adjective, as chart 19.32 illustrates. Bear in mind, however, that not all adjectives can be transformed into adverbs by adding *-ment*.

• Exercise 19.33 gives you practice changing adjectives into adverbs. Complete the sentences by writing the appropriate adverb.

√ Check your answers in key 19.33 at the back of the workbook.

• In exercise 19.34, study the examples given in the workbook, then answer the questions you hear with the appropriate adverb, choosing among the four adverbs listed.

Audio cues (for reference):
19.34 Activation orale: Naturellement, malheureusement, heureusement, énormément

1. Est-ce qu'on fait du français dans les écoles françaises?
2. Vous étiez nulle en maths?
3. Vous étiez bonne en maths?
4. Vous avez beaucoup d'amis?
5. Est-ce qu'on fait de l'anglais dans les écoles anglaises?
6. Est-ce qu'on parle chinois en Chine?
7. Oh! Vous avez raté votre bac?
8. Vous étiez nul en chimie?
9. Mais la chimie était obligatoire?
10. Vous étiez bonne en français?
11. Vous avez réussi à votre examen?
12. Vous avez eu votre bac?
13. Vous avez beaucoup travaillé?
14. Il y a beaucoup de travail au lycée?
15. On étudie beaucoup de matières au lycée?

19.35 Activation: Dialogue between Mireille and the waiter

Listen to the conversation between Mireille and the waiter at the Closerie des Lilas and memorize the Mireille's lines, imitating and repeating as usual.

TOWARD FREE EXPRESSION

19.36, 19.37 Words at large

In 19.36, answer the questions you see using expressions you have studied in this lesson. (You may give other answers as well if you like.)

In 19.37, proceed as usual. (If necessary, refer to lesson 3 for directions.)

19.38 Role-playing and reinvention of the story

You have made the acquaintance of Mireille or Robert in Paris. The two of you have spent an afternoon together, and you are telling another friend how it went. Report to your friend, using the suggestions in the workbook to get started. If you work with a partner, pretend that one of you met Mireille, the other Robert, and compare notes.

• **Suggested written assignment.** Write out a version of your encounter with Robert or Mireille in 19.38, and send it to your instructor along with summary quiz 19. Write six to eight sentences. (See the course syllabus for details.)

DOCUMENT

At the end of the textbook chapter for lesson 19 you will find two short passages for reading practice.

The first is a traditional ditty about oil paints and watercolors that French schoolchildren sing.

The second is from *Les Cerveaux brûlés* by Norge (see the commentary on the document for lesson 18 in this guide). "L'Histoire" criticizes an approach to learning history that used to be widespread in French schools: rote memorization of dates, battles, the names of kings, and so on.

SELF-TESTING EXERCISES

- Complete and check exercises 19.39-19.42 as usual.

SUMMARY QUIZ

Consult the course syllabus or check with your instructor for information about completing and handing in summary quiz 19.

LESSON 20

Entering school zone II

The story

Mireille is going on about her Greek art professor when Robert suddenly knocks over his glass, dumping his kir in her lap. When everything is cleaned up, Robert brings their conversation back to her general attitude toward the university. She loves it. She loves the relative freedom. There is time for her to read. Lately she's been reading Hemingway.

The waiter, hearing that name, goes into raptures about both the man—who used to sit at that very table—and his works. It turns out, however, that he has no first-hand knowledge of either. Robert orders more drinks.

Then, in response to Mireille's questions, Robert says he is taking time out from school to "find himself," to decide what he really wants to do in life. Mireille teases him about this. Her joking attitude toward his identity crisis appears to irritate Robert greatly (or is he just trying to impress her?), for he launches into a mighty diatribe against traditional education, which he proclaims to be out of tune with modern life. It's not that Robert hasn't been a good student—he has. He even admits (without being asked) that he is what is known as gifted. At this, the irrepressible Mireille gets in a one-liner about how he must have won prizes for modesty, too. Then she denies that she is making fun of him. On the subject of education, Robert's sense of humor seems to have deserted him. His tirade will no doubt continue.

Notes on culture and communication

• **La Closerie des Lilas** is a Left Bank literary café and restaurant much frequented by the writers and artists of the neighborhood, Montparnasse. It was one of the favorite haunts of American writers of the Lost Generation, among them F. Scott Fitzgerald, Gertrude Stein, and Ernest Hemingway.

• **Pour me trouver.** After the waiter has helped clean up the spilled kir, we witness a scene of culture conflict. The French have difficulty understanding the American custom of allowing students a year off from college to "find themselves," for several reasons. First, there is the traditional French concept of time and career: you choose your career early on, and once the decision is made there is little opportunity to deviate from it. Second, since advancement depends upon seniority, a young person who really wants to get ahead cannot afford to take time off and lose ground in the career race.

Then there is the very notion of "finding oneself," which Mireille finds a bit ridiculous. She is not alone. The French seem to have a more definite concept of personality than Americans, and one's career is considered quite distinct from from one's personality. What you are going to do and who you are have little to do with each other. So no matter what the motive, taking time off is not much different from goofing off! Little wonder, then, that Mireille is sarcastic, and Robert hurt.

Content and learning objectives of lesson 20

This lesson shows how French speakers apologize and excuse others, express surprise, and refer to best and worst. It also shows how they poke fun at each other.

The following points are highlighted in lesson 20 (you should concentrate on sections marked with a √):

√• Verb forms (20.8-20.10, 20.28)
• Stressed pronouns, review
√• *Ne . . . jamais*, *ne . . . rien* (20.17-20.20)
√• *Mettre*, *boire* (20.29, 20.30)
√• *Passé composé* and pronouns (20.31-20.37)

ASSIMILATION OF THE TEXT

20.1-20.3 Text work-up, aural comprehension, and oral production

Proceed as usual in these sections. (Refer to lesson 3.1-3.3 for directions, if necessary.) Work with the text and illustrations in the textbook, as in previous lessons.

TOWARD COMMUNICATION

20.4-20.7 Observation and activation: Pronunciation; the sounds /a/ and /ã/

The French /a/ is very different from most of the sounds associated with the letter *a* in English (/e/ in A, *B*, *C*, /æ/ in *dad*, /ə/ in *ahead*). It is closer to the /a/ in *father*, although it is pronounced more in the front of the mouth than the English /a/. The nonnasal vowel /a/ must be clearly distinguished from the nasal vowel /ã/.

• Repeat the examples of /a/ you hear in 20.5, and of /a/ and /ã/ in 20.6. In 20.7, determine whether the sentences you hear contain the verb *attendre* (/a/) or *entendre* (/ã/) and mark the appropriate box on the grid in your workbook.

20.8-20.10 Observation and activation: *Attendre* and *entendre*

Chart 20.8 lists the forms of *attendre* and *entendre* in the present and *passé composé.* The two verbs are conjugated in exactly the same way. Note that the auxiliary in the *passé composé* is *avoir.*

• Exercise 20.9 gives you practice using *attendre* in the present. You will be asked whether various people are staying. Say yes, they are waiting for someone, using the present tense of *attendre.*

Audio cues (for reference):
20.9 Activation orale: Attendre; présent de l'indicatif

1. Tu restes là?
2. Vous restez là, vous deux?
3. Elle reste là?
4. Tes parents restent là?
5. Tu restes là?

• Exercise 20.10 will help you practice using *attendre* in the *passé composé.* You will be asked whether various people left. Say no, they waited, using the *passé composé* of *attendre.*

Audio cues (for reference):
20.10 Activation orale: Attendre; passé composé

1. Tu es parti?
2. Vous êtes partis, vous deux?
3. Il est parti?
4. Elles sont parties?
5. Tu es parti, toi?

20.11 Observation: Excusing oneself

Chart 20.11 presents some conversationally useful expressions for excusing yourself and for responding when others apologize.

The first three responses indicate that you think no harm was done. The last two are used when someone tries to rectify the mistake and you don't want anyone to bother (for example, when a waiter attempts to dry off your dress after your conversation partner has dumped his drink on it).

20.12 Observation: Surprise and disbelief

The phrases in chart 20.12 can be used when someone tells you something unbelievable, such as that he or she just saw Hemingway. (Needless to say, the responses "Vous avez bu!" and "Vous buvez trop!", referring to an alleged state of intoxication on the part of your interlocutor, must be used with extreme caution.)

20.13 Observation: Denial

Chart 20.13 groups together a number of phrases that can be used to deny a negative intention someone has attributed to you—for instance, when you are accused of making fun of an earnest young man who goes about proclaiming he wants to find himself.

20.14-20.16 Observation and activation: Making fun of people; *se moquer de*

Se moquer is a reflexive verb (see lesson 11) that is usually followed by a noun or a stressed pronoun: "Mireille se moque de **Robert**," "Mireille se moque de **lui**."

• Exercises 20.15 and 20.16 review the use of *se moquer de* in positive and negative expressions. In 20.15, you will hear that various people are not happy. Say it's because Mireille is making fun of them, using *se moquer* and the appropriate stressed pronouns.

Audio cues (for reference):

20.15 Activation orale: Se moquer de; pronoms accentués (révision)

1. Robert n'est pas content...
2. Il n'est pas content...
3. Colette n'est pas contente...
4. Les gens ne sont pas contents...
5. Mes amis et moi, nous ne sommes pas contents...
6. Vous non plus, vous n'êtes pas contents...
7. Tu n'es pas content...
8. Les amies de Mireille ne sont pas contentes...

• In 20.16, you will be asked why various people are making fun of others. React with (mock) astonishment, rejecting the suggestion that anyone is being laughed at. You will need to use two stressed pronouns in your responses, one to express your surprise that you or others are being accused of ridiculing someone (*moi?*, *lui?*, etc.), and the other to refer to those who are being ridiculed (or, as you maintain, **not** ridiculed).

Audio cues (for reference):
20.16 Activation orale: Se moquer de; pronoms accentués (révision)

1. Pourquoi tu te moques de moi, comme ça?
2. Pourquoi est-ce que tu te moques de Robert comme ça?
3. Pourquoi est-ce que tu te moques de tes soeurs comme ça?
4. Pourquoi est-ce que tu te moques des gens comme ça?
5. Pourquoi est-ce que Mireille se moque de moi comme ça?
6. Pourquoi est-ce que Mireille se moque de Robert comme ça?
7. Pourquoi est-ce que Mireille se moque des gens comme ça?
8. Pourquoi est-ce que ces gens se moquent de moi comme ça?
9. Pourquoi est-ce que ces gens se moquent de Robert comme ça?

20.17-20.20 Observation and activation: *Jamais/toujours, rien/quelque chose, personne/tout le monde*

Section 20.17 reviews the negative expression *ne . . . jamais* in its function as the opposite of *toujours.*

In the last example in the list, notice the presence of **two** negative expressions, *jamais* and *personne*, introduced by a single *ne.* You will see other double negatives in exercises 20.19 and 20.20.

• In exercise 20.18, you will hear that certain things are always true of certain people. Take issue with these statements and say that just the opposite is true, using *ne . . . jamais* in place of *toujours.*

Audio cues (for reference):
20.18 Activation orale: Jamais/toujours

1. Il a toujours de bonnes notes.
2. Vous avez toujours de bonnes notes!
3. Mais si, vous avez toujours eu de bonnes notes!
4. Vous vous moquez toujours de moi!
5. Elle se moque toujours de lui!
6. Elle se moque toujours de nous!
7. Elle fait toujours ce qu'elle veut!
8. Vous faites toujours ce que vous voulez!
9. Vous avez toujours aimé les maths!
10. Vous êtes toujours en vacances!

• 20.19 will familiarize you with the combination of *rien* as the opposite of *quelque chose*, and *jamais* as the opposite of *toujours.* You will hear negative statements combining *jamais* and *rien.* Take issue with these statements and say the opposite, using the *toujours quelque chose* combination.

Audio cues (for reference):
20.19 Activation orale: Jamais/toujours; rien/quelque chose

1. Vous n'avez jamais rien à faire!
2. Elle n'a jamais rien à faire!
3. Je n'ai jamais rien à dire!
4. Il n'a jamais rien à faire!
5. Il n'a jamais rien à voir!
6. Il n'a jamais rien d'intéressant!

• 20.20 will give you practice using the negative combination *jamais personne.* You are surprised to hear certain kinds of behavior attributed to various people. Question the speaker to make certain you've understood correctly who is being talked about, using stressed pronouns. Then disagree, replacing *toujours* with *ne . . . jamais* and *tout le monde* with *personne.*

Audio cues (for reference):
20.20 Activation orale: Jamais/toujours; personne/tout le monde

1. Elle se moque toujours de tout le monde.
2. Tu te moques toujours de tout le monde!
3. Vous vous moquez toujours de tout le monde, vous deux!
4. Tu connais tout le monde!
5. Tu parles à tout le monde!
6. Tu parles toujours à tout le monde!

20.21, 20.22 Observation and activation: Learning

The verb *apprendre* can be used to refer to learning something, such as a subject, or to learning how to do something. In the first instance, *apprendre* is used with a direct object noun ("elle apprend **ses leçons**"); in the second, it is used with an infinitive introduced by *à* ("elle apprend **à nager**").

• Exercise 20.22 reflects both uses. You will be asked whether various people have certain kinds of knowledge. Say yes, they learned all by themselves, using *apprendre* with a noun when the question is about a subject, and with an infinitive when it is about a skill.

Audio cues (for reference):
20.22 Activation orale: Apprentissage

1. Robert sait lire?
2. Robert sait le français?
3. Robert sait jouer du violon?
4. Il sait jouer aux échecs?
5. Il sait l'anglais?
6. Et vous, vous savez l'anglais?
7. Vous savez le français?
8. Vous savez conduire?
9. Et Robert, il sait conduire?
10. Vos enfants savent nager?

20.23 Observation: The best and the worst

The expressions in chart 20.23 show how the spectrum of quality can be divided into different degrees, from worst through average to best.

20.24-20.27 Observation and activation: Time; no time for oneself

The sentences in section 20.24 contain three useful ways to express the familiar sentiment that there is too much to do and never enough time for oneself. Note the use of the stressed pronoun after *à* in "on n'a pas une minute **à soi**" and its variants.

Soi is the stressed pronoun that corresponds to the subject pronoun *on*, referring to everybody generally and nobody in particular. Recall that the stressed pronouns for *il* or *elle* are *lui* and *elle*; for *ils* and *elles* the stressed forms are *eux* and *elles*.

• In exercise 20.25, you will be asked why various people don't do various things. Answer that they haven't the time to do them, using *avoir le temps* and the infinitive of the verb you hear.

Audio cues (for reference):
20.25 Activation orale: Avoir le temps de...

1. Pourquoi est-ce que le garçon de la Closerie ne lit pas?
2. Pourquoi est-ce que tu ne lis pas?
3. Pourquoi est-ce que vous ne lisez pas, vous deux?
4. Pourquoi est-ce que vos enfants ne lisent pas?
5. Pourquoi est-ce que votre fille ne lit pas?
6. Pourquoi est-ce que vos parents ne partent pas en vacances?
7. Pourquoi est-ce que vous ne faites pas du karaté?

• In 20.26, you will be asked why certain people don't read much. Answer that they don't have a minute to themselves, using the appropriate stressed pronoun.

Audio cues (for reference):
20.26 Activation orale: Ne pas avoir une minute à soi

1. Pourquoi est-ce que le garçon de la Closerie ne lit pas?
2. Pourquoi est-ce que tu ne lis pas?
3. Pourquoi est-ce que vos parents ne lisent pas?
4. Pourquoi est-ce que vos filles ne lisent pas?
5. Pourquoi est-ce que vous ne lisez pas, vous deux?
6. Pourquoi est-ce que votre fils ne lit pas?

• In 20.27, you will be asked why people don't take the time to read. By now you are a little tired of all these questions, and you point out that people can't just do what they want.

Audio cues (for reference):
20.27 Activation orale: Faire ce qu'on veut

1. Pourquoi est-ce que le garçon de la Closerie ne prend pas le temps de lire?
2. Pourquoi est-ce que tu ne prends pas le temps de lire?
3. Pourquoi est-ce que vos parents ne prennent pas le temps de lire?
4. Pourquoi est-ce que vous ne prenez pas le temps de lire, vous deux?

20.28 Observation: *Réfléchir, choisir, finir*

The chart shows that these three verbs are conjugated in the same way.

Note that in the present, all three singular forms of each verb are pronounced identically. In all three plural forms an added consonant sound /s/ appears at the end of the stem. This means that the /s/ sound will also appear in all forms of the imperfect, since they are derived from the *nous* form of the present.

In the *passé composé*, the auxiliary used is *avoir*, and the past participles end in *-i*. (Hence the past participle **and** all three singular forms of the present are pronounced in the same way.)

20.29 Observation: *Mettre*

Chart 20.29 shows various forms of *mettre* in the present and the past.

Notice that *mettre* can be used reflexively: "je me suis mis en congé."

The auxiliary of *mettre* in the *passé composé* is *avoir*: "**J'ai** mis une jupe." Note, however, that the auxiliary of *mettre* when it is used **reflexively** in the *passé composé* is *être*: "Je me **suis** mis en congé." This is not an isolated case: *être* is the auxiliary for **all** reflexive verbs in the *passé composé*.

Note that the imperfect (*mettait*) is derived, predictably, from the *nous* form (**mett***ons*).

20.30 Observation: *Boire*

The chart lists forms of *boire* in the present and in both past tenses. Notice the change of vowel sound in the stem in the *nous* and *vous* forms of the present. This makes the imperfect sound quite different from the present (*je b***u***vais* versus *je b***oi***s*), since the stem of the imperfect is, as usual, that of the *nous* form of the present (*buv-*).

20.31-20.33 Observation and activation: *Passé composé* and pronouns

Up to this point the great majority of verbs you have seen in the *passé composé* have *avoir* as their auxiliary. This is true of most verbs in the language. *Avoir* is even the auxiliary of auxiliaries: it is used with *être* and with *avoir* itself, as the second part of chart 20.31 demonstrates. Remember, however, that the auxiliary of **reflexive verbs** is always *être*.

Chart 20.32 shows the position of pronouns (and *en*) in relation to the verb.

Recall that in the present (and in all the tenses that have single forms: the imperfect, the future, and so forth), object pronouns (as well as *y* and *en*) are placed in front of the verb: "il **la** regarde," "elle **lui** plaît," "j'**en** ai assez." Notice that in the *passé composé* and other compound tenses they are placed in front of the **auxiliary**. Clearly the auxiliary, as the part that is conjugated, can be considered the active verbal element in a compound tense.

• Study chart 20.32 carefully, and review the examples in exercise 20.33 before beginning it. Then answer the questions you hear, replacing nouns with appropriate pronouns, *y*, or *en*. In choosing appropriate replacements, be on the alert for indirect objects, and remember that *de* + noun is replaced by *en*.

Audio cues (for reference):

20.33 Activation orale: Passé composé et pronoms

1. Vous avez choisi vos cours?
2. Vos enfants ont fait des maths?
3. Il a parlé à Mireille?
4. Vous avez choisi vos cours, vous deux?
5. Tu as fini tes devoirs?
6. Mireille a eu son bac?
7. Elle a raté son interro de maths?
8. Vos enfants ont fait du français?
9. Ils sont allés en France?
10. Vous avez entendu parler de Saint-Tropez?
11. Vous y êtes allé?
12. Tu as bu ton kir?
13. Vous avez parlé aux parents de Mireille?

20.34-20.37 Observation and activation: *Passé composé*, pronouns, and negation

In a negative expression in the *passé composé*, *ne* and *pas* surround the auxiliary, as chart 20.34 illustrates. The object pronoun is still placed directly in front of the auxiliary (**between** *ne* and the auxiliary).

• In exercise 20.35, various people have left. Say they didn't wait, using the *passé composé* in negative sentences. Your task is simply to position *ne* and *pas* correctly in relation to the two parts of the verb (auxiliary and past participle).

Audio cues (for reference):
20.35 Activation orale: Passé composé et négation

1. Nous sommes partis...
2. Ils sont partis.
3. Je suis parti.
4. Mireille est partie.
5. Robert est parti.

• In 20.36, people have gone, leaving others behind. Say they didn't wait for them, using the *passé composé* and the appropriate direct object pronoun. The problem is the same as in the preceding exercise, with the added complication of a direct object pronoun to be placed between *ne* and the auxiliary.

Audio cues (for reference):
20.36 Activation orale: Passé composé, négation et pronoms

1. Nous sommes partis sans Robert.
2. Nous sommes partis sans Robert et Mireille.
3. Nous sommes partis sans eux.
4. Je suis parti sans Mireille.
5. Ils sont partis sans elle.
6. Ils sont partis sans nous.

• In 20.37, answer no to the questions you hear, replacing nouns with pronouns, *y*, or *en*, as necessary.

Audio cues (for reference):
20.37 Activation orale: Passé composé, négation et pronoms

1. Vos enfants ont fait de l'allemand?
2. Vous avez fini vos devoirs, vous deux?
3. Est-ce que Mireille a eu le prix de mathématiques?
4. Tu as lu les romans d'Hemingway, toi?
5. Est-ce que le garçon de la Closerie a connu Hemingway?
6. Est-ce qu'il l'a lu?
7. Est-ce que vous avez entendu parler de Marienbad?
8. Est-ce que vous y êtes allé?
9. Est-ce que vos filles ont fait de l'histoire de l'art?
10. Est-ce que Robert a parlé aux parents de Mireille?

20.38 Activation: Dialogue between Robert and Mireille

Listen to the conversation between Robert and Mireille and memorize Mireille's lines, imitating and repeating as usual.

TOWARD FREE EXPRESSION

20.39, 20.40 Words at large

In 20.39, answer the questions you see using expressions you have studied in lesson 20. Review the situations and questions printed in your workbook, then listen to them on the audio recording and answer.

In 20.40, proceed as in previous versions of this exercise.

• **Suggested oral assignment.** Record your answers to 20.40 and send them to your instructor on the cassette you use for summary quiz 20. (See the course syllabus for details.)

20.41 Role-playing and reinvention of the story

You are seated at Robert's and Mireille's table at the Closerie des Lilas. The subject is you, your occupation, your studies. Say as much as you can, using the suggestions in the workbook to get started. If you work with a partner, one of you can play Robert or Mireille and ask questions, react, etc. Or you can each talk about yourselves. You may tell the truth, or invent an imaginary character.

SELF-TESTING EXERCISES

• Complete and check exercises 20.42, 20.43, and 20.44 as usual.

SUMMARY QUIZ

Consult the course syllabus or check with your instructor for information about completing and handing in summary quiz 20.

LESSON 21
Entering school zone III

The story

They're on their third kir and Robert is getting up a real head of antiintellectual steam. First, helped by computers and calculators, he dismisses all of mathematics. Chemistry is next (here, Mireille agrees; she doesn't like the smell of the chemicals). Physics follows. Robert fell from a balcony when he was ten and spent three weeks in a hospital. Knowledge of the laws of falling bodies would not have helped him. Then come Latin (who speaks it?), literature (artificial), history (distorted to suit nationalistic purposes), and modern languages (too much emphasis on grammar).

Always game for a brisk argument, Mireille has countered Robert's opinions, but her objections have been brushed aside. For instance, she argues that someone has to program the computers, that Latin provides intellectual discipline, that classical literature is beautiful, and that modern languages are useful. At the end, he calls her comment about culture "sententious" and invites her to lunch, not because of her sententiousness, but because it's almost noon, he's hungry, and he assumes that she is, too. Besides, he'd like to continue their conversation. Mireille must decline. She's expected at home, where she has lunch every day. Upon learning the time, she rushes off, claiming that she's going to be late.

Notes on culture and communication

• **Le Quartier Latin.** The Latin Quarter is one of the oldest neighborhoods in Paris. It was the cradle of the university of Paris in the thirteenth century. Today it is the home of many colleges, universities, and institutes, several prestigious professional schools, numerous bookstores, libraries, publishing houses, and so on. It is the heart of academic and intellectual life in Paris.

• **Tragédies en vers.** French seventeenth-century tragedies were written in Alexandrine verse, (lines of poetry twelve syllables long), as in this example from one of the best-known poets of the period, Jean Racine:

> Oui, puisque je retrouve un ami si fidèle,
> Ma fortune va prendre une face nouvelle. . . .

• **Robert the Bold.** Galled and provoked by Mireille's assumption that by taking a leave of absence from college he is just goofing off, and no doubt fortified by his three kirs, Robert explodes, taking out his hurt feelings on the whole educational curriculum. His diatribe against education is exaggerated and childish, yet Mireille looks curiously pleased and relieved. Robert had been almost too sweet and agreeable. Was he just another affable American, smiling and nodding, avoiding argument at any cost? Here Robert's mother's Frenchness comes to the fore. His whole bearing becomes French. He becomes argumentative. He leans forward toward Mireille with every verbal jab. He gesticulates more, expressing his impatience by expelling his breath through pouting lips. Not in the least persuaded by his arguments, Mireille smiles at Robert indulgently, affectionately—and with renewed interest.

Content and learning objectives of lesson 21

This lesson will familiarize you with ways of describing things as useful, specifying what they are useful for, and talking about know-how. It shows how French speakers use *avoir* to refer to being hungry, being right or wrong, and other common situations.

The following points are highlighted in lesson 21 (you should concentrate on sections marked with a √):

√• Masculine and feminine forms, review and extension (21.7-21.10)
√• *Faire rire*, *faire croire*
• *Recevoir*
√• *Savoir* and infinitives (21.16-21.19)
√• Agreement of past participles with *avoir* (21.27, 21.28)

ASSIMILATION OF THE TEXT

21.1-21.4 Text work-up, aural comprehension, and oral production

Proceed as usual in these sections. (Refer to lesson 3.1-3.3 and lesson 4.3 for directions, if necessary.) Work with the text and illustrations in the textbook, as in previous lessons.

TOWARD COMMUNICATION

21.5, 21.6 Observation and activation: Pronunciation; open syllables (review)

You saw in lesson 2 that the stream of speech is divided into syllables. Most French syllables begin with a consonant sound and end in a vowel sound (*fa-ti-gué*); they are **open syllables**. In the example given in

21.5, all the syllables are open except the last, *-rrasse*, which ends in a consonant sound, /s/.

• Repeat the words and expressions you hear in 21.6, separating the syllables slightly, as in the examples.

21.7-21.10 Observation and activation: Masculine and feminine

The charts in 21.7 show masculine and feminine forms for words that end in *-el* and *-al*.

You saw in lesson 4 that the gender of a word is part of the word itself. It is not dictated by any male or female aspect of the thing the word refers to (remember *une victime*, *un juge*). The gender of a word is sometimes reflected in the **ending** of the word. Sections 21.8 and 21.9 show how you can predict the gender of certain words by looking at their endings.

In 21.8, you see a number of words that have the same ending, *-tion*. If you look at the articles that accompany these words (*une*, *la*) you will see that they are all feminine. It happens, for reasons that have to do with the way French evolved from Latin, that nearly **all** French nouns ending in *-tion* are feminine.

The same is true of nouns ending in *-ie*, like *philosophie* and *tragédie*.

• In exercise 21.10, complete the sentences with the masculine or feminine form of the article, depending on whether the noun is masculine or feminine. In cases where you cannot tell the gender of the noun from its ending, look at the ending of an accompanying adjective.

√ Check your answers in key 21.10 at the back of the workbook.

21.11-21.13 Observation and activation: Usefulness

The verb *servir* is used to say that something is useful, as the first chart in 21.11 demonstrates. The purpose a particular thing is useful for is introduced by *à*.

Notice that the forms of *servir* behave like those of *sortir*, *partir*, and *sentir*. In all these verbs (and many others as well), there is a consonant sound in the three persons of the plural that is not heard in the singular.

• In exercise 21.12, you will be asked whether various items are useful. A partial answer to each question is given in your workbook. If the answer is *oui*, say what the item is useful for, using *servir à* and the infinitive you see. If the answer is *non*, say that the item serves no useful purpose, using *servir à* and *rien*.

Audio cues (for reference):
21.12 Activation orale: Utilité

1. Une calculatrice, est-ce que c'est utile?
2. Une fleur, est-ce que c'est utile?
3. Des lunettes, est-ce que c'est utile?
4. Un crayon, est-ce que c'est utile?
5. Et fumer (une cigarette), est-ce que c'est utile?
6. Une calculatrice, est-ce que c'est utile?
7. Une cravate, est-ce que c'est utile?
8. Une montre, est-ce que c'est utile?

• 21.13 will give you practice in using *servir à* to talk about what various people and things are useful for. You will hear sentences containing *être utile*. Express the same idea using *servir à*.

Audio cues (for reference):
21.13 Activation orale: Utilité; servir

1. Est-ce que les mathématiques sont utiles?
2. Non, les mathématiques ne sont pas utiles.
3. Est-ce que l'histoire de l'art est utile?
4. Non, ce n'est pas utile.
5. Est-ce que les professeurs sont utiles?
6. Les professeurs ne sont pas utiles.
7. Est-ce que nous sommes utiles, nous?
8. Nous ne sommes pas utiles.

21.14, 21.15 Observation and activation: *Faire croire, faire rire*

If I laugh, it is because you **make** me laugh. Robert is trying to **make** Mireille believe he is super-gifted. *Faire* can be used with an infinitive like *croire*, *rire*, and so forth to express this kind of causation.

Notice that with *faire rire* the person who ends up laughing is the **direct object** of *faire:* "ça **la** fait rire," "tu **me** fais rire."

• In exercise 21.15, you will hear that various people find other people funny. Restate each sentence using *faire rire.* Note that the subject of the sentence you hear will become the direct object of *faire rire*, and vice versa.

21.16-21.19 Observation and activation: Expressions with *avoir*

Chart 21.16 presents a number of expressions, new and old, that use *avoir* to refer to age, hunger, wealth, health, and a host of other situations. Three of them appear in the exercises that follow.

Note that in many idiomatic expressions such as those that appear in the chart (*avoir faim*, *avoir raison*, and so on), the noun that follows *avoir* is not accompanied by any article.

• In 21.17, you will be told that a number of people are mistaken. Say no, they're right, using *avoir raison.*

Audio cues (for reference):
21.17 Activation orale: Avoir raison

1. Vous vous trompez!
2. Mireille se trompe.
3. Les manifestants se trompent.
4. Je me trompe, moi?
5. Vous vous trompez, vous deux!

• In 21.18, you will hear that various people can't stand certain things. Say they're wrong, using *avoir tort.*

Audio cues (for reference):
21.18 Activation orale: Avoir tort

1. J'ai horreur du latin!
2. Mireille a horreur de la chimie.
3. Jean-Pierre a horreur des maths.
4. Nous avons horreur de la philosophie.
5. Mes parents ont horreur du cinéma.

• In 21.19, you have doubts about the accuracy of certain statements you have heard. Express your scepticism, using *avoir l'air.*

Audio cues (for reference):
21.19 Activation orale: Avoir l'air

1. Mireille n'est peut-être pas pressée...
2. Tu ne t'ennuies peut-être pas...
3. Mireille n'est peut-être pas fragile...
4. Tu n'aimes peut-être pas ça...
5. Il n'a peut-être pas faim...
6. Vous n'avez peut-être pas faim...
7. Ils ne savent peut-être pas ce qu'ils font...
8. Tu ne sais peut-être pas ce que tu fais...

21.20, 21.21 Observation and activation: *Recevoir*

Chart 21.20 shows the similarities in the conjugation of *recevoir* and *devoir* in the present and *passé composé.*

Note. In the past participle *reçu* and three of the forms of the present—*reçois*, *reçoit*, and *reçoivent*—the *c* is written with a special mark called a **cedilla:** *ç* (*c cédille*). In French, the letter *c* is **soft** (that is, it is pronounced /s/) before *e* and *i* (**C**é*cile*) and **hard** (pronounced /k/) before *a*, *o*, and *u* (**c***afé*, **c***ombien*, **c***ubain*). In the case of a verb like *recevoir*, where the stem of the infinitive has a soft *c*, the cedilla comes into play in front of an ending beginning with *a* or *o* to indicate that the *c* represents a soft sound, even though it is followed by an ending spelled with an *a*, a *u*, or an *o*: *reçoivent*, for example. It is not needed in *recevons* or *recevez*, since *c* followed by *e* is always pronounced /s/.

• In exercise 21.21, you will hear that a number of people are cultivated. Agree, pointing out that they got a good education. Use appropriate forms of *recevoir*.

Audio cues (for reference):
21.21 Activation orale: Recevoir

1. Elle est très cultivée.
2. Hubert est très cultivé.
3. Que vous êtes cultivés, vous deux!
4. Mireille et ses soeurs sont très cultivées.
5. Que tu es cultivé!

21.22, 21.23 Observation and activation: *Savoir* and infinitives

Chart 21.22 illustrates how *savoir* is used with an infinitive to refer to skill, ability, or know-how. Notice that *savoir* is followed immediately by the infinitive, with nothing placed in between them: *elle sait* **lire.**

• In exercise 21.23, you will hear that various people are going to be taught how to do certain things. Answer that they have known how to do them for some time, using the appropriate form of *savoir* and the infinitive representing the skill in question. (You will hear the infinitive after the verb *apprendre*.)

Audio cues (for reference):
21.23 Activation orale: Savoir + infinitif

1. Je vais vous apprendre à lire.
2. Nous allons lui apprendre à écrire.
3. Nous allons lui apprendre à nager.
4. Je vais vous apprendre à faire des explosifs.
5. Je vais vous apprendre à jouer aux échecs.
6. Je vais leur apprendre à conduire.
7. Mireille va t'apprendre à danser.
8. Robert va t'apprendre à faire de la planche à voile.

21.24-21.26 Observation and activation: *S'y mettre*

Chart 21.24 shows how *mettre* is used reflexively (**se** *mettre*) to talk about applying yourself to something—putting your mind to it and beginning it. *Se mettre* is used with *à*, followed by the activity that is being undertaken. The activity can be expressed either as a noun (*il s'est mis* **au travail**) or an infinitive (*il s'est mis* **à parler**).

As the second chart shows, *à* and its object can be replaced by *y*, which comes right after the reflexive pronoun.

• In exercise 21.25, say that people can be a certain way when they really get into it, using *s'y mettre.*

Audio cues (for reference):
21.25 Activation orale: S'y mettre

1. Ce que vous êtes drôle.
2. Ce que Robert est cérémonieux!
3. Ce que Mireille est sentencieuse!
4. Ce que vous êtes embêtants, tous les deux!
5. Ce que tu es agaçant!
6. Ce que les professeurs sont embêtants!
7. Ce que vous êtes spirituels, tous les deux!
8. Ce que les parents sont autoritaires!

• In 21.26, you will be asked whether people are undertaking various activities. Say yes, they are beginning to, using *s'y mettre.*

Audio cues (for reference):
21.26 Activation orale: S'y mettre

1. Tu commences l'italien?
2. Tu te mets à l'informatique?
3. Tu te mets au bridge?
4. Robert se met aux échecs?
5. Vous vous mettez au latin, tous les deux?
6. Les soeurs de Mireille se mettent au ski, maintenant?
7. Les Belleau se mettent aux mots croisés, maintenant?

21.27, 21.28 Observation and activation: Agreement of the past participle with *avoir*

In compound tenses such as the *passé composé*, the past participles of verbs conjugated with the auxiliary *avoir* agree in gender and number with any direct object that comes before the verb.

As you have seen, direct object **nouns** normally come **after** the verb: "Robert a invité **Hubert**." There is no agreement with direct object nouns that come after the verb.

Pronouns, however, are placed **in front** of the verb: "Il **les** a invités." There **is** agreement with direct object pronouns that come before the verb. The past participle *invité***s** has an *-s* at the end because it agrees with *les* (= Mireille and Hubert).

In the case of an *-er* verb like *inviter*, whose past participle ends in a vowel (*invit***é**), there is no change in the pronunciation of the various forms of the past participle: *invité* and *invitées* are pronounced identically. But in the case of a verb like *mettre*, whose past participle ends in a consonant (*mis*), the feminine form ends in *-se*, pronounced /z/.

• In exercise 21.28, complete the past participles where necessary. Remember that unless a direct object pronoun comes **before** the past participle, there will be no agreement. Note, too, that whenever there is a direct object pronoun in front of the verb the stage is set for an agreement, **but** if the pronoun is masculine singular, this agreement will not be reflected in any ending added to the past participle: "Il a invité Robert; il **l'**a invité."

21.29 Activation: Dialogue between Robert and Mireille

Listen to the conversation between Robert and Mireille and memorize Robert's lines, imitating and repeating as usual.

TOWARD FREE EXPRESSION

21.30 Words at large

Proceed as usual. (If necessary, refer to lesson 3 for directions.)

21.31, 21.32 Role-playing and reinvention of the story

In 21.31, you are Mireille listening to Robert's blanket condemnation of every field of knowledge. Answer his criticisms, out loud, using the suggestions in the workbook as a point of departure. If you work with a partner, take parts and complete the exercise, then switch roles and do it again.

In 21.32, tell (out loud) the untold story of Robert's fall from a balcony in New Orleans when he was 10 years old. You may use the alternatives in the workbook to get started, or you may invent the whole story yourself. If you work with a partner, tell parallel stories, each one giving his or her version of each scene. Or collaborate on a single story, describing alternate scenes in turn.

• **Suggested written assignment.** Write out a version of the story of Robert's mishap in New Orleans (21.32), and send it to your instructor with summary quiz 21. (See the course syllabus for details.) Write at least ten sentences.

DOCUMENTS

At the end of the textbook chapter for lesson 21 you will find a short passage and a poem for reading practice.

Raymond Queneau (1903-1976) was a linguist and a mathematician in addition to being a poet and a novelist. A member of the surrealist movement, he was interested in the "automatic writing" of the unconscious mind—a topic that also interested the subject of this poem, the American writer Gertrude Stein. In his poem, Queneau imitates Stein's abstract style, with its strange yet oddly consistent logic, and writes a series of variations on her most famous line, "A rose is a rose is a rose."

SELF-TESTING EXERCISES

- Complete and check exercises 21.33-21.35 as usual.

SUMMARY QUIZ

Consult the course syllabus or check with your instructor for information about completing and handing in summary quiz 21.

LESSON 22
Fishing for an invitation I

The story

Noon: Marie-Laure goes home for lunch reciting one of those rhyming chants so popular with little girls on both sides of the Atlantic.

12:05: Robert asks about making a phone call, has a little difficulty comprehending how the public phone works, finally understands, buys the necessary token, wrestles again briefly with the phone, and gets through to the Courtois's apartment. The Portuguese maid who answers tells him that Madame is out walking Minouche. He will have to call again in a half-hour.

Robert pays the café tab. It seems high, but at least the 15 percent tip is included. Robert roams rather aimlessly until about 12:30 and then, with considerable help from a passerby, manages to phone Mme Courtois. A world-class talker, Mme Courtois inquires after Mrs. Taylor (Robert's mother and her childhood friend), laments over the illness of Minouche (her cat), complains about her husband's excessive devotion to work, and invites Robert to dinner in two days' time—all in the same breath.

After lunch in a café-restaurant, Robert returns to the Luxembourg Garden to keep his appointment with Marie-Laure. She has no English homework for him to help with after all, but she does notice the man in black who's been following our young friend. Robert remembers seeing him earlier. It's all very strange!

Notes on culture and communication

• **Le déjeuner.** Traditionally in France, mealtime is a family occasion when everyone sits down at the table to share a cooked meal. This ritual applies to lunch as well as dinner when the family members' work schedules permit.

• **Le service.** In France, a service charge is usually included in café, restaurant, and hotel bills.

• **Pièces, cartes magnétiques, jetons.** On the street, public telephones work either with coins or, more often now, magnetic cards that can be purchased at the post office or the tobacconist's shop. In cafés and restaurants, tokens are sometimes necessary; they can be bought from the bartender or at the cash register.

• **Telephones and the breakdown of communication.** In this lesson, Robert learns how to operate French public telephones. He has his problems, but once he figures out the system he finds that it works efficiently and well. His real difficulties stem from the fact that on the telephone you cannot see the person you are talking to. Deprived of nonverbal cues, Robert discovers that communication in a foreign country can be unexpectedly complicated. In every culture, certain facial expressions govern taking turns when you talk. In France, the person who wishes to have a turn raises his head slightly, wrinkles his forehead a bit, raises his eyebrows and opens his mouth as if to speak. When Madame Courtois asks Robert a question, he prepares to take his turn and makes the appropriate facial expression. She cannot see him, however, so she follows her natural inclination to keep talking. Small wonder that Robert cannot get a word in edgewise!

Content and learning objectives of lesson 22

This lesson contains basic vocabulary for talking about meals, making telephone calls, and talking about being late. It also shows how French speakers express pleasure.

The following points are highlighted in lesson 22 (you should concentrate on sections marked with a √):

√• The *passé composé* of reflexive verbs (22.16-22.18)
√• Agreement of past participles; reflexive verbs (22.19, 22.20)
√• Verbs conjugated with *avoir* or *être* (22.21-22.25)
√• Agreement of past participles; verbs conjugated with *être* (22.26, 22.27)
• *Faire plaisir*

ASSIMILATION OF THE TEXT

22.1-22.3 Text work-up, aural comprehension, and oral production

Proceed as usual in these sections. (Refer to lessons 3.1, 3.2, and 4.3 for directions, if necessary.) Work with the text and illustrations in the textbook, as in previous lessons.

TOWARD COMMUNICATION

22.4 Activation: Pronunciation; the sound /y/

• Repeat the words and expressions you hear.

22.5-22.7 Observation and activation: Meals

The three main meals of the day are the subject of chart 22.5. Notice that, in name, the morning meal (**petit** *déjeuner*) is a small-scale version of the noon meal (*déjeuner*). The noon and evening meals have corresponding verbs: *le déjeuner* (noun) ⇒ *déjeuner* (verb), *le dîner* (noun) ⇒ *dîner* (verb). For the morning meal, however, there is no separate verb; the noun is used with the verb *prendre*.

• In exercise 22.6, you will be told what time it is. Say it's time for the corresponding meal, using the nouns *petit déjeuner*, *déjeuner*, or *dîner*.

Audio cues (for reference):
22.6 Activation orale: Repas

1. Il est 8 heures du matin!
2. Il est midi!
3. Il est 8 heures du soir!
4. Il est 8 heures du matin!

• In 22.7, you will be asked what Mireille is going to do at various times of day. Say she's going to have the appropriate meal, using the verbs *déjeuner* or *dîner*, or the expression *prendre le petit déjeuner*.

Audio cues (for reference):
22.7 Activation orale: Repas

1. Il est midi. Qu'est-ce que Mireille va faire?
2. Il est 8 heures du matin. Qu'est-ce que Mireille va faire?
3. Il est 8 heures du soir. Qu'est-ce que Mireille va faire?
4. Il est midi. Qu'est-ce que Mireille va faire?
5. Il est 8 heures du matin. Qu'est-ce que Mireille va prendre?
6. Il est midi. Qu'est-ce qu'elle va faire?
7. Il est 8 heures du matin. Qu'est ce qu'elle va faire?

22.8, 22.9 Observation and activation: Telephone calls

Chart 22.8 presents useful phrases for two essential telephone situations: answering a call when it is for you, and answering when it is for someone else.

Notice that in an informal situation, Mireille answers simply, "C'est moi!" In a more formal situation, Mme Courtois says, "C'est moi-même!"

Note the use of the verb *quitter* in the negative ("Ne **quittez** pas!") to ask a caller to wait.

• Complete exercise 22.9, listening first to each dialogue, then playing the part of the person who answers, as in the example.

22.10-22.11 Observation and activation: Telephone calls; *appeler*, *rappeler*

If the person you are calling on the telephone is not there, you may wish to call again. Note that *rappeler* is the verb *appeler* with the added prefix *r-* indicating repetition. (With other verbs the prefix may be written *re-*: *retéléphoner*, *reprendre*, and so forth.)

Notice that the infinitive and the *nous* and *vous* forms of *rappeler* are written with a single *l*, while the other forms have two. This spelling change reflects a change in vowel sound. The *-e-* in the stem of *rapp***e***ler* is an /ə/ sound; it occurs in an open syllable (a syllable that ends in a vowel sound: *ra*-**ppe**-*ler*).

The *-e-* of *rapp***e***llent*, on the other hand, is in a closed syllable (a syllable that ends in a consonant sound: *ra*-**ppelle**). It is pronounced /ɛ/.

• In exercise 22.11, answer the phone, telling the caller to try again.

Audio cues (for reference):
22.11 Activation orale: Communications téléphoniques; appeler et rappeler

1. Allô, je peux parler à Mireille?
2. Allô, je peux parler à Robert?
3. Allô, je peux parler à ta soeur?
4. Allô, je peux parler à tes parents?
5. Allô, je peux parler à ton père?

22.12-22.15 Observation and activation: As time goes by; *se dépêcher*, *être en retard*

Section 22.12 presents two useful expressions for talking about being late and hurrying up. Notice that *se dépêcher* is a reflexive verb: *je* **me** *dépêche*.

• In exercise 22.13, tell various people why they should or shouldn't hurry, using *être en retard*.

Audio cues (for reference):
22.13 Activation orale: Le temps qui passe; se dépêcher, être en retard

1. Dépêchez-vous!
2. Ne vous dépêchez pas!
3. Dépêche-toi!
4. Dépêchons-nous!
5. Ne te dépêche pas!
6. Ne nous dépêchons pas!
7. Dépêchez-vous!
8. Ne vous dépêchez pas!

• In 22.14, if people are late, tell them to hurry up; if they are not late, tell them not to rush. Use *se dépêcher.*

Audio cues (for reference):
22.14 Activation orale: Le temps qui passe; se dépêcher, être en retard

1. Vous êtes en retard!
2. Vous n'êtes pas en retard!
3. Tu es en retard!
4. Nous sommes en retard!
5. Nous ne sommes pas en retard!
6. Tu n'es pas en retard!
7. Vous n'êtes pas en retard!
8. Vous êtes en retard.

• In 22.15, various people are late. Say they are hurrying.

Audio cues (for reference):
22.15 Activation orale: Le temps qui passe; se dépêcher, être en retard

1. Je suis en retard.
2. Mireille est en retard.
3. Robert est en retard.
4. Nous sommes en retard.
5. Robert et Mireille sont en retard.
6. Mireille et Marie-Laure sont en retard.

22.16-22.18 Observation and activation: The *passé composé* of reflexive verbs

Note that the verbs in 22.16 are all used with a reflexive pronoun; they are known therefore as **reflexive verbs.** The reflexive pronoun, like all object pronouns, is placed **before** the auxiliary: *elle* **s'***est arrêtée.*

Recall from lesson 19 that most **nonreflexive** verbs are conjugated with *avoir* in compound tenses, You will notice that the **reflexive** verbs in chart 22.16 are conjugated with the auxiliary *être.* **All** reflexive verbs are conjugated with *être* in the compound tenses.

• Exercise 22.18 gives you Robert and Mireille's meeting in instant replay. They are about to take the crucial steps that lead up to their first encounter. At each action, say they've done what we knew they'd do, using the *passé composé.* Remember to place the pronoun *se* immediately in front of the auxiliary *être.*

22.19-22.20 Observation and activation: Agreement of the past participle of reflexive verbs

As you saw in lesson 21, the ending of a past participle will reflect the gender and number of the direct object when the direct object is placed **in front** of it. In "il **les** a invit**ées**," *les* = Mireille and Colette; the past participle **agrees** with the direct object. (There is no agreement when the direct object **follows** the verb: "il a invité **Mireille et Colette**".)

In the case of reflexive verbs, the same pattern applies: "elle s'est arrêtée." Whenever the reflexive pronoun is the direct object of the verb, as it often is, the past participle will agree with it, since the pronoun always precedes the verb.

Remember that in order to figure out whether there should or shouldn't be agreement two things need to happen. (1) You need to know what the **direct object** of the verb is (is it the reflexive pronoun or not?). (2) Assuming that you've decided the reflexive pronoun is in fact the direct object, you need to determine what or whom this reflexive pronoun stands for, since *me*, *te*, *se*, *nous*, and *vous* can stand for either a masculine or a feminine, and *se* and *vous* can stand for either a singular or a plural.

If the whole matter of agreement seems unreasonably complicated, keep the following in mind:

1. In **spoken** French, few past participle agreements make any difference in sound: *invité*, *invitée*, and *invitées* are all pronounced the same. There is a difference in pronunciation only in the feminine forms of past participles that end in a written consonant (*elle s'est assise*, for example). In all other cases, no listener will ever know whether you remembered to make the past participle agree or not.

2. More and more French speakers, including well-educated ones, tend to ignore the refinements of past participle agreements. So if you miss a few yourself you will technically be in error, but you will also be in very good company.

• In exercise 22.20, add the appropriate ending to the past participles unless none is needed.

√ Check your answers in key 22.20 at the back of the workbook.

22.21-22.25 Observation and activation: Verbs conjugated with *avoir* or *être* in compound tenses

You have just seen that **most** nonreflexive verbs are conjugated with *avoir* in the compound tenses, and that **all** reflexive verbs are conjugated with *être*.

A **few** nonreflexive verbs are also conjugated with *être*. Most of them are shown in chart 22.21. This small group of verbs conjugated with *être* is made up of verbs that cannot be used with a direct object. Such verbs are known in general as **intransitive** verbs.

The verbs in chart 22.21 have a further characteristic: they all refer either to **movement** (up, down, in, out, and so forth: *monter*, *descendre*, *entrer*, *sortir*, etc.), to **lack of movement** (*rester*), or to **change of status** (being born, becoming, dying: *naître*, *devenir*, *mourir*). There are fifteen or so of these verbs in all.

Chart 22.22 illustrates the fact that only some intransitive verbs are conjugated exclusively with *être*, since the same verb—*passer*—is conjugated with *être* when it is used in an intransitive way (a way that does not allow it to take a direct object) and with *avoir* when it is used in a transitive way (a way that does allow it to take a direct object).

We can summarize this business of conjugation with *être* and *avoir* as follows:

Conjugated with *avoir:* most verbs, including **all** nonreflexive verbs used with a direct object.

Conjugated with *être:* (1) **all** reflexive verbs; (2) a small group of (nonreflexive) intransitive verbs of movement.

• In exercise 22.23, Robert is about to make a phone call from a café. As he completes each step, say he has done what you predicted he'd do, using the *passé composé*. (Choice of the auxiliary is simplified by the fact that all the verbs you need to use belong to that small group of intransitive verbs conjugated with *être*.)

Audio cues (for reference):
22.23 Activation orale: Passé composé; auxiliare être

1. Vous allez voir! Robert va téléphoner.
2. Il descend au sous-sol.
3. Il entre dans la cabine.
4. Il sort de la cabine.
5. Il remonte dans la salle.
6. Il revient dans la cabine.
7. Il ressort de la cabine.

• In 22.24, various people weren't at home last night. Explain that they were out, that they went to the movies, using the *passé composé* of *sortir* and *aller*—two prominent members of that small group of intransitive verbs conjugated with *être*.

Audio cues (for reference):
22.24 Activation orale: Passé composé; auxiliare être

1. Vous n'étiez pas chez vous, hier soir!
2. Tu n'étais pas chez toi, hier soir!
3. Robert n'était pas chez lui, hier soir!
4. Vous n'étiez pas chez vous, hier soir, tous les deux.

5. Colette et Mireille n'étaient pas chez elles, hier soir!
6. Ils n'étaient pas chez eux, hier soir!

• In 22.25, various people may or may not be coming along. Point out that there's no reason to, since they've already been twice, using the *passé composé* of *venir* (another of that limited group conjugated with *être*).

Audio cues (for reference):
22.25 Activation orale: Passé composé; auxiliare être

1. Vous allez venir?
2. Tu vas venir?
3. Je vais venir, si tu veux.
4. Il va venir?
5. Nous allons venir, si tu veux.
6. Ils vont venir?

22.26, 22.27 Observation and activation: Agreement of past participles; verbs conjugated with *être*

You have seen that past participles **agree** with direct objects when the direct object comes **before** the verb. This is true whether the verb is used reflexively (conjugated with *être*) or not (conjugated with *avoir*): "Elle **s'**est assis**e**," "elle **les** a invit**és**." If the direct object comes after the verb there will be no agreement: "Elle a invité **les Courtois**." This pattern is followed by the overwhelming majority of verbs in French.

As chart 22.26 illustrates, agreement in the small group of **intransitive** verbs of movement that don't take direct objects and are conjugated with *être* is simplicity itself: they **all** agree in gender and number with the **subject** of the verb.

• In exercise 22.27, complete the verb forms you see, supplying endings for the past participles that show agreement with the subject.

√ Check your answers in key 22.27 at the back of the workbook.

22.28, 22.29 Observation and activation: *Faire plaisir*

The examples in section 22.28 show how the expression *faire plaisir* can be used to refer to people, things, and situations that provide pleasure.

Faire plaisir can be used with a noun or pronoun when you want to specify what thing is pleasing someone: "**Ta lettre** nous a fait plaisir;" "**elle** nous a fait plaisir."

It can also be used with *de* and an infinitive to indicate what action or circumstance is producing pleasure: "Ça m'a fait plaisir **de recevoir** ta lettre."

In such cases, the subject of *faire plaisir* will be *ça* (which stands for *recevoir ta lettre*).

In both situations, *faire plaisir* is used with an indirect object to indicate who is being pleased: "Ta lettre a fait plaisir **à Mireille**," "ça **lui** a fait plaisir de recevoir ta lettre."

• In exercise 22.29, people have received certain items. Say that each item pleased whoever got it, using *faire plaisir* with the appropriate pronouns. Remember that the thing received will be the subject of *faire plaisir*, and that the recipient will be its indirect object.

Audio cues (for reference):
22.29 Activation orale: Faire plaisir

1. Ils ont reçu ta lettre.
2. J'ai reçu ton cadeau.
3. Nous avons reçu tes chocolats.
4. Robert a reçu mon coup de téléphone.
5. Mireille a reçu votre télégramme.
6. Les Belleau ont reçu ma lettre.

22.30 Activation: Dialogue between Robert and the waiter

Listen to the conversation between Robert and the waiter at the Closerie des Lilas. Take the waiter's role, being as patient as you can with our slightly confused foreigner, and imitate and repeat as usual.

TOWARD FREE EXPRESSION

22.31 Words at large

Proceed as usual. (If necessary, refer to lesson 3 for directions.)

22.32, 22.33 Role-playing and reinvention of the story

In 22.32, you have taken a job at the Closerie des Lilas, and Robert is your customer. He is asking about using the telephone. Answer him (out loud). You may imitate dialogue from the story, or make up your own.

In 22.33, Robert has succeeded in phoning Mme Courtois. Imagine their conversation, using the suggestions in the workbook to get started.

• **Suggested oral assignment.** Record a version of the dialogue between Robert and the waiter in 22.32, and send it to your instructor on the cassette you use for summary quiz 22. (See the course syllabus for details.)

SELF-TESTING EXERCISES

- Complete and check exercises 22.34 and 22.35 as usual.

SUMMARY QUIZ

Consult the course syllabus or check with your instructor for information about completing and handing in summary quiz 22.

LESSON 23

Fishing for an invitation II

The story

Mireille arrives and finds both her sister and Robert with odd looks on their faces. To change the subject, Robert reports on his two calls to Mme Courtois. Mireille tells him that Concepcion, the Courtois's maid, is a superb cook, as is Mme Courtois herself.

We learn more about the Courtois. Monsieur is an optimist; Madame is a pessimist. They have no children. Madame is crazy about cats, while Monsieur is a dedicated gourmet. Unfortunately, Mireille doesn't know if she'll be able to act on Robert's suggestion and get herself invited to dinner on the same night. Suddenly, looking at the time, she dashes off. Where to? Marie-Laure offers her familiar, impenetrable "Mystery . . . and gumdrops!"

Wondering all the while whether Mireille will be at the Courtois's, Robert does what he can to kill time until his appointment. He takes in the Louvre, where a father's answers to his son's questions don't do much for the little boy's understanding of art history. He moves on to Beaubourg. He starts getting ready for dinner hours too early, but just the same events conspire to make him late. The métro, which most people navigate so easily, takes Robert to the other end of Paris. When he has asked his way and discovered where he is, he chooses to cross the city on foot rather than risk his fate any further in the subway. At last, at 7:30, having found the right apartment building but rung at the wrong door, Robert finds the Courtois's apartment and reaches out to press the doorbell.

Notes on culture and communication

• **La bonne.** In some bourgeois and upper middle-class families, maids are still a cherished part of the standard of living, though increasingly difficult to find and to afford. Over the past two decades, the majority of Parisian maids have been women of Portuguese or Spanish origin.

• **Le Métro, le R.E.R.** The Paris subway began operation in 1891. Its network covers the whole of Paris and the surrounding suburbs, and it was recently expanded to serve the outskirts of the capital with the Réseau Express Régional (R.E.R.), which has faster trains that make fewer stops.

• **Lost in the métro.** Robert's dinner date is for seven-thirty. He is dressed and on his way at three. Normally to go from the Quartier Latin to the Quai de Grenelle would take fifteen minutes by taxi, a half-hour by subway, and no more than forty-five minutes on foot. Robert takes the subway and manages to end up in Montmartre, about three miles from the Quai de Grenelle. This sets some kind of record, for no one, but no one, ever gets lost in the Paris subway. It is so logically laid out, and the maps are so clear, that the métro is famous for being easy to navigate, as compared to, say, the New York subway. Anyway, Robert manages to make it to the Quai de Grenelle on the dot of seven-thirty. This is a social blunder in France, where no one is expected for dinner on time. (Notice that Mireille arrives fashionably late.) The rule of thumb is that fifteen minutes is the minimum delay.

Content and learning objectives of lesson 23

In this lesson, you will see how French speakers excuse themselves and respond to others who ask to be excused. The lesson also shows ways of referring to unexpected encounters, expressing uncertainty and worry, and talking about the future.

The following points are highlighted in lesson 23 (you should concentrate on the section marked with a √):

• *Se demander*, *s'en faire*
√• The future tense (23.19-23.25)

ASSIMILATION OF THE TEXT

23.1-23.4 Text work-up, aural comprehension, and oral production

Proceed as usual in these sections. (Refer to lesson 3.1-3.3 and lesson 4.3 for directions, if necessary.) Work with the text and illustrations in the textbook, as in previous lessons.

TOWARD COMMUNICATION

23.5 Observation and activation: Pronunciation; tonic stress (review)

• Repeat the words and expressions you hear. Remember that no syllable should receive a stress **except** the last syllable of each rhythmic group.

23.6, 23.7 Observation and activation: Politenesses

Chart 23.6 presents a number of useful expressions for expressing and responding to apologies.

• In exercise 23.7, you will hear a number of situations in which a response is needed. Answer with the most appropriate expression among the alternatives you see in the workbook, and circle the corresponding letter, as in the example.

Audio cues (for reference):
23.7 Activation orale: Réponses à donner

1. Excusez-moi.
2. Si Robert vous dit: "Est-ce que je peux vous inviter à déjeuner?", qu'est-ce que vous répondez?
3. Vous êtes un bon vivant. On vous demande: "Vous aimez manger dans les bons restaurants?" Qu'est-ce que vous répondez?
4. Vous êtes Robert. Vous voulez aller chez les Courtois, mais vous vous trompez de porte. Le voisin des Courtois vous dit: "Non, Monsieur. Madame Courtois, ce n'est pas ici. C'est la porte à côté." Qu'est-ce que vous dites?
5. Un ami vous dit: "J'ai décidé de faire médecine." Vous trouvez que c'est une excellente idée. Qu'est-ce que vous dites?

23.8, 23.9 Observation and activation: Appearances and reality

There are various ways of describing how others strike us; the left hand column of chart 23.8 shows two of them.

These interpretations are of course open to challenge. The right hand column shows two ways of telling others that their version of reality is off the mark.

• In exercise 23.9, react to the statements you hear with a correction. For instance, if you are told that one person looks mean and another has a foreign accent, say it's not really so. Note that the correction is introduced here by *pourtant*.

Audio cues (for reference):
23.9 Activation orale: Apparences et réalité

1. Il a l'air bizarre.
2. Il a un accent américain.
3. Il a l'air stupide.
4. Elle a l'air intelligent.
5. Ils ont l'air sportif.
6. Elles ont l'air riche.
7. Elle a l'air fragile.
8. Nous avons l'air costaud.
9. Elle a l'air anglais.
10. Elle a l'air mexicain.
11. Il a l'air portugais.
12. Elle a un accent portugais.
13. Elle a un accent français.
14. Elle a un accent américain.
15. Elle a un accent allemand.
16. Elles ont un accent japonais.
17. Elles ont un accent suédois.
18. Elle a un accent étranger.

23.10, 23.11 Observation and activation: Encounters

The three expressions in 23.10 are used to refer to chance encounters. *Tomber sur* stresses the unexpected nature of an encounter. Of course, when the object of *tomber sur* is expressed as a pronoun, the **stressed** pronoun is used, since it follows a preposition (*sur*).

• The purpose of exercise 23.11 is to practice using the proper form of *tomber sur* (conjugated with *être* in compound tenses) and the proper object pronoun after the preposition *sur*. You will be asked whether you have seen various people. Say yes, you just ran into them, using *tomber sur*. The choice of location is up to you.

Audio cues (for reference):
23.11 Activation orale: Rencontres; tomber sur

1. Tu as vu Hubert?
2. Tu as vu Mireille?
3. Tu as vu mes parents?
4. Vous avez vu les soeurs de Mireille?
5. Vous avez vu ma soeur?
6. Ils ont vu les Courtois?
7. Ils ont vu Tante Georgette?

23.12-23.15 Observation and activation: Uncertainty, worry

These sections feature ways of expressing uncertainty and foreboding.

Se demander (23.12) expresses uncertainty, often tinged with worry: Robert is curious (and anxious) to know whether Mireille will be at the Courtois's dinner.

Etre inquiet, *s'en faire*, and *ne pas être tranquille* (23.14) express worry. They are favorite expressions of Mme Courtois, who is the worrying type.

• In exercise 23.13, various people are in the dark about events. Say they are wondering about what is happening or going to happen, using *se demander*.

Audio cues (for reference):
23.13 Activation orale: Incertitude, inquiétude; se demander

1. Je ne sais pas ce qui va se passer.
2. Il ne sait pas si Mireille sera là.
3. Nous ne savons pas si Mireille sera là.
4. Ils ne savent pas si Mireille sera là.
5. Je ne sais pas pourquoi ils font ça.
6. Nous ne savons pas où est Mireille.
7. Robert ne sait pas où elle est.
8. Nous ne savons pas ce qui va se passer.
9. Je ne sais pas si Mireille va venir.
10. Elle ne sait pas comment tout ça va finir.

• In 23.15, certain people are nervous. Say they're worried, using *s'en faire*.

Audio cues (for reference):
23.15 Activation orale: Inquiétude; s'en faire

1. Elle n'est pas tranquille du tout.
2. Robert n'est pas tranquille.
3. Nous ne sommes pas tranquilles du tout.
4. Tes parents ne sont pas tranquilles du tout.
5. Je ne suis pas tranquille du tout!

23.16-23.18 Observation and activation: Optimism, pessimism

The tug-of-war of personalities between M. and Mme Courtois inspired chart 23.16, which sets forth a series of optimistic and pessimistic expressions for all occasions.

• Play the role of an optimist, then that of a pessimist, in exercises 23.17 and 23.18, repeating the optimistic or pessimistic statement in the dialogues you hear, as indicated. Since the object of the game is to catch the phrases you hear and repeat them right away, audio cues are not given for these exercises.

23.19-23.25 Observation and activation: The future tense

You have already seen and used one way of expressing the future in French. It was one of the very first points presented in lesson 2: "Nous **allons apprendre** le français." This is the **immediate future**, used to present actions as about to happen in what the speaker considers to be a relatively short time. It is formed by combining *aller* and an infinitive.

Chart 23.19 introduces the regular **future** tense, used to indicate that actions will occur at a time considered to be relatively distant.

Chart 23.20 shows that the future forms have a characteristic *r* (in pronunciation and in spelling) just before the verb ending: *finirai*, *finiront*. This feature is of great help in recognizing the future tense.

Charts 23.21 and 23.22 show how the future of regular verbs is formed.

Finir*ai*, **trouver***ai:* the **stem** of the future of regular verbs in *-ir* and *-er* is the **infinitive**. Notice that both infinitives end in the characteristic *r* of the future.

Comprendr*ai:* the stem of the future of verbs in *-re* is the infinitive minus the final *e*. Again, *r* is the last consonant before the ending.

The **endings** of the future are easy to remember: they are identical to the endings of the present tense of *avoir*.

• Exercise 23.23 will give you practice in recognizing the future. Determine whether the sentences you hear are in the future or the present, and mark the grid in your workbook accordingly.

√ Check your answers in key 23.23 at the back of the workbook.

• In 23.24, you will hear that various actions are to take place right away. Respond by saying they can be done later, using the future.

Audio cues (for reference):
23.24 Activation orale: Futur

1. Je vais téléphoner tout de suite.
2. Je vais finir tout de suite.
3. Tu vas finir tout de suite?
4. Vous allez finir tout de suite?
5. Ils vont partir tout de suite?
6. Nous allons partir!
7. On va manger tout de suite?
8. Tu vas apprendre ta leçon tout de suite!
9. Tu vas rentrer tout de suite?
10. Vous allez vous décider tout de suite?

• In 23.25, you will hear someone wondering whether various things are about to happen. Reassure the speaker by saying that they will happen eventually. Use the future.

Audio cues (for reference):
23.25 Activation orale: Futur

1. Je me demande si Mireille va être là.
2. Je me demande si elle va téléphoner.
3. Je me demande s'ils vont finir ce soir.
4. Je me demande si je vais comprendre.
5. Je me demande si ça va s'arranger.
6. Je me demande si elle va trouver le temps!
7. Je me demande s'ils vont partir.
8. Je me demande si je vais dormir.
9. Je me demande si ça va marcher.

23.26 Activation: Dialogue between Robert and a passerby

Listen to the conversation between Robert and the passerby. Memorize the lines of the passerby, imitating and repeating as usual.

TOWARD FREE EXPRESSION

23.27 Words at large

Proceed as usual. (If necessary, refer to lesson 3 for directions.)

23.28, 23.29 Role-playing and reinvention of the story

In 23.28, the Courtois's cat, Minouche, has fallen ill, and the pessimistic Mme Courtois and her optimistic husband discuss the situation. Reconstruct their conversation out loud, using the suggestions in the workbook as a point of departure.

In 23.29, Mme Courtois is telling Robert her life story. Imagine what she says, using the suggestions in the workbook to get started. If you work with a partner, share Mme Courtois's monologue, each speaker telling a different part of the story.

• **Suggested written assignment.** Write out a version of the dialogue between M. and Mme Courtois about Minouche's health in 23.28, and send it to your instructor along with summary quiz 23. (See the course syllabus for details.)

SELF-TESTING EXERCISES

• Complete and check exercises 23.30-23.32 as usual.

SUMMARY QUIZ

Consult the course syllabus or check with your instructor for information about completing and handing in summary quiz 23.

LESSON 24
Bills of fare I

The story

Mme Courtois greets Robert at length. But Mireille is nowhere to be seen. In a flashback, we learn that Mireille did call and has been invited. Fortunately, she arrives before Robert's disappointment at her absence becomes terminal. Mme Courtois introduces the young people, who say nothing about having met before. This, as the professor points out, condemns them to eternal secrecy. Nothing is simple!

M. Courtois arrives. There is cordial small talk. He offers drinks from his well-stocked bar, making a time-worn joke when Robert asks for a "finger" of port (is that a vertical or a horizontal finger? Ho, ho.) The conversation turns to fast-food restaurants, which M. Courtois, a gourmet, naturally despises. Robert is about to die of hunger by 8:30, when dinner is served.

The "simple" meal consists of gazpacho, trout, a leg of lamb, salad, cheese, and dessert, each main dish accompanied by an excellent wine. M. Courtois outlines a tour of France for Robert, a tour in which gastronomy looms much larger than history or scenic beauty.

To get away, Robert pleads jet lag and Mireille an early departure to the family's country house in the morning. M. Courtois will not be dissuaded from driving them home, so they have just a moment alone. In that moment, Mireille tells Robert to call her on Monday. He forgets her number right away, but no matter; it's got to be in the phone book.

Notes on culture and communication

• **Dîner chez les Courtois: l'heure.** The French start dinner later than Americans, usually between 7:00 and 8:30 p.m.

• **Dîner chez les Courtois: le repas.** Formal meals in France tend to be more elaborate and highly structured than similar meals in English-speaking countries. The Courtois dinner is a typical example of this ritual. Before the actual meal, an apéritif is served which is usually not a cocktail, but a specialty drink, often wine-based. The meal itself starts with an appetizer, which at dinner-time may be soup. Then comes a fish course, followed by meat or poultry with vegetables. Salad is served next, as a separate course, followed by cheese and dessert. White wine usually accompanies fish; red wine is reserved for meat and cheese. After-dinner coffee is usually served in the living room, followed by brandy or liqueurs.

• **Gastronomy and the middle class.** Monsieur Courtois belongs to an older generation of middle-class French businessmen—prosperous, hardworking, patriarchal, and bon vivant. He brings out a tray of bottles and begins an evening of social drinking during which he talks incessantly about food. The French have always been devoted to good food and wine, which they consider as much as expression of culture as art and literature, and they like to talk about eating and drinking during meals, but M. Courtois's obsession with gastronomy seems to reflect another age.

Content and learning objectives of lesson 24

This lesson shows how French speakers compliment others and say thank-yous when they are the guests of others. It also illustrates further ways of talking about the future.

The following points are highlighted in lesson 24 (you should concentrate on sections marked with a √):

- √• *Servir* (24.12, 24.13)
- √• Future of irregular verbs (24.14-24.17)
- • Relative pronouns *qui* and *que*

ASSIMILATION OF THE TEXT

24.1-24.4 Text work-up, aural comprehension, and oral production

Proceed as usual in these sections. (Refer to lessons 3.1, 3.2, and 4.3 for directions, if necessary.) Work with the text and illustrations in the textbook, as in previous lessons.

TOWARD COMMUNICATION

24.5, 24.6 Observation and activation: Pronunciation; unstable /ə/

The sound /ə/, known as **unstable** /ə/, is often shortened considerably and sometimes nearly eliminated. You saw examples of situations where /ə/ is shortened or dropped in lesson 22.10: *rappe̸lez*, *rapp'lez*.

This unstable /ə/ is **often** shortened when it is preceded by a single consonant sound: *samedi* ⇒ *sa***m'***di*, *sûrement* ⇒ *sû***r'***ment*. Mireille, telling Hubert to call her back, would say, "N'oublie pas de rapp'ler!"

Unstable /ə/ is **never** dropped or severely shortened when eliminating it would bring three consonant sounds together: *ven***dre***di*, *ju***stem***ent*.

When French speakers are making a conscious effort to speak carefully and distinctly, they will tend not to curtail or eliminate /ə/. Mireille, telling a long-distance caller her father will be back soon, would likely say, "Rappølez dans une heure."

• In exercise 24.6, repeat the words and expressions you hear. Observe whether the /ə/ is fully sounded or not.

24.7-24.9 Observation and activation: Compliments and recommendations

Charts 24.7 and 24.8 contain a number of useful dinner-table expressions. For guests, there are appreciative comments that compliment the host or hostess on the quality of the fare. For hosts, there are recommendations that guests try some particular specialty or delicacy.

• Exercise 24.9 will give you practice in making sense of small-talk at the dinner table. Decide whether the expressions you hear in exercise 24.9 are appreciative comments or recommendations, marking your choices on the grid in your workbook.

√ Check your answers in key 24.9 at the back of the workbook.

24.10, 24.11 Observation and activation: Thank-yous

Chart 24.10 gives several very common expressions to use when thanking a host or hostess at the end of the evening, before saying *au revoir*. The first four phrases may be used singly or in any combination. *Merci encore*, since it repeats your thanks, should come after an earlier *merci!*, and is generally one of the last things said before leaving.

• Study 24.10 carefully before doing the dictation exercise in 24.11. Then listen and complete the sentences in your workbook with the appropriate expressions of thanks.

√ Check your answers in key 24.11 at the back of the workbook.

24.12, 24.13 Observation and activation: About service

The examples in section 24.12 group together expressions using the verb *servir* (lesson 21) or the noun *service.* They refer to situations that range from service in restaurants and at the butcher shop to helping oneself or one's guests at the dinner table.

• Study 24.12 carefully before beginning exercise 24.13. First, read each incomplete sentence and guess what it is about. Then complete it with *service* or a form of the verb *servir*, as appropriate.

√ Check your answers in key 24.13 at the back of the workbook.

24.14-24.17 Observation and activation: The future; irregular verbs

You saw in lesson 23 how the future of regular verbs in *-ir* is formed with the infinitive as stem and the endings of the present tense of *avoir*. You also saw that this basic pattern applies, with minor modifications, to regular verbs in *-er* and *-re* as well.

Charts 24.14 and 24.15 present a number of common verbs that have irregular **stems** in the future. In 24.15, the future forms of verbs that have similar irregularities (*être* and *faire*—**sera, fera**—for example) are grouped together.

Notice that despite the irregularity of their stems, these verbs have two features that **all** verbs share in the future: (1) endings that are those of the present tense of *avoir*, and (2) an /r/ sound just before the ending. The /r/ sound is spelled with one *r* (in special cases, two *r*s).

As a result, if you know only one form of the future of these verbs, you can easily figure out what all the others must be, and use them without a second thought.

• In exercise 24.16, various people are wondering whether certain things will happen. Say of course they will, using the future of the verbs you hear.

• In 24.17, you will be asked whether various things are going to happen. Say no, they won't, using the future.

Audio cues (for reference):
24.17 Activation orale: Futurs irréguliers

1. Mireille et Robert vont aller au cinéma?
2. Robert va s'ennuyer chez les Courtois?

3. Robert va mourir de faim?
4. Les Courtois vont savoir que Mireille et Robert se connaissent?
5. M. Courtois va apprécier les fast foods américains?
6. Mme Courtois va servir le café à table?
7. La bonne portugaise va renverser la crème renversée?
8. Robert va reprendre de l'Armagnac?
9. Robert va pouvoir partir seul avec Mireille?

• The statements in 24.18 say that various things cannot be done, and they give the reasons why. Say that these things will be done when they can. Use the future both to say that things will be done and to say when they will be done. Note that *quand*, which indicates when things will happen, will be followed by the future.

24.19-24.23 Observation and activation: Relative pronouns *qui* and *que*

Relative pronouns take their name from their function: they link parts of a sentence by **relating** them through a noun they have in common. In the English sentences "The person who just called is Ghislaine" and "The kir that Robert spilled ruined Mireille's skirt," *who* and *that* are relative pronouns. They refer to the nouns *person* and *skirt*, which are known as their **antecedents**.

The relative pronouns *qui* and *que* in French can refer to people or things. Their antecedents can be masculine or feminine, singular or plural—that is, a single form represents a masculine as well as a feminine, a singular as well as a plural; such forms are **invariable.**

Qui functions as the **subject** of the verb that follows it, as chart 24.19 shows. *Qui* does not elide with words that begin with a vowel sound.

Que functions as the **direct object** of the verb that follows, as chart 24.21 demonstrates. It does elide to *qu'* with words that begin with a vowel sound.

Note that in English, the direct object relative pronouns *that* and *whom* can be dropped: "The kir Robert spilled," "the person Mireille saw." This never happens in French: "Le kir **que** Robert a renversé," "la personne **que** Mireille a vue." The relative pronoun is always expressed.

• Complete exercise 24.20 by combining the two sentences you hear into a single sentence with the relative pronoun *qui*, as in the example.

• In the written exercises in 24.22 and 24.23, supply the appropriate relative pronoun. The first step is to determine what noun it will represent. This will be helpful in figuring out the meaning of the sentence. Then you will need to decide whether the relative pronoun will be the subject or the direct object of the verb that follows. If it is the subject you will use *qui*. If it is the direct object you will use *que* (*qu'* in front of vowel sounds).

√ Check your answers in keys 24.22 and 24.23 at the back of the workbook.

24.24 Activation: Dialogue between Mme Courtois and Robert

Listen to the conversation between Mme Courtois and Robert. Memorize Robert's lines, imitating and repeating as usual.

TOWARD FREE EXPRESSION

24.25 Words at large

Proceed as usual. (If necessary, refer to lesson 3 for directions.)

24.26, 24.27 Role-playing and reinvention of the story

In 24.26, imagine you are Robert answering M. and Mme Courtois's questions. Answer out loud, using the suggestions in the workbook as a point of departure. If you work with a partner, take parts and complete the exercise, then switch roles and do it again.

In 24.27, make up a totally different version of the dinner scene at the Courtois's, using the suggestions in the workbook to get started and bringing in your own ideas. If you work with a partner, take turns narrating the episode.

• **Suggested oral assignment.** Record a version of the conversation between Robert and M. and Mme Courtois in 24.26, and send it to your instructor on the cassette you use for summary quiz 24. (See the course syllabus for details.)

SELF-TESTING EXERCISES

• Complete and check exercises 24.28 and 24.29, as usual.

SUMMARY QUIZ

Consult the course syllabus or check with your instructor for information about completing and handing in summary quiz 24.

LESSON 25
Bills of fare II

The story

Robert gets up, performs his ablutions, and orders breakfast. Tea? Hot chocolate? After some hesitation, he settles on *café au lait*. He takes a leisurely walk, during which he is tempted by a display of cheeses at an open-air market. The teacher is obliged to remind him that he has just had breakfast. Later, he does buy a sandwich. The vendor cannot change Robert's 500-franc note, but he gets help from a co-worker.

Still later, Robert sits down in a restaurant where, by pure chance, we find Mireille's Aunt Georgette. Georgette is a tough customer, and plagues her hapless waiter with a long series of complaints. Several items in her place setting are unacceptable. She has her heart set on a nice plate of calf's head, but the kitchen is out of it. She finally settles on a lamb chop, which is served too rare and sent back. It reappears burned to a crisp (waiter's revenge?). The peas are fresh . . . from the can. The cheeses? They're either too young or too old, and the bread was fresh a week ago.

As she leaves, Georgette wants us to understand she's not fussy by nature. But there are limits!

Notes on culture and communication

• **Bleu, saignant, à point.** In France, special attention is paid to degrees of doneness for red meat. The choices range from *bleu* (extra rare) and *saignant* (rare to medium-rare) to *à point* (medium rare) and *bien cuit* (well-done). The French rarely order beef or lamb *bien cuit*. The leg of lamb served by Mme Courtois in lesson 24 was *à point* on the outside and *saignant* inside, to satisfy all tastes.

• **The martyrdom of the street vendor.** When Robert orders a nine-franc *croque-monsieur* and tries to pay for it with a five hundred-franc note, the vendor gives us a magnificent example of French nonverbal communication. He utters a deeply-felt "Oh là là!" As he does so, he lifts his head upward, rolls his eyes as far back as they can go, and with his arms raised in prayerful appeal calls on Heaven (and whatever bystanders happen to be paying attention) to witness this outrageous test of his patience and good will.

Content and learning objectives of lesson 25

This lesson reviews commands and shows how French speakers talk about grooming and personal hygiene. It will also familiarize you with ways of talking about food and ordering at a restaurant.

The following points are highlighted in lesson 25 (you should concentrate on sections marked with a √):

- The imperative, review
- √ The imperative with pronouns, *en*, and *y* (25.15-25.17)
- √ Partitive *en*, review (25.18-25.19)
- √ The imperative with indirect object pronouns, review (25.20-25.22)
- √ Position of *en* with personal pronouns (25.23)
- *En* used with determinatives
- Demonstrative and indirect object pronouns, review

ASSIMILATION OF THE TEXT

25.1-25.5 Text work-up, aural comprehension, and oral production

Proceed as usual in these sections. (Refer to lesson 3.1-3.3 and lesson 4.3 for directions, if necessary.) Work with the text and illustrations in the textbook, as in previous lessons.

TOWARD COMMUNICATION

25.6, 25.7 Observation and activation: Pronunciation; release of final consonants

Final consonants in French are followed by a brief release. That is, the rhythmic group that contains a final consonant does not grind to a halt on the consonant sound. After closing on the consonant sound the mouth relaxes and opens, releasing a barely perceptible /ə/ sound.

- Repeat the words and expressions you hear in 25.7, listening for and repeating the slight release on final consonants.

25.8, 25.9 Observation and activation: *Frais, fait, en conserve*

Chart 25.8 shows three situations in which the adjective *frais* is applied to food.

In referring to the freshness of meat, fish, or bread, the opposite of *frais* is *pas frais.*

In referring to the degree of ripeness of a soft or semisoft cheese, the opposite of *frais* is *fait.*

In contrasting fresh and canned vegetables, the opposite of *frais* is *en conserve.*

• In exercise 25.9, you will hear statements about stale, overripe, or canned foods. Match them with the protests you see on the grid in your workbook.

√ Check your answers in key 25.9 at the back of the workbook.

25.10 Observation: The imperative (review)

Chart 25.10 reintroduces the imperative, first presented in lesson 5.

Recall that, for most verbs, the forms of the imperative (for example, "**Bois** quelque chose!") are identical to the corresponding forms of the present indicative ("Tu ne **bois** pas?").

Remember that while the *tu* form of the indicative of *-er* verbs ends in *-s* ("Tu ne **manges** pas?"), the corresponding imperative is written **without** an *-s* ("**Mange** quelque chose!").

25.11, 25.12 Observation and activation: Meals

You saw the names of the main meals of the day and the approximate times at which they are served in lesson 22. Chart 25.11 adds traditional afternoon refreshments for children (*le goûter*) and for adults (*le thé*).

• In exercise 25.12, people are reminded what time of day it is. Tell them to come and take the appropriate meal or refreshment.

Audio cues (for reference):
25.12 Activation orale: Repas

1. Marie-Laure, il est 7 heures du matin!
2. Les enfants, il est midi et demi.
3. Les enfants, il est 4 heures.
4. Marie-Laure et Mireille, il est 8 heures du soir.
5. Robert, qu'est-ce que tu fais au lit, il est presque 9 heures du matin.
6. Mireille, les invités sont là depuis une demi-heure. Il est 5 heures et demie...
7. Chéri, il est midi et demi.

25.13, 25.14 Observation and activation: Grooming

In talking about the everyday activities of personal hygiene and grooming, the verb is used reflexively: "Il **se brosse** les dents." The noun identifying the part of the body being groomed is used with the definite article (**les** *dents*).

• In exercise 25.14, you will hear Mme Belleau complaining that Marie-Laure and others have not yet done what they are supposed to do. Tell them to do it, using the imperative. Note that what they must do is expressed by a reflexive verb (*réveille-toi!*). This reflexive verb occasionally has as its direct object a part of the body; remember that it is used with a **definite** article (*lave-toi* **les** *mains*).

Audio cues (for reference):
25.14 Activation orale: Toilette

1. Marie-Laure! Tu n'es pas réveillée!
2. Tu n'es pas levée!
3. Tu ne t'es pas lavée!
4. Tu ne t'es pas lavé les mains!
5. Tu ne t'es pas brossé les cheveux!
6. Tu ne t'es pas brossé les dents!
7. Alors, les enfants, vous n'êtes pas réveillées!
8. Alors, les enfants, vous n'êtes pas habillées!
9. Alors, les enfants, vous ne vous êtes pas brossé les dents!
10. Alors, les enfants, vous ne vous êtes pas coupé les ongles!

25.15-25.17 Observation and activation: Imperative with pronouns, *en*, and *y*

Charts 25.15 and 25.16 show the position of pronouns, *en*, and *y* when they are used with an imperative.

When you are giving a **positive** command, pronouns, *en*, and *y* all **follow** the verb: "Allez-y!" When the command is **negative**, they come **before** it: "N'y allez pas!"

"Manges-**en**!" There is always an *-s* in the second person singular of the imperative in front of *y* and *en*, even in the case of *-er* verbs.

"Mange!" "Manges-**en**!" You saw a reminder in 25.10, above, that the second person singular of the imperative of *-er* verbs (*mange!*) does not have the *s* of the *tu* form of the indicative (*tu mange*s). But when the second person imperative is followed by *en* or *y*, there is always an *s*. Example: "*va* au restaurant!" (no *s*), but "*Va*s-y!" (with *s*).

• In exercise 25.17, someone will ask your approval to do various things. Give it, using the imperative of the verb you hear and *y* or *en*, as appropriate.

Audio cues (for reference):
25.17 Activation orale: Impératif; 2ème personne du singulier; en, y

1. Je peux manger des fruits?
2. Je peux aller au cinéma ce soir?
3. Je peux prendre des pommes de terre?
4. Je peux prendre de la salade?
5. Je peux manger du fromage?
6. Je peux manger des fruits?
7. J'achète de la viande?
8. J'achète du vin?
9. J'achète des oeufs?
10. Je peux aller chez les Courtois?
11. Je peux aller à la plage?
12. Je peux aller au café?

25.18-25.19 Observation and activation: Partitive *en* (review)

You have already seen how *en* can stand in for a partitive expression (lessons 9 and 15). Chart 25.18 reviews the position of *en* with verbs in the indicative and the imperative.

En behaves like a direct object pronoun. It comes in front of most forms of the verb, including negative imperatives: "Il **en** reprend," "N'**en** reprenez pas!" But it comes **after** the verb in the case of a positive imperative: "Reprenez-**en**!"

• In exercise 25.19, you will be asked whether various items are still available or still needed. Say no, using *en* to replace the name of the item, as in the example.

Audio cues (for reference):
25.19 Activation orale: En partitif

1. Il reste encore de la tête de veau?
2. Il leur reste encore du fromage?
3. Il vous reste encore des pieds de porc?
4. Vous avez encore du lapin à la moutarde?
5. Vous avez encore du gigot?
6. Il te reste du pain?
7. Il lui reste des boules de gomme?
8. Tu veux encore des petits pois?
9. Vous voulez encore des haricots verts?
10. Robert veut encore de la viande?

25.20-25.22 Activation: Imperative and indirect object pronouns (review)

These exercises will help you review imperatives and refresh your memory of indirect object pronouns.

• In 25.20, you and other restaurant customers want a number of things. Order them brought, using the imperative of *apporter* and the indirect object pronoun corresponding to each customer.

Audio cues (for reference):
25.20 Activation orale: Impératif et pronoms personnels objets indirects (révision)

1. Je veux une fourchette propre!
2. Elle veut une côtelette à point.
3. Nous voudrions des pieds de porc.
4. Ce monsieur veut de la tête de veau.
5. Ces dames veulent le plateau de fromages.
6. Ces messeurs voudraient du pain.
7. Je veux un couteau qui coupe!

• In 25.21, the customers complain about various defective items. Ask on their behalf that the offending items be changed, using the imperative of *changer* and the indirect object pronoun corresponding to each customer.

Audio cues (for reference):
25.21 Activation orale: Impératif et pronoms personnels objets indirects (révision)

1. L'assiette de cette dame est sale!
2. Mon assiette est sale.
3. Les verres de ces messieurs sont pleins de rouge à lèvres!
4. La nappe de ces dames est déchirée.
5. La serviette de cette dame est déchirée.
6. Le couteau de ce monsieur ne coupe pas.

• Exercise 25.22: this time, ask that the customers be given what they want, using the imperative of *donner* and the proper indirect object pronoun.

Audio cues (for reference):
25.22 Activation orale: Impératif et pronoms personnels objets indirects (révision)

1. Elle veut une autre assiette.
2. Cette dame veut une autre serviette.
3. Je veux une autre assiette.
4. Nous voulons d'autres verres!
5. Ces messieurs veulent une autre nappe.
6. Ce monsieur veut un autre verre.
7. Je veux une autre table!

25.23 Observation: Position of *en* with personal pronouns

"Je vous **en** apporte!" The chart illustrates an important characteristic of *en*. When it occurs with a pronoun, *en* is always placed **after** the pronoun.

25.24-25.26 Observation and activation: *En* used with determinatives

You have seen *en* used to replace nouns used partitively. Since partitives by themselves do not refer to specific quantities or numbers (**du** *vin*, **des** *côtelettes*, **des** *verres*), nouns are often accompanied by **determinatives**—

expressions that specify these quantities: **une bouteille de** *vin*, **deux** *côtelettes*, **un autre** *verre*. *En* can stand in for partitive nouns in these circumstances, too.

When *en* replaces the noun, the noun disappears, of course, but the determinative does not. It stays in place, preceded by *en*.

• In exercise 25.25, ask for replacements for various unsatisfactory items, using *en* and the appropriate form of *un autre*, as in the example.

Notice that *un autre*, *une autre*, and the plural, *d'autres*, are used with nouns that refer to units that can be counted, such as *verres*, *côtelettes*, or *truites*. With substances like *pain*, *vin*, or *beurre* that are not counted the form *d'autre* is used.

Audio cues (for reference):

25.25 Activation orale: En + un autre, une autre, d'autre, ou d'autres

1. Cette côtelette est carbonisée!
2. Le verre est sale!
3. Ma fourchette n'est pas propre!
4. Nos serviettes sont déchirées!
5. La serviette de cette dame est déchirée!
6. Le pain de ces messieurs n'est pas frais!
7. Mon couteau ne coupe pas.
8. Nos couteaux ne coupent pas.
9. La côtelette de Tante Georgette est carbonisée.
10. Les petits pois de ces messieurs ne sont pas frais.

• In 25.26, proceed as in 25.25, writing the proper forms in your workbook.

√ Check your answers in key 25.26 at the back of the workbook.

25.27 Observation: Expletives

Tante Georgette's indignation at the service she receives in the restaurant is unmistakable, but just in case the waiter has missed the point she hammers it home by using the pronoun *moi* in a special way. *Moi* is not needed in these sentences; Georgette adds it as a way of imposing herself, of drawing attention to the imperative nature of her requirements.

25.28, 25.29 Activation: Demonstrative pronouns; indirect object pronouns (review)

• In exercise 25.28, you have asked the waiter to bring replacement items to various people. Tell him why the original will not do, using *plaire*, indirect object pronouns, and appropriate forms of the demonstrative pronoun *celui-ci* to refer to the items being replaced.

Audio cues (for reference):
25.28 Activation orale: Pronoms démonstratifs; celui-ci, celle-ci, ceux-ci, celles-ci; Pronoms objets indirects (révision)

1. Apportez-moi un autre verre.
2. Apportez-moi un autre pied de porc.
3. Apportez un autre pied de porc à cette dame.
4. Apportez-moi d'autres petits pois.
5. Apportez-moi une autre côtelette.
6. Apportez-moi un autre plateau de fromages.
6. Apportez un autre plateau de fromages à ces messieurs.
7. Apportez-nous d'autres haricots verts.
8. Apportez donc une autre tête de veau à ce monsieur.

• In 25.29, proceed as in 25.28, writing the appropriate forms in your workbook.

√ Check your answers in key 25.29 at the back of the workbook.

25.30 Activation: Dialogue between Tante Georgette and the waiter

Listen to the conversation between Tante Georgette and the waiter. Memorize Georgette's lines, imitating and repeating as usual.

TOWARD FREE EXPRESSION

25.31 Words at large

Proceed as usual. (If necessary, refer to lesson 3 for directions.)

25.32, 25.33 Role-playing and reinvention of the story

In 25.32, you are Tante Georgette at the restaurant. Give the waiter a piece of your mind, out loud, using the suggestions in the workbook as a point of departure.

In 25.33, the waiter is quicker on his feet, and has the presence of mind (and the cheek) to indulge in a little witty repartee with Georgette. Imagine the scene, using the suggestions in the workbook to get started.

• **Suggested written assignment.** Write out a version of the dialogue between Georgette and the waiter in 25.32, and send it to your instructor along with summary quiz 25. (See the course syllabus for details.)

SELF-TESTING EXERCISES

- Complete and check exercises 25.34–25.37 as usual.

SUMMARY QUIZ

Consult the course syllabus or check with your instructor for information about completing and handing in summary quiz 25.

LESSON 26
Bills of fare III

The story

Late Sunday morning, in a pastry shop, Robert chooses one of the many varieties of pastry and eats it. Then he looks around for a restaurant. This time, he ends up in the same establishment as a young couple. He notices that the woman, whose back is turned to him, is blonde. He wonders whether it might be Mireille, but he can't tell. The young man is very attentive to his blonde companion, and together they discuss the menu. They are struck by the number of dishes on the menu named "Mireille." The waiter explains that the chef once loved a woman named Mireille who died of indigestion. Since then, he has named his finest creations after her. Touching.

By this time, Robert has overheard the name "Mireille," and begun to think that the blonde really is the Mireille he knows. This does not improve his digestion.

Meanwhile, we eavesdrop on the young couple's choices for what turns out to be a substantial meal, from oysters and salmon through grilled meats, cheeses, and sweets, with well-chosen wines at the right moments. The young woman's first reaction to the dessert cart is resistance, but she soon yields to the temptation of a particularly gooey specialty.

When the couple gets up to leave, Robert realizes that the young woman is not Mireille. (In fact, she is Mireille's sister, Cécile, out for Sunday lunch with her husband, Jean-Denis. Robert has never met them.) But what an amazing coincidence!

Notes on culture and communication

• **Dimanche à Paris.** Sunday is the great day for family gatherings in France. At about one in the afternoon, Paris starts to become a lonely place for single people. The outdoor markets, which have been busy since early morning, close. The few people who go to mass on Sunday have gone home. Many people have fled to their *résidence secondaire* in the country. Pastry shops, like the one where Robert buys his *religieuse*, stay open to supply fancy desserts for the big family dinners. Some restaurants close, but many stay open for families who want to "go out." Robert ends up in one such restaurant.

• **Les fromages.** France boasts an extraordinary variety of cheeses—365 different kinds of cheese, or one for each day of the year, according to popular tradition. (New types are being created all the time.)

• **The restaurant ritual.** The restaurant scene with Cécile and Jean-Denis opens a window on a number of aspects of French life related to food and dining. One is ritual behavior in matters of ordering wine, tasting it, and dealing with the waiter. A second is traditional facial expressions that show your reaction to a wine or your enjoyment of a certain dish. A third is the French preoccupation with degrees of doneness, particularly the national taste for foods that are served raw (salmon, oysters) or barely-cooked (the steak that Jean-Denis orders *bleu*).

Content and learning objectives of lesson 26

This lesson shows how French speakers order food and wine at a restaurant, and how they talk about various ingredients, dishes, and preparations.

The following points are highlighted in lesson 26 (you should concentrate on sections marked with a √):

√• *Ne . . . que* (26.11-26.12)
• Definite article versus partitive article
√• Expressions of quantity (26.17-26.20)
√• Vowel change e/è (26.21-26.23)
√• Endings of the present indicative, review (26.26-26.28)

ASSIMILATION OF THE TEXT

26.1-26.3 Text work-up, aural comprehension, and oral production

Proceed as usual in these sections. (Refer to lessons 3.1, 3.2, and 4.3 for directions, if necessary.) Then work with the text and illustrations in the textbook, as in previous lessons.

TOWARD COMMUNICATION

26.4, 26.5 Observation and activation: Pronunciation; No explosion after /p/, /k/, and /t/

In English, the consonant sounds /p/, /k/, and /t/ tend to end in a release of air, a little puff of breath between the consonant sound and the following vowel sound that makes the consonant slightly percussive: **p**<*it*, **k**<*it*, t<*op*. This puff of air is not heard when /p/, /k/, and /t/ are preceded by *s:* s*pit*, s*kit*, s*top*.

The French /p/, /k/, and /t/ sounds are never followed by a puff of breath. In this respect, they are similar to the corresponding sounds in *spit*, *skit*, and *stop*.

• Repeat the words and expressions you hear in exercise 26.5, saying the vowel sound immediately after the consonant sound, with no puff of air in between.

26.6 Observation: Pronunciation; /s/ and /z/ (review)

In French words, an *s* between two vowels is always pronounced /z/: *poison*, *désert*. A double *s* is always pronounced /s/: *poisson*, *dessert*.

The distinction between these two sounds is no insignificant matter. As the examples show, the meaning of a word can depend on it.

26.7 Observation: Ordering in a restaurant

The sentences in 26.7 show half a dozen useful expressions for ordering a *steak au poivre* (or anything else) in a restaurant. As the chart indicates, the **future** is often used in this kind of situation, as opposed to the imperative (more commonly used by speakers of English).

26.8-26.10 Observation and activation: Degrees of doneness (red meat); culinary discrimination

Chart 26.8 shows expressions for the various degrees of doneness of beef and other red meats, from raw (degree 0) through extra well-done (charred, degree 5). Absolutely fresh raw beef is served in French restaurants, either ground (*steak tartare*) or in extremely thin slices (*carpaccio*). People who like their beef extra rare will order it *bleu*. Red meat that is well done is considered unappetizing and tough.

Meat is never actually ordered *carbonisée;* if it arrives that way at the table it is usually sent right back to the kitchen.

• In exercise 26.9, determine which degree of doneness is referred to in the sentences you hear, checking the answer on the grid in your workbook.

• Exercise 26.10 gives you practice in identifying different foods. In a restaurant, you are offered a number of dishes; some may be familiar to you, some not. As always, you will need partly to guess what you are being offered. Decide which kind of food each one probably represents, say your answer, and check the corresponding box on the grid.

√ Check your answers in keys 26.9 and 26.10 at the back of the workbook.

26.11, 26.12 Observation and activation: Restriction; *ne . . . que*

If Cécile, lunching with her husband, wants only an omelette, she can draw attention to the limited extent of her desires by using the expression *ne. . . que*. *Ne. . . que* is a negation (Cécile doesn't want anything . . .), but it is not a total negation (Cécile doesn't want anything **except** a little omelette).

Similarly, Georgette might use *ne . . . que* to comment on a selection of cheeses she finds shockingly limited. The cheese tray is not empty, but it might as well be; what little it does contain is pitifully inadequate.

As in all negative expressions, *ne* comes before the verb. *Que* is placed in front of the item that represents the exception.

• In the first three items of exercise 26.12, say that you were very reasonable in ordering at the restaurant. Use *ne . . . que* to indicate that you only took one thing.

In the next three numbers, say that there isn't much choice of things to eat—in fact, all there is is a single item.

In items 7-10, say that the Belleaus have fewer children and cars—and that Marie-Laure is younger—than one might think.

Audio cues (for reference):
26.12 Activation orale: Restriction; ne...que

1. Qu'est-ce que vous avez pris, à part le cassoulet?
2. Qu'est-ce que tu prends, à part le cassoulet?
3. Qu'est-ce que tu as pris avec la choucroute?
4. Qu'est-ce qu'il y a comme viande, à part le steak?
5. Qu'est-ce que vous avez comme fromage, à part le Cantal?
6. Qu'est-ce qu'il reste comme dessert, à part la mousse au chocolat?
7. Mireille a deux soeurs ou trois soeurs?
8. Les Belleau ont 3 enfants ou 4 enfants?
9. Ils ont une voiture ou deux voitures?
10. Marie-Laure a dix ans ou onze ans?

26.13, 26.14 Observation and activation: *Porter, apporter, rapporter, emporter, remporter*

The chart and the examples in 26.13 show a group of related verbs, all based on the verb *porter*.

When the waiter is its subject, *porter* refers to the basic task of carrying dishes, without specifying from where or to where he is carrying them.

Apporter and *emporter*, on the other hand, tell you in which direction he is carrying them. **Ap***porter* indicates he is carrying them to a given point (the customer's table, for example). **Em***porter* indicates he is carrying them away from that given point. (Recall *mener*, **a***mener*, and **em***mener* from lesson 15.)

Finally, **rap***porter* and **rem***porter* indicate repetitions, further trips to (*rapporter*) or from (*remporter*) the customer's table (or any other point of reference). (*R-* and *re-* are prefixes that often indicate a repetition of the same action: *prendre* ⇒ **re***prendre*, *appeler* ⇒ **r***appeler*, téléphoner ⇒ **re***téléphoner*, and so forth.)

• In exercise 26.14, determine which verb related to *porter* makes the most sense in each of the sentences you see in the workbook, and write it in the space provided.

√ Check your answers in key 26.14 at the back of the workbook.

26.15, 26.16 Observation and activation: Whole, part

You saw in lesson 8 how the partitive articles *du*, *de la*, *de l'*, and *des* are used to refer to part of a whole. Chart 26.15 contrasts these partitive articles, used to refer to parts, with definite articles, used to refer to wholes.

• In exercise 26.16, the participants at the Courtois's dinner are enjoying what they are eating and drinking. Point out that they're having more, using *reprendre* and the partitive article.

Note. In the sentences you hear, the **definite article** is used with verbs like *trouver* and *aimer*. This is because these verbs express an **attitude** toward something, and attitudes tend to apply to the whole thing rather than to some limited quantity of it. With *reprendre*, however, the **partitive article** is used because in this context *reprendre* refers to **taking** a certain quantity of whatever is offered. (Robert takes a second helping of lamb, not the entire leg of lamb.)

Audio cues (for reference):
26.16 Activation orale: Totalité, partie

1. Robert trouve le gigot excellent.
2. Il trouve le gazpacho délicieux.
3. Mireille trouve la soupe délicieuse.
4. Robert trouve l'Armagnac extraordinaire.
5. Il aime bien le porto.
6. M Courtois trouve la truite excellente.
7. Mireille trouve le Camembert particulièrement bon.
8. Mme Courtois trouve les pommes de terre très bonnes.
9. Mireille adore la crème renversée.
10. Robert trouve le Bordeaux excellent.

26.17-26.20 Observation and activation: Expressions of quantity

Charts 26.17 and 26.18 present a series of quantities expressed in terms of various weights, volumes, measures, numbers, and containers. Some of these expressions of quantity are **nouns**, some are **adverbs**. Notice that **all** are followed by *de* (or its elided form *d'*), with no definite article.

• In exercise 26.19, say you'll have a little bit of various things to eat and drink, using *un peu de* (*d'*) and the noun you hear.

Audio cues (for reference):
26.19 Activation orale: Expressions de quantité

1. De la sauce?
2. Du pain?
3. De l'eau?
4. Du potage?
5. De la salade?
6. Du fromage?
7. De la crème?
8. Du café?

• In 26.20, approve the purchase of a bottle of each of various liquids, using *une bouteille de* (*d'*) and the noun you hear.

Audio cues (for reference):
26.20 Activation orale: Expressions de quantité

1. J'achète du vin?
2. J'achète du Porto?
3. J'achète de l'eau minérale?
4. J'achète de l'Armagnac?
5. J'achète du whisky?
6. J'achète de l'huile?
7. J'achète du Cognac?
8. J'achète du Cinzano?

26.21-26.23 Observation and activation: Alternation of /ə/ and /ɛ/ (review)

You saw in lesson 15 that the stems of verbs like *appeler* and *promener* have an /ə/ sound in an open syllable that changes to /ɛ/ in a closed syllable. That pattern extends to the verb *acheter* as well, as chart 26.21 illustrates.

Note that *acheter* acts like *promener:* in writing, the /ɛ/ sound is spelled *è: j'achète.*

With *appeler* and verbs like it, on the other hand, the /ɛ/ is written as *e* followed by a doubled consonant: *j'appe***ll***e.*

• In exercise 26.22, answer the questions with the appropriate form of the verb you hear, paying close attention to the vowel sound in the form you say.

Audio cues (for reference):
26.22 Activation orale: Alternance

1. Vous vous rappelez le numéro de Mireille?
2. Vous vous promenez souvent au Luxembourg?
3. Vous avez acheté le journal?
4. Vous vous rappelez l'adresse de Mireille?
5. Alors, qu'est-ce que vous achetez?

• In 26.23, say you have no desire whatever to do various things you are told to do, using the appropriate form of the verb you hear. Again, pay particular attention to the vowel sound in the stem of the verb.

Audio cues (for reference):
26.23 Activation orale: Alternance

1. Appelle Ghislaine!
2. Appelle-moi ce soir!
3. Lève-toi!
4. Achète le journal!
5. Promène-toi!
6. Amène Fido au Luxembourg!
7. Achète-toi une robe!
8. Achète-toi des boules de gomme!
9. Achète des boules de gomme à Marie-Laure!

26.24, 26.25 Observation and activation: Substances and preparations

Chart 26.24 contains the names of a number of foods and dishes. Each is composed of two nouns.

In the series titled *substance*, the second noun indicates the make-up or origin of the first: *de la graisse* **d'***oie* comes from a goose, *une purée* **de** *thon* is made from tuna. The noun indicating origin is introduced by *de*.

In the series titled *préparation*, the second noun indicates the garnish, flavor, or seasoning of the first. In *des oeufs* **à la** *neige*, custard is served with eggwhites that are beaten to look like snow; *un éclair* **au** *café* is filled with coffee-flavored pastry cream; *une tarte* **aux** *fraises* is flavored and garnished with strawberries. The second noun is introduced by *à* and the **definite article**.

• In exercise 26.25, determine whether the second noun in each pair of nouns you see describes the origin of the first or the way in which it is prepared, and write the appropriate connecting word in your workbook.

√ Check your answers in key 26.25 at the back of the workbook.

26.26–26.28 Observation and activation: Endings of the present indicative (review)

The charts in 26.26, 26.27, and 26.28 review the characteristic endings of the present tense, grouping together verbs whose forms show similar patterns in the present.

• In each verb group, study the model verb and write in the missing forms of the other verbs in the group.

Note. This is an excellent opportunity to do a review of verbs. Be sure to give yourself enough time to do these exercises thoroughly.

√ Check your answers in keys 26.26, 26.27, and 26.28 at the back of the workbook.

26.29 Activation: Dialogue between the waiter and Cécile

Listen to the conversation between the waiter and Cécile. Memorize Cécile's lines, imitating and repeating as usual.

TOWARD FREE EXPRESSION

26.30 Words at large

Proceed as usual. (If necessary, refer to lesson 3 for directions.)

26.31, 26.32 Role-playing and reinvention of the story

In 26.31, Robert is at a restaurant, quizzing a waiter about the dishes he sees listed on the menu. Imagine their dialogue, out loud, using the suggestions in the workbook as a point of departure.

In 26.32, Robert is ordering. Imagine his exchange with the waiter, using the suggestions in the workbook to get started.

• **Suggested oral assignment.** Record a version of Robert's dialogue with the waiter in 26.31, and send it to your instructor on the cassette you use for summary quiz 26. (See the course syllabus for details.)

DOCUMENT

At the end of the textbook chapter for lesson 26, you will find a poem for reading practice, "Pour un art poétique," by Raymond Queneau (see lesson 21).

Queneau here uses cookbook language in a playful way to describe the process of writing a poem. He places the step-by-step, how-to instructions of a recipe (*faites cuire . . . , prenez un petit bout/un grand morceau . . .*) side by side with the abstractions of poetry (*sens*, *innocence*). The result is funny, but it also suggests that the raw materials of a poem—words—have a double nature. They belong to both the material world (of cooking) and the spiritual world (of poetic beauty). The way to move from one world into the other, Queneau suggests, is through writing.

SELF-TESTING EXERCISES

• Complete and check exercises 26.33-26.36 as usual.

SUMMARY QUIZ

Consult the course syllabus or check with your instructor for information about completing and handing in summary quiz 26.

Name ______________________________

Instructor ________________ Section ____

SUMMARY QUIZ 2

I. You will hear five sentences. Each will contain one of the terms listed below. Indicate which it is by checking the appropriate box. (5 pts.)

	1	2	3	4	5
malade					
bibliothèque					
restaurant					
pressé					
non					

II. Before continuing, review the list of expressions below. You are to play the part of Mireille in a series of encounters. On the recording, you will hear what the other person says to you in each encounter. Select the appropriate response from the list below and write it on the corresponding line. (10 pts.)

Ça va.
Au revoir, monsieur.
Pas mal.
Salut!
Bonjour, monsieur.
Très bien, merci, et vous-même?
Je vais bien, et toi?
Ça va, vous deux?
Tu es malade?
Au revoir.

A. Mireille rencontre un professeur.

1. ______________________________

2. ______________________________

3. ______________________________

B. Mireille rencontre Hubert.

4. ______________________________

5. ______________________________

C. Mireille rencontre Tante Georgette.

6. ______________________________

7. ______________________________

8. ______________________________

D. Mireille rencontre Catherine et Marc.

9. ______________________________

10. ______________________________

III. Complete the following sentences by writing in the appropriate word, as indicated. (There is no audio segment for this exercise.)

A. Complete with the appropriate form of the verb *aller*. (6 pts.)

1-2. Salut, Ousmane. Comment __vas__-tu?

3-4. —Bonjour, Mademoiselle Belleau. Où __allez__-vous?

—Je __vais__ à la fac.

5. Marc et Catherine __vont__ au restau-U.

6. Nous __allons__ apprendre le français.

B. Complete with the appropriate subject pronoun. (4 pts.)

1. —Tu es malade?

—Non, __je__ suis fatigué!

2. —Est-ce que Tante Georgette est pressée?

—Mais non, __elle__ n'est pas pressée.

3. Voilà Hubert et Catherine. __Ils__ sont pressés.

4. Bonjour, monsieur. __Vous__ êtes le professeur de français?

Name ________________________________

Instructor ____________________ Section _____

SUMMARY QUIZ 3

I. You will hear a series of questions based on the text of lesson 3. Check the most appropriate answer to each question. (8 pts.)

	1	2	3	4	5	6	7	8
oui								
non								
nous								
une histoire								
parce que ça va être utile								

II. Determine if the sentences you hear refer to a man (masculine) or a woman (feminine). (5 pts.)

	1	2	3	4	5
masculine					
feminine					

III. (12 pts.)

A. Complete with the appropriate form of the indefinite article (*un, une, des*) or the definite article (*le, la, l', les*).

Nous allons inventer __une__ histoire. Ça va être

__une__ histoire de deux jeunes gens. Nous allons choisir

un jeune homme et une jeune fille. Le jeune

homme va être américain. La jeune fille va être

française. Les jeunes gens vont avoir des amis.

B. In each of the exchanges below, the two speakers can agree on the nationality but not on the sex of their fictional characters. Complete each sentence with the masculine or feminine form as appropriate.

1. —Pour l'histoire, tu préfères une Américaine?

   —Non, je préfère un Américain.

2. —Tu préfères un Anglais?

   —Non, une Anglaise.

3. —Une Norvégienne?

   —Non, un Norvégien.

4. —Pourquoi pas un Africain?

   —Non, je préfère une Africaine.

Name ______________________________

Instructor ________________ Section _____

SUMMARY QUIZ 4

I. You will hear a series of questions about the text of lesson 4. Select the best answer from the possible answers listed below. First write the number of each question you hear next to the corresponding answer. Then complete the answer by writing in the appropriate word. (10 pts.)

____ Il __________ à la Cité universitaire.

____ Ça va __________ un roman.

____ Il __________ à l'aéroport.

____ Ils __________ la douane.

____ Non, il __________ brésilien.

II. Listen and write in the missing words or letters. (6 pts.)

Dans _une_ histoire, _une_ jeune____ fille____ __________

être amusante____.

III. Write in the appropriate form of the verb indicated. (9 pts.)

A. être

1-3. Je _suis_ américain et tu _es_ français. Mais nous

sommes amis.

4. Vous _êtes_ japonais?

B. parler

5. Vous _parlez_ espagnol?

6-7. Les Brésiliens ___sont___ portugais mais nous, nous ___sommes___ français.

C. **étudier**

8-9. —Qu'est-ce que tu ___étudies___ ?

—J' ___étudie___ le français.

IV. Oral Production. Record the following exercises on an audiocassette for submission to your instructor. Before you begin, record your name and today's date.

A. Read the following sentences. (5 pts.)

Bonjour! Nous allons inventer une histoire.
Ça va être un roman.

B. Record your version of the story so far as suggested in section 4.38. You may use your imagination but do not stray from the sentence structures outlined in section 4.38. Five to eight sentences are about right. (20 pts.)

Name ______________________

Instructor ______________ Section ____

SUMMARY QUIZ 5

I. Before listening to the tape, review the list of questions below. You will hear answers to the questions. Write the number of the answer in the space provided in front of the corresponding question. (5 pts.)

____ Pourquoi est-ce qu'il faut donner un prénom aux jeunes gens?

____ Où est-ce que la mère de Mireille travaille?

____ Quel âge a Marie-Laure, la soeur de Mireille?

____ Est-ce que Robert a des frères ou des soeurs?

____ Est-ce que les parents de Robert sont pauvres?

II. Listen and complete with forms of the verb *avoir* and numbers. Use figures for the numbers. (Don't write them as words.) (10 pts.)

1-3. —Quel âge __as__ -tu?

—J' __ai__ __58__ ans.

4-7. —Vous __avez__ des enfants?

—Oui, nous __avons__ __2__ fils et __3__ filles.

8-10. J'habite __3__ rue d'Alésia, Paris __18__ème. J'ai

__2__ enfants.

III. Write negative answers to the following questions. (6 pts.)

1. —Vous travaillez?

—Non, nous __ne travaillons pas__.

2. —Tu vas à la bibliothèque?

—Non, je ne vais pas à la bibliothèque.

3. —Vous êtes français?

—Non, je ne suis pas français.

IV. Replace each statement with an order, using the imperative form of the verb. (4 pts.)

1. Vous pouvez passer. passez!

2. Tu peux aller au cinéma. Va au cinéma!

3. Tu peux parler. Parle!

4. Nous pouvons continuer. continuons!

Name ____________________

Instructor ____________ Section ____

SUMMARY QUIZ 6

I. Listen and complete the portrait of Mireille as you hear it by adding endings to the adjectives, as appropriate. (6 pts.)

1. Mireille est blonde___. Elle a les cheveux longues.

2. Elle a les jambes longues et finES.

3. Elle n'a pas la taille épaisE___.

4. Elle a les yeux bleuS___.

II. Dictation (9 pts.)

A. Write the numbers you hear, using figures. (5 pts.)

Cette dame a _______ ans. Elle habite _______, rue de Seine, Paris _______ème. Elle a _______ chats et _______ chiens.

B. Give the total for each arithmetic problem you hear, using figures. (4 pts.)

1. __________

2. __________

3. __________

4. __________

III. Complete by writing the appropriate form of the expression *faire de*. (10 pts.)

1. Mireille adore la natation. Elle fait de natation tous les jours.

2. Ses soeurs préfèrent le cheval. Elles faisent du cheval.

3. —Tu aimes l'aviron?

   —Oui, je fais de l' aviron.

4. —Vous aimez le ski?

   —Oui, nous faisons des ski.

5. Nous aimons beaucoup la voile. Nous faisons de la voile tous les weekends.

IV. Oral Production. Record the following exercises on an audiocassette for submission to your instructor. Before you begin, record your name and today's date.

A. Read these verses. (5 pts.)

On a le monde quand on est blonde.
On a la lune quand on est brune.
La vie est douce quand on est rousse.

B. Answer each of the following questions, giving at least four possibilities for each one. Say the questions before giving your answers. (20 pts.)

1. Qu'est-ce qu'une jeune fille peut être?
2. Qu'est-ce qu'une jeune fille peut avoir?
3. Qu'est-ce qu'une jeune fille peut faire?

Name ______________________________

Instructor ________________ Section _____

SUMMARY QUIZ 7

I. You will hear a series of statements describing Mireille. Rewrite them so they describe Robert instead. Since Mireille and Robert are really quite different, this will mean choosing new words to describe him. (10 pts.)

1. Robert est ________________________.

2. Il est __________.

3. Il a ________________________.

4. Il a ________________________.

5. Il est ____________________.

II. Listen and write the numbers you hear, using figures. (5 pts.)

1. Cécile a ______ ans. Elle habite ______, rue des Cerisiers à Colombes.

2. Guillaume Belleau a ______ ans. Il habite ______, rue de Courcelles, Paris ______ème.

III. Complete by writing the appropriate form of *aimer* or *faire* as the context demands. (10 pts.)

1-3. —Mademoiselle Belleau, vous __________ du ski?

—Non, je ne __________ pas de ski parce que je n'________ pas les sports d'hiver.

4-5. Oncle Guillaume n'__________ pas l'exercice, alors il ne ________ pas de sport.

Name ______________________________

Instructor ____________________ Section _____

SUMMARY QUIZ 8

I. Listen and complete the answers to the questions you hear about Mireille's genealogy, using the possessive adjectives *son, sa, ses.* (10 pts.)

1. Ce sont ________ parents.

2. C'est ________ soeur.

3. C'est ________ oncle.

4. C'est ________ tante.

5. C'est ________ cousine.

II. Dictation (15 pts.)

1. Guillaume Belleau _________________________. Il a _______

_______ fortune et ______ loisirs. Georgette Belleau ______

__________ fortune. _________________________ enfants.

2. Dates historiques: La révolution de _______

L'appel du 18 juin _______

III. Oral Production. Record the following exercises on an audiocassette for submission to your instructor. Before you begin, record your name and today's date.

A. (5 pts.)
Read the following dates.

1912
1937
1980

Now give two dates that are important in your life (birth, marriage, birth of a child, etc.). Write them below and say them out loud.

____

____

B. Describe a new character for the story, quite different from Robert and Mireille. You may use the suggestions in section 7.34 if you wish. Say what what this character looks like and what he or she does. Also give an idea of his or her personality. Five sentences are about right. (20 pts.)

Name ______________________________

Instructor ____________________ Section _____

SUMMARY QUIZ 9

I. Listen and determine who or what is being described, then check the appropriate box. (6 pts.)

	1	2	3	4	5	6
la Bretagne						
le jeu des portraits						
Oncle Guillaume						
Tante Georgette						
Marie-Laure						
Madame Belleau						

II. Listen and complete the following sentences, writing the possessive adjective appropriate to the sentence you hear. (9 pts.)

1. _______ amis sont très sympathiques.
2. _______ fils est charmant.
3. _______ soeur est agaçante.
4. _______ fille est très sympathique.
5. _______ cousine est très gentille.
6. _______ frère est agaçant.
7. _______ parents sont fatigants.
8. _______ enfants sont charmants.
9. _______ oncle est généreux.

III. Complete, by writing in the appropriate forms of *faire de* or *jouer à*. Use *jouer à* whenever it is possible. (10 pts.)

1. —Vous aimez la natation?

   —Oui, nous ________________________ natation.

2. J'adore le ski. Et toi, tu ___________ ski?

3. —Tu aimes le poker?

   —Oui, je ___________ poker.

4. —Vous ______________________ alpinisme?

   —Oui, j'aime l'alpinisme.

5. —Tes amis aiment les échecs?

   —Oui, ils ______________________ échecs.

Name ______________________________

Instructor ________________ Section _____

SUMMARY QUIZ 10

I. Listen and determine which of our characters is being described. (5 pts.)

	1	2	3	4	5
Mireille					
Robert					
Monsieur Belleau					
Oncle Guillaume					
Tante Georgette					

II. Listen, then rewrite the comparisons you hear as in the example. (10 pts.)

Example: You hear: Mireille est moins grande que Robert.
You see: Robert est __________ grand qu' _______.
You write: Robert est plus grand qu'elle.

1. Mireille est __________ sportive que __________.

2. Robert est __________ riche que __________.

3. Mireille est __________ moqueuse que __________.

4. Robert est __________ intelligent que __________.

5. Robert est __________ grand que __________.

III. Write in the correct form of the verb indicated. (3 pts.)

A. Choose between *savoir* or *connaître*.

Georges fait le portrait de quelqu'un que personne ne

_______________. Les autres ne _______________ pas de qui il

parle parce qu'ils ne _______________ pas M. Delapierre.

B. *venir*

Mireille (à ses soeurs): Alors, vous _____________?

Jean-Denis (à Mireille): Non, elles ne _______________ pas,

elles sont occupées.

IV. Oral Production. Record the following exercises on an audiocassette for submission to your instructor. Before you begin, record your name and today's date (in French, if you wish, now that you know how).

A. Read the following passage. (5 pts.)

En 1964, François Belleau épouse Madeleine Pothier. Ils ont trois enfants, trois filles: Cécile, Mireille, et Marie-Laure.

B. Describe someone in your family or at work as if you were playing "portraits". Say four or five sentences, starting with the most ordinary characteristic and working up to the most unusual. At the end, identify the person you are describing. (20 pts.)

Name ______________________

Instructor ______________ Section ____

SUMMARY QUIZ 11

I. You will hear a series of statements about the text of the lesson. Indicate whether each is true (*vrai*) or false (*faux*) by marking the appropriate box. (5 pts.)

	1	2	3	4	5
C'est vrai.					
C'est faux.					

II. Dictation (10 pts.)

1. —Nous ____________ _______ Etats-Unis.

   —Vous ____________ _______ arriver?

   —Oui. Nous ____________ à Paris ____________ hier.

2. _______ _______ _________! ___________ ciel bleu!

III. You will hear five questions about the text of the lesson. Complete the answer to each with the appropriate pronoun (*le, la, l'*, or *les*). (5 pts.)

1. Oui, elle _______ voit.
2. Oui, il _______ remarque.
3. Oui, il _______ remarque.
4. Oui, elle _______ aime.
5. Elle _______ trouve ennuyeux.

IV. Write the appropriate reflexive or non-reflexive form of the verb indicated. (5 pts.)

1. *présenter, se présenter*

Le jeune homme ____________________ à Mireille.

2–3. *appeler, s'appeler*

Il ____________________ Jean-Pierre Bourdon.

Tante Georgette ____________ son chien: "Viens, Fido!"

4. *lever, se lever*

Mireille ____________ les yeux.

5. *habiller, s'habiller*

Je ____________________ chez Dior.

Name ______________________

Instructor ______________ Section _____

SUMMARY QUIZ 12

I. You are in a contrary mood. As you hear a series of exclamations about the weather, respond to each one by marking the opposite of what you hear. (5 pts.)

	1	2	3	4	5
Il fait chaud.					
Il fait beau.					
Le ciel est bleu.					
Il n'y a pas un nuage.					
Il y a du soleil.					

II. (10 pts.)

A. Listen and respond to each question with a command.

Example: You hear: Je me lève?
You write: Oui, lève-toi!

1. Oui, ______________________!

2. Oui, ______________________!

B. Now contradict each command you hear.

Example: You hear: Lève-toi!
You write: Non, ne te lève pas!

3. Non, ______________________!

4. Non, ______________________!

III. Complete the following sentences, using the same verb you find in the first part of the sentence. (10 pts.)

1. Si vous pouvez, je ____________ moi aussi.

2. Si vous suivez les manifestants, je les ____________ moi aussi.

3. —Vous faites du sport?

—Oui, je ____________ du patin.

4. Si j'ai le temps, vous ____________ sûrement le temps aussi.

5. Si nous pouvons, ils ____________ eux aussi.

6. Je suis prête. Vous ____________ prêts aussi?

7. —Qu'est-ce que vous apprenez?

—J'____________________ le français.

8. Si vous sortez, je ____________ moi aussi.

9. Nous avons trois filles, mais les Courtois n'____________

pas d'enfants.

10. Si je pars, les enfants ____________ avec moi.

IV. Oral Production. Record the following exercises on an audiocassette for submission to your instructor. Before you begin, record your name and today's date.

A. Read the following sentences. (5 pts.)

Elles ont deux soeurs.
Il pleut.
Elle pleure.
Il est vieux.

B. Answer these questions, giving at least five possiblities for each question. Say short, complete sentences: don't just list nouns or verbs. (20 pts.)

1. Qu'est-ce qu'on peut prendre?
2. Qu'est-ce qu'on peut faire quand il fait beau?

Name ____________________

Instructor ____________ Section ____

SUMMARY QUIZ 13

I. Someone is trying to strike up a conversation with you. Check off the appropriate answer to each initiative you hear. (5 pts.)

	1	2	3	4	5
Non, je préfère l'hiver.					
Non, je ne fume pas.					
De la sociologie.					
Non, il fait mauvais.					
Oui, je suis américain(e).					

II. Complete by writing in the appropriate adjective or pronoun, using either an interrogative (*quel, lequel*) or a demonstrative (*ce, celui*). (14 pts.)

1. Les yeux de Mireille sont bleu-gris. __________ de Marie-Laure sont bleus.

2-3. —Vous connaissez une des soeurs de Mireille? __________ connaissez-vous, la grande ou la petite?

—Je connais __________ qui est mariée, Cécile.

4. Vous aimez le cinéma? __________ films préférez-vous, les films suédois ou les films anglais?

5. —Quand est-ce que vous allez à Saint-Tropez? La semaine prochaine?

—Non, j'y vais ___________ semaine.

6-7. —Tu vois ___________ fille?

—___________? La blonde ou la rousse?

III. Complete by writing in the appropriate form of *attendre* or *faire*. (6 pts.)

1-2. —Vous ___________?

—Bien sûr, puisque nous ___________ la queue!

3-4. Depuis combien de temps est-ce qu'Annick ___________ la queue?

5. Eh là, pas de resquille! Vous allez ___________ la queue comme tout le monde!

6. J'___________ l'autobus.

Name ______________________________

Instructor ____________________ Section _____

SUMMARY QUIZ 14

I. Listen to the conversation between Robert and Mireille on the audio recording for summary quiz 14. As you listen, check off the facts you learn. Be careful! All the facts listed below are true, but you are only to check the ones you learn from the conversation you hear. (5 pts.)

_____ Il y a une manifestation.

_____ Mireille fait de l'histoire de l'art.

_____ Robert est américain.

_____ Robert parle très bien français.

_____ Robert est fils unique.

_____ La mère de Robert est française.

_____ Robert vient d'arriver en France.

II. Complete with the masculine or feminine form, as appropriate, of the adjective you hear on the audio recording. (10 pts.)

Example: You hear: Quelle robe ravissante!
You see: Quel tailleur ______________!
You write: ravissant

1. Mireille est __________.

2. Quel ___________ pantalon!

3. C'est une idée ______________________.

4. Il est ______________________.

5. Cette chambre est ______________________.

6. Cette maison est __________.

7. Robert est ____________.

8. Mais sa soeur n'est pas _________________ du tout.

9. Son costume est _________________.

10. Et nous, nous partons le mois _________________________.

III. Complete by writing in the appropriate form of *parler* or *dire*. (5 pts.)

1-3. —Pardon, Madame, __________-vous anglais?

—Qu'est-ce que vous ____________, jeune homme? Les

jeunes ne ____________ pas assez fort!

4. Je ____________ toujours la vérité.

5. Jean-Pierre Bourdon est très bavard. Il ____________ beaucoup.

IV. Complete by writing in the correct form of the imperfect (past tense), choosing between *avoir* and *être*, as appropriate. (5 pts.)

—Quand Robert ____________ petit, il ____________ l'habitude de

passer ses vacances aux Bermudes ou en Amérique Latine. Et vous?

Où est-ce que vous ____________ l'habitude de passer vos vacances?

—Quand j'____________ petit, j'____________ l'habitude d'aller

à la Martinique.

V. Oral Production. Record the following exercises on an audiocassette for submission to your instructor. Before you begin, record your name and today's date.

A. Read these dates and prices. (5 pts.)

le 23 octobre
lundi 15 septembre 1986
6 francs 50

B. Complete the dialogue below by writing in appropriate lines for Robert. Then record both parts on your audiocassette. Say the name of each character before you read his or her line. (20 pts.)

Mireille: Quelle belle matinée!

Robert:

Mireille: Vous êtes étudiant à la Sorbonne?

Robert:

Mireille: Vous n'êtes pas français?

Robert:

Mireille: Eh bien, vous n'avez pas d'accent du tout pour un étranger!

Robert:

Mireille: Il y a longtemps que vous êtes en France?

Robert:

Mireille: Vous venez souvent en France?

Name ________________________

Instructor ________________ Section _____

SUMMARY QUIZ 15

I. Indicate whether the statements you hear about the text of the lesson are true or false. (5 pts.)

	1	2	3	4	5
C'est vrai.					
C'est faux.					

II. Jot down the numbers you hear, using figures. (5 pts.)

1-2. _______ francs _______.

3. Un billet de _______ francs.

4-5. Donnez-moi _______ pièces de _______ centimes, s'il vous plaît.

III. Complete the answers to the questions you hear, providing the appropriate form of *aller* or *venir* and a preposition. (10 pts.)

1. Elle ______________ fac.
2. Je ____________________ bibliothèque.
3. Ils ______________ Luxembourg.
4. Nous ______________ cinéma.
5. Ils ________________ Louvre.

IV. Complete as appropriate. (5 pts.)

—C'est quand, la Fête Nationale aux Etats-Unis? En automne?

—Non, c'est _______ juillet.

—Ce n'est pas _________ Noël?

—Mais non, idiot, c'est _______ mois _______ juillet!

-C'est _______ 4 juillet.

Name ____________________

Instructor ______________ Section ____

SUMMARY QUIZ 16

I. Listen to the sentences, and identify the place being referred to in each one. Check the appropriate box. (5 pts.)

	1	2	3	4	5
Belle-Ile-en-Mer					
Chartres					
le Pays Basque					
La Rochelle					
le bassin du Luxembourg					

II. Listen and complete the answers to the questions you hear, using the verb you hear and *y* or *en* as appropriate. (10 pts.)

1. Oui, elle ________________.

2. Oui, nous ________________ envie.

3. Oui, j'____________________.

4-5. Oui, ils ________________ profiter pour ________________.

III. Listen and complete the answers to the questions you hear. (3 pts.)

1. Oui, je ________________ Marie-Laure.

2. Mais oui, je la ________________.

3. Oui, j'________________ son bateau.

IV. Complete by writing in the correct form of *savoir* or *connaître* as appropriate. (7 pts.)

1-2. —Où est le bateau de Marie-Laure?

—Je ______________ où il est! (Mais Marie-Laure ne

______________ pas!)

3-5. Robert ne ____________________ pas Madame Courtois. Les parents

de Mireille la ___________________ (évidemment!), mais nous ne

la ___________________ pas.

6-7. —Je ne __________________ pas la Sorbonne.

—Mais vous _______________ où c'est, n'est-ce pas?

V. Oral Production. Record the following exercises on an audiocassette for submission to your instructor. Before you begin, record your name and today's date.

A. Read the following sentences. (5 pts.)

Ils sont deux garçons.
Ils ont deux garçons.
Je préfère ça.
C'est la meilleure amie de ma mère.

B. Start up a conversation with someone. Comment on the weather. Ask the kinds of questions you might ask anyone to get them talking. Ask at least five questions. (20 pts.)

Name ______________________

Instructor ______________ Section _____

SUMMARY QUIZ 17

I. Listen and determine who is speaking in each of the statements you hear. (5 pts.)

	1	2	3	4	5
Robert					
Mireille					
Robert ou Mireille					

II. Imagine you are Mireille, answering Robert's questions about your family. Listen and complete the answers to his questions, choosing between *c'est* and *il/elle est*. (5 pts.)

1. ____________ ma soeur.

2. Non, ______________ mariée.

3. ____________ son mari.

4. ____________ professeur.

5. ____________ sympathique.

III. (10 pts.)

A. You will hear a series of statements about the present. Write a contrasting statement about the past, using the imperfect.

Example: You hear: Je n'aime plus les romans policiers.
You see: Mais autrefois, j'____________ les romans policiers.
You write: aimais

1. Mais autrefois, elle ______________ être infirmière.

2. Mais autrefois, ils ________________ du vélo.

3. Mais autrefois, nous ________________ en Bretagne tous les étés.

4. Mais autrefois, je ________________ espagnol avec ma mère.

5. Autrefois, vous ________________ aux boules!

B. Now do just the reverse. Substitute the present for the imperfect.

6-7. Maintenant, je ____________ grand et je ________________

anglais.

8-9. Maintenant, Mireille ne _____________ plus de voile

parce qu'elle ne _______________ plus en Bretagne.

10. Et maintenant, tu ______________ être banquier?

IV. Write the masculine or feminine form of each profession below, as appropriate. (5 pts.)

1. Elle est infirmière. Il est ______________________.

2. Il est médecin. Elle est ______________________.

3. Il est pharmacien. Elle est ______________________.

4. Elle est actrice. Il est ______________________.

5. Il est fermier. Elle est ______________________.

Name ______________________________

Instructor ________________ Section ____

SUMMARY QUIZ 18

I. You will hear descriptions of various professions. Mark the one being described by checking the appropriate box. (5 pts.)

	1	2	3	4	5
les militaires					
un bouvier					
un boucher					
une étudiante					
un professeur					

II. Rewrite the statements you hear, by changing the verb to agree with the subject *on*. (5 pts.)

1. En France, on ______________ français.

2. Nous, on ______________ au Quartier Latin.

3-4. On ______________ des idées bizarres quand on

______________ petit.

5. En France, on ___________ bien manger.

III. Complete the answers to the questions you hear with the appropriate pronoun. (5 pts.)

1. Non, vous ne ____________ dérangez pas.

2. Non, elle ne ____________ répond pas.

3. Oui, elle ____________ voit.

4. Oui, il ____________ parle.

5. Non, ça ne ____________ intéresse pas.

IV. Listen to the statements, then complete each command with the appropriate pronoun. (5 pts.)

1. Ecoute-_________!

2. Réponds-_________!

3. Téléphonez-_________!

4. Parlez-_________!

5. Ne _________ dérange pas!

V. Complete by writing in the appropriate form of the stressed pronoun. (5 pts.)

1. Nous allons rentrer chez _________.

2. Robert est rentré chez _________.

3. Les manifestants refusent de rentrer chez _________.

4. Marie-Laure et Mireille sont toujours chez _________.

5. Vous rentrez chez _________?

VI. Oral Production. Record the following exercises on an audiocassette for submission to your instructor. Before you begin, record your name and today's date.

A. Read the following exchange. (5 pts.)

—Qu'est-ce que vous aimiez faire quand vous étiez petit? Qu'est-ce que vous vouliez être?
—J'aimais jouer. Je voulais être marin ou pompier.

B. Explain how Robert and Mireille arrive in their meeting place at the courtyard of the Sorbonne. Trace the route of each one, giving about four sentences for each. (20 pts.)

Name ______________________________

Instructor ________________ Section _____

SUMMARY QUIZ 19

I. Listen and determine what is being referred to in each statement you hear. (5 pts.)

	1	2	3	4	5
la Closerie des Lilas					
l'apéritif					
l'histoire					
la botanique					
le bac					

II. Listen and mark the times you hear. (5 pts.)

	1	2	3	4	5
12h00					
12h15					
12h30					
12h45					
13h00					

III. Complete the answers to the questions you hear with the correct form of the auxilliary verb (*avoir* or *être*).

1. Oui, je ______________ parti.

2. Oui, nous ______________ pris un kir.

3. Oui, nous nous ______________ amusés.

4. Oui, j'______________ passé la douane.

5. Nous l'______________ trouvé gentil.

IV. Answer the questions using *plaire* and the appropriate indirect object pronoun. (10 pts.)

1. —Comment trouvez-vous les Parisiennes?

   —Elles ______________________ assez. . . .

2. —Est-ce que Mireille trouve Robert sympathique?

   —Oui, il ______________________ beaucoup.

3. —Est-ce que vos parents ont aimé Paris?

   —Oui, ça ______________________ beaucoup plu.

4. —J'aime beaucoup Jean-Pierre Bourdon.

   —Comment?! Il ______________________?

5. —Est-ce que tu aimes le kir?

   —Oui, ça ______________________ assez. . . .

Name ______________________________

Instructor __________________ Section _____

SUMMARY QUIZ 20

I. With characteristic modesty, Robert is telling us about himself, but he can't seem to finish his sentences. Help him out. Choose the word or expression from the list below that best completes each incomplete sentence you hear and write it on the corresponding line. (5 pts.)

doué	en congé
faire le point	tout seul
de bonnes notes	

1. . . . ____________________________.

2. . . . ____________________________.

3. . . . ____________________________.

4. . . . ____________________________.

5. . . . ____________________________.

II. Contradict each statement you hear, using the appropriate negative expression: *jamais, rien, personne.* (5 pts.)

1. Non, il n'a ______________ à faire.

2. Non, elle ne connaît ________________.

3. Mais non, ils ne sont ________________ pressés.

4. Non, au contraire, elle ne se moque de ______________.

5. Non, je n'entends ________________.

III. Complete the answers to the questions you hear. (7 pts.)

A. Present tense

1. Je ____________________ un kir.

2. Oui, oui, nous ________________________.

3. Je ____________________ ma jupe rouge.

B. Passé composé

4. Oui, j'________________________.

5. Si, nous ______________________.

IV. Answer each question using the *passé composé* and the appropriate object pronoun. (8 pts.)

1. —Est-ce que Mireille apprend l'anglais à la fac?

—Non, elle ___________________________ en Angleterre.

2. —Tu lis ce roman?

—Non, je ___________________________ l'été dernier.

3. —Est-ce que Robert et Mireille traversent le jardin du Luxembourg maintenant?

—Non, mais ils ___________________________ pour aller à la Closerie des Lilas.

4. —Tu vois ce type?

—Oui, je ________________________ à la fac hier.

V. Oral Production. Record the following exercises on an audiocassette for submission to your instructor. Before you begin, record your name and today's date.

A. Read the following sentence. (5 pts.)

Transportée d'admiration, j'ai entrepris de couvrir de fresques les murs de ma chambre.

B. You stop a stranger on a Paris street. Excuse yourself politely and request the following things (one or two sentences each is enough). (10 pts.)

1. The time of day.
2. A light for your cigarette

C. Read the following sentences and respond to each one with an appropriate expression, as suggested. (10 pts.)

1. —Vous fumez? (emphatic negative answer)
2. —J'ai appris à lire et à écrire tout seul! (astonishment)

Name ____________________

Instructor ______________ Section ____

SUMMARY QUIZ 21

I. Listen and decide which subject is being referred to. Then check the appropriate box. (5 pts.)

	1	2	3	4	5
la chimie					
l'histoire					
la physique					
le latin					
la littérature					
les mathématiques					

II. Listen and complete the sentences below, using the verb you hear. (8 pts.)

Example: You hear: Je suis français.
You see: Elles _______ françaises elles aussi?
You write: sont

1. Tu ne ____________________ rien?

2. Vous ____________________ aussi?

3. Il ____________________ lui aussi?

4. Je ____________________ beaucoup de lettres.

5. Où est-ce que vous ____________________?

6. Oui, vous ____________________ travailler.

7. Ils ne ______________________________ pas lire?

8. A quoi ______________________________ la chimie?

III. Rewrite the sentences you hear, replacing the direct object by a direct object pronoun and adding agreement to the past participle if necessary. (7 pts.)

1. Mireille ________ a toujours aimé_____.

2. Je ________ ai mis_____.

3. Il ________ a rencontré_____.

4. Vous ________ avez fini_____?

IV. Masculine or feminine? Complete with *le/la* or *un/une*, as appropriate. (5 pts.)

1-2. Mireille suit ________ cours d'art grec. Elle n'étudie pas ________ philosophie.

3. L'histoire ne dit pas ________ vérité.

4-5. Robert aime ________ géométrie parce que c'est ________ très bon exercice mental.

Name ______________________________

Instructor ________________ Section _____

SUMMARY QUIZ 22

I. Which time is given or alluded to in each sentence you hear? Mark the appropriate box. (5 pts.)

	1	2	3	4	5
07h30					
11h07					
11h55					
17h30					
20h00					

II. It's time to summarize what you know about Robert and Mireille. Listen and complete the following dictation. (8 pts.)

Mireille ________________ étudiante. Elle ________________ de l'histoire de l'art. Robert la ________________ à la Sorbonne où elle ________________ un cours. Les deux jeunes gens ________________ l'apéritif ensemble à la Closerie des Lilas. Ils ________________ de leurs familles. Par une étrange coïncidence, ils ________________ tous les deux une certaine Madame Courtois. Nous ne ________________ pas s'ils ________________ aller la voir.

III. Add agreement to the past participles if necessary. (5 pts.)

Mireille est entré____ dans la cour de la Sorbonne et Robert l'a remarqué____. Les deux jeunes gens sont allé____ à la Closerie des Lilas où ils se sont assis____ à la terrasse. Un homme en noir les a suivi____.

IV. Complete with the appropriate form of *avoir* or *être*. (7 pts.)

1. Robert ________ arrivé à Paris.
2. Il ________ trouvé un hôtel.
3. Le lendemain il ________ décidé d'aller explorer le Quartier Latin.
4. Il ________ rencontré une jeune fille charmante.
5. Ils ________ engagé la conversation.
6. Puis ils se ________ promenés au Luxembourg.
7. Ils ________ restés longtemps à bavarder.

V. Oral Production. Record the following exercises on an audiocassette for submission to your instructor. Before you begin, record your name and today's date.

A. Read the following verse. (5 pts.)

La peinture à l'huile
C'est plus difficile,
Mais c'est bien plus beau
Que la peinture à l'eau.

B. Describe yourself as you are now, contrasting past and present. You may talk about your appearance, your profession, your family, your likes and dislikes. Compare with how you looked, what you did, what you liked and disliked when you were younger. Six to eight sentences are sufficient. (20 pts.)

Name ______________________________

Instructor ____________________ Section ____

SUMMARY QUIZ 23

I. Listen and determine who or what is being referred to in each of the sentences you hear. Check the appropriate box. (6 pts.)

	1	2	3	4	5	6
Minouche						
Madame Courtois						
la bonne de Madame Courtois						
la Tour Totem						

II. Who is speaking, an optimist or a pessimist? Check the appropriate box. (9 pts.)

	1	2	3	4	5	6	7	8	9
optimiste									
pessimiste									

III. Listen to the following questions, then answer them using the future tense. (10 pts.)

Example: You hear: Elle a trouvé son chien?
You see: Non, mais elle le __________ sûrement.
You write: trouvera

1. Non, mais je ____________________ bientôt.

2. Non, mais ils ____________________ un jour ou l'autre.

3. Non, nous ______________________________ ce soir.

4. Mais vous ______________________________ demain, n'est-ce pas?

5. Non, elle ne ______________________________ pas ce soir.

Name ______________________________

Instructor ____________________ Section _____

SUMMARY QUIZ 24

I. You will hear two responses to each statement or question below. Only one response is appropriate. Indicate which it is by circling A or B. (5 pts.)

1. Excusez-moi de vous avoir dérangé. Je suis désolé. A B

2. Qu'est-ce que je peux vous offrir? A B

3. Je vous présente ma fille. A B

4. J'espère que vous m'excuserez, mais il faut que je rentre. A B

5. Pardon, Mademoiselle. La Tour Totem, s'il vous plaît? A B

II. Dictation. (5 pts.)

1. Le ______________ est compris.

2-3. C'est un libre-______________. On se ______________ soi-même.

4. Vous avez faim? ______________-vous!

5. Laissez-moi vous ______________.

III. Rewrite the sentences you hear, putting the verb into the future tense. (7 pts.)

1-2. Vous ______________? Nous ______________ un jeune Américain à dîner.

3-4. On ______________ à Chartres quand il ______________ beau.

5. Il ______________ en France.

6. Je ______________ malade demain aussi.

7. Tu ______________!

IV. Complete by writing in the appropriate relative pronoun (*qui*, *que*, or *qu'*). (8 pts.)

Madame Courtois, ____________ est la marraine de Mireille, l'a invitée à dîner chez elle en même temps que Robert, le jeune homme ____________ Mireille a rencontré dans la cour de la Sorbonne. Madame Courtois, ____________ est une amie de la mère de Robert, n'a pas d'enfants, mais elle a une chatte ____________ elle adore. Son mari, ____________ voyage beaucoup pour ses affaires, est un gourmet ____________ connaît tous les restaurants de Paris. Pour des raisons ____________ nous ignorons, (et ____________ ne nous intéressent pas), il va faire un voyage aux Etats-Unis.

V. Oral Production. Record the following exercises on an audiocassette for submission to your instructor. Before you begin, record your name and today's date.

A. Read the following sentences. Be careful where you place the stress. (5 pts.)

Il voyage.
Il voyage beaucoup.
Il voyage beaucoup pour ses affaires.

B. What could you serve to M. Courtois if he came to dinner? List the ingredients of a meal. Remember that he will expect a dinner in the French style (with a first course, wine, and cheese). (10 pts.)

C. What would you say in each of the following situations? A sentence or two is enough for each. (10 pts.)

1. You ask someone to have lunch with you.
2. You bump into someone on the street. Excuse yourself.
3. Express your appreciation to your hostess after a good meal.
4. Cheer up a gloomy friend with a selection of optimistic phrases.

Name ______________________________

Instructor ____________________ Section _____

SUMMARY QUIZ 25

I. Nothing goes quite right when Tante Georgette goes out to eat. Listen and check off the items she complains about by marking the appropriate box. (5 pts.)

	1	2	3	4	5
la serviette					
la fourchette					
la cuillère					
le couteau					
l'assiette					
le verre					

II. You will hear a series of statements in the future tense. Make them more forceful by putting the verb into the imperative. (5 pts.)

1. ____________________ quelque chose!

2. ____________________ avec nous!

3. ____________________ la carte des vins!

4. ____________________ cette assiette!

5. ____________________ votre café!

III. Complete the answers to the questions you hear, choosing the appropriate direct or indirect object pronoun, *y* or *en*. (7 pts.)

1. Non, elle n'_______ est pas.

2. Oui, téléphone-_______.

3. Non, merci, je n'_______ veux pas.

4. Oui, je _______ aime beaucoup.

5. Si, je _______ ai parlé.

6. Oui, je _______ ai vu.

7. Oui, apportez-_______.

IV. Complete by writing the answers to the questions or commands below, using *en* and personal pronouns. (8 pts.)

1. —Vous avez servi du vin à cette dame?

   —Oui, je _____________ ai servi.

2. —Je vous donne du pain?

   —Oui, donnez-_____________.

3. —Le garçon t'a donné de la moutarde?

   —Oui, il _____________ a donné.

4. —Garçon! Apportez du pain à ces clients!

   —Bien, monsieur, je _____________ apporte tout de suite.

Name ________________________________

Instructor ____________________ Section _____

SUMMARY QUIZ 26

I. You will hear a meal being ordered. Unfortunately the order of the dishes is scrambled. Help the waiter by putting the dishes in the proper order (shown below). Simply write the number of the dish on the corresponding line. (5 pts.)

_____ hors d'oeuvre

_____ plat de viande

_____ fromage

_____ dessert

_____ café

II. You will hear a series of commands. Make them less direct by rewriting the verb in the future tense. Don't forget to include pronouns where necessary. (5 pts.)

1. Vous ____________________ plus fort.

2. Vous ___________________________ le menu.

3. Vous ____________________ du pain, s'il vous plaît.

III. Listen and complete the sentences below using the verb you hear in the present indicative. (8 pts.)

1. Vous _______________ ici?

2. Moi aussi, j'_______________ des romans.

3. Vous _______________ quelque chose?

4. Nous ne _________________ rien.

5. Qu'est-ce que vous ____________________?

6. Je ne ____________________ personne.

7. Tu ____________________?

8. Elle ne ______________ pas, non plus.

IV. Complete. (7 pts.)

1. Vous avez ________ huîtres?

2. Non, je regrette, nous n'avons pas ________ huîtres.

3. Apportez-moi une douzaine ________ huîtres.

4. Vous voulez des ________ haricots?

5-6. Oui, beaucoup ________ haricots, s'il vous plaît. J'adore ________ haricots.

7. Tout le monde prend ________ café?

V. Oral Production. Record the following exercises on an audiocassette for submission to your instructor. Before you begin, record your name and today's date.

A. Read the following sentences, taking care not to let the consonants "explode" at the beginning of a word. (5 pts.)

Pas de poulet pour moi.
Je préfère la purée de thon aux tomates.

B. You are in Paris and you dial the phone number Mireille gave Robert in lesson 24. To your astonishment, she answers. Ask her to join you for dinner. Specify the time and the date (tomorrow, for instance). Tell her what kinds of good things they have on the menu at the restaurant you have chosen. End the call appropriately. (20 pts.)